The Light Extended
A Journal of the Golden Dawn

PRAISE FOR THIS BOOK

"At a time when so much writing on occultism lumbers along well-worn trails in the foothills of magic, it's refreshing to encounter a journal that leaps for the heights. *The Light Extended* is such a journal. Its contents include material from across the spectrum of Golden Dawn work, from unpublished Order documents to the cutting edge of the modern tradition. No one interested in serious Golden Dawn magic can afford to be without it."

— John Michael Greer,
editor of *The Golden Dawn* (Seventh Edition)
and author of *Circles of Power*

"An impressive launch to a brand new journal of Golden Dawn and Western Mysteries, *The Light Extended* leaps right out of the gate with some of the biggest names in modern Hermeticism; with in-depth entries offered by the Ciceros (giving their view on goetia and fallen angels), the Forrests (exploring Egyptian symbolism in both modern and ancient occultism), Darcy Kuntz (a ritual involving the Enochian Watchtower of Fire), as well as Jayne Gibson, Tony Fuller, Alex Sumner, and more. You can hardly go wrong with this 300+ page compendium of modern esotericism."

— Aaron Leitch,
author of *Secrets of the Magickal Grimoires*

The Light Extended
A Journal of the Golden Dawn

CHIC & TABATHA CICERO,
ADAM FORREST,
M. ISIDORA FORREST,
TONY FULLER,
DARCY KÜNTZ,
SAMUEL SCARBOROUGH,
FRATER YSHY,
JAYNE GIBSON,
ALEX SUMNER,
SOROR DPF,
FRATER D,
FRATER YECHIDAH

KERUBIM PRESS

DUBLIN 2019

Copyright © 2019 Chic Cicero and S. Tabatha Cicero, Samuel Scarborough, Frater YShY, Tony Fuller, Jayne Gibson, Adam P. Forrest, Soror DPF, Alex Sumner, Frater D, M. Isidora Forrest, Darcy Küntz, Frater Yechidah

All rights reserved. No part of this publication may be reproduced, stored in a retrieval system, or transmitted, in any form or by any means, electronic, mechanical, photocopying, recording or otherwise, without the prior permission of the publisher.

Any person who makes any unauthorised act in relation to this publication may be liable for criminal prosecution and civil claims for damages.

The Moral Rights of the Authors have been asserted.

Cover design by Kerubim Press

First Edition 2019

ISBN 978-1-908705-16-7

Published by Kerubim Press
Dublin, Ireland

www.kerubimpress.com
enquiries@kerubimpress.com

CONTENTS

How the Mighty Have Fallen: A Golden Dawn Perspective on the Fallen Angels, Goetic Spirits, and the Qlippoth — 009
by Chic Cicero and S. Tabatha Cicero

The Lesser Ritual of the Pentagram: The Foundational Ritual of the Golden Dawn Tradition — 047
by Samuel Scarborough

The Lord of the Universe — 088
by Frater YShY

Private Ritual for Influencing a Person for Good: or to Correct Evil Habits (Stella Matutina) — 114
with an Introduction by Tony Fuller

Theurgy and the Body of Light — 120
by Jayne Gibson

On the 42 Assessors of the Hall of the Two Truths: A Supplemental Z Libellus on the Enterer of the Threshold for the Study and Practice of the Adepta Major — 139
by Adam P. Forrest

Ἑκάς ἑκάς ἐστε βέβηλοι (Hekas Hekas Este Bebeloi) — 205
by Soror DPF

❀	Skrying in Theory & Practice	210
	by Alex Sumner	
❀	Thelema and the Golden Dawn: Spatting Siblings or Kissing Cousins?	228
	by Frater D	
❀	"I Have Put On the Cloak of the Great Lady; I Am the Great Lady": The Assumption of Godforms and the Key to Egyptian Magic	247
	by M. Isidora Forrest	
❀	The Fire Tablet Ritual	306
	with an Introduction by Darcy Küntz	
❀	The Enochian Alphabet: Golden Dawn Versus Dee Purist Letter Forms	313
	by Frater Yechidah	

How the Mighty Have Fallen

A Golden Dawn Perspective on the Fallen Angels, Goetic Spirits, and the Qlippoth

by Chic Cicero and S. Tabatha Cicero

It should come as no surprise that a large portion of the Golden Dawn system involves working with angels, archangels, intelligences, and spiritual beings of all stripes. Outer Order students first learn of the four mighty archangels Michael, Gabriel, Raphael and Uriel in their daily practice of the Lesser Ritual of the Pentagram. As they advance through the various grades of the First Order, they learn many more names of angels, rulers, and spirits attributed to the Elements, the Planets, and the Sephiroth.

In his paper entitled "Angels: Jewish, Christian and Pagan" printed in the S.R.I.A.'s *Transactions of the Metropolitan College*, Dr. W. Wynn Westcott writes:

> "The word angel meant a messenger, and so the human idea of an angel is that of a spiritual being from a higher plane sent by Divine Authority to give instruction or to carry out some work of an exception and superhuman nature [...] The Fathers of the Christian Church have held various views of the functions of Angels..." Some of the Church Fathers "have affirmed that Angels are in constant action in the world guiding and guarding men, cities, nations and churches."[1]

In the same paper Westcott examines the equivalent of angels in the Pagan religions:

---
1 Gilbert, R.A., *The Magical Mason*, 124.

THE LIGHT EXTENDED

"The pagan faiths of ancient Greece and Rome taught the existence of higher beings as guardians of their cities and sacred places, and they recognized spiritual and incorporeal personalities as presiding over seas, mountains and forest, and rulers of the elemental forces of the Fire, Earth, Air, and Water. There were special groups of such spiritual Elementals, and rulers definite personality were believed in and addressed by names, and they were often worshiped and propitiated by ceremonies, offerings, libations and incense."[2]

In the Qabalah, archangels and angels are considered specific aspects of God, each with a particular purpose and jurisdiction. Nearly all of the Hebraic angels have the suffixes "el" or "yah" at the end of their names, indicating that they are "of God." The word *angel* comes from the Greek *angelos* which is itself a translation of the Hebrew word *melakh* (מלאך) meaning "messenger." Angels have been described as "messengers of the soul." A more precise definition states that an angel is "an intermediate Intelligence between the human and the One in the Great Chain of Being."[3] The magician, too, is a part of this uninterrupted chain and is linked to a divine hierarchy headed by the Ineffable One, the highest transcendent aspect of God. This hierarchy includes various facets of divinity or "essences" of God which can be identified as the many divine names of God in the Qabalistic tradition, or as the many celestial deities known in the pantheons of different religions. After the highest aspects of divinity, archangels, angels, and intelligences follow next in the hierarchical progression. Human beings are ranked in the middle of this divine hierarchy, before the lower spirits and elementals. We are positioned in this sequence by virtue of the human soul and the Higher Genius, sometimes referred to as the Holy Guardian Angel,[4] one's personal angelic contact with the higher realms. Working with angels and archangels enhances the relationship between the human magician

---

2 Ibid.
3 Forrest, Adam, "This Holy Invisible Companionship, *The Golden Dawn Journal: Book Two: Qabalah: Theory and Magic*, (St. Paul, MN: Llewellyn Publications, 1994), 188.
4 Some consider these terms synonymous, while others believe they are two distinct entities.

and his Higher and Divine Genius, and it is this relationship that "attunes the Adept in greater harmony with the Angelic Plane of Yetzirah, and prepares him in innumerable ways for the Angelic Epiphany, the Golden Dawn of the Angelic Knowledge and Conversation."[5]

Golden Dawn practitioners adhere to this chain of command whenever they perform magical ceremonies. In a divine universe, the Sacred must be petitioned through the proper channels, from the highest to lowest spiritual ranks. Therefore in any ritual the Theurgist first invokes the highest divine names of God before invoking any lesser aspects of divinity or celestial deities. Following these, archangels, angels, and other intelligences are invoked. The magician works primarily with archangels and angels as "divine intermediates," in both directions of the hierarchical ranks, requesting them to command the lesser spirits, rulers, and elementals to carry out the goal of the magical working. Working in this way, angelic beings are seen as companions on the Theurgist's path, working together in the Great Chain of Being; colleagues who stand ready to aid the sincere magician with their transformative power. They are the dwellers of the unseen worlds through which the pilgrim travels on his journey.

Heinrich Cornelius Agrippa spoke of the helpfulness of angels: "Magicians teach that celestial gifts may through inferiors being conformable to superiors be drawn down by opportune influences of the heaven; and so also by these celestial (gifts), the celestial angels, as they are servants of the stars, may be procured, and conveyed to us."[6] The angels themselves communicated to John Dee and seer Edward Kelly that they are open to those magicians who call upon them in amity and with respect, "All those before spoken of are subject to thy call of friendship."[7]

But there are other angels who, according to our tradition are not friends to humanity. In medieval times they were called fallen angels, devils and demons. Belief in evil spirits was certainly not new, nor was it unique to medieval Europe, it dates to the very beginnings of civilization. "The demon-lore of ancient Egypt and Mesopotamia is extremely complex and detailed, and includes quite a range of

---

5 Ibid.
6 Agrippa, *Three Books of Occult Philosophy*, Book I, (part 2), 112.
7 Quoted in Forrest, 231.

blood-curdling entities."⁸ Nevertheless, by the Middle Ages the terms "devil" and "demon" were considered interchangeable.

It was not always so, however. In antiquity, the word Greek word *demon*, or more correctly *daemon* or *daimon* (δαίμων), simply meant "spirit," without any connotation of being good, bad, or indifferent. A daemon was regarded as an intermediary between gods and humans, comparable to an angel or a saint in the Christian hierarchy. According to Plato, the name daemon was derived from "knowing" indicating that these beings were possessed of a greater intelligence than humanity. A similar word, *daimoniakos*, signified "divinely influenced" and was used to describe a number of the gods.⁹ As time passed, however, the word "demon" was gradually used to indicate more of a malevolent influence. "Evil at last triumphed in monopolizing the name, and *demon* became synonymous with *devil*."¹⁰

The influence of Neoplatonic theurgy in the magical work of the Golden Dawn has lead modern practitioners to separate the terms daemon and demon, reclaiming the original meaning of *daemon* to mean simply "spirit" (and oftentimes a helpful spirit), while using the word *demon* to indicate a malicious or qlippothic entity.

The word demon is also used to indicate a spiritual entity that has undergone a separation from the Divine and a downgrade from their previously exalted position—a fall from grace, so to speak. This *fall* appears in various traditions that have found their way into the Western Esoteric Tradition, but the most common motifs are those of the fallen angels of Judeo-Christian lore and the broken vessels from the Qabalah. In this brief essay, we will examine three types of fallen entities: the nephilim, goetic spirits, and the qlippoth.

The Nephilim

The nephilim were the monstrous offspring of the first Fallen Angels to debut in Jewish lore.¹¹ The term *nephilim* (נפלים), is sometimes

---

8 Greer, *The New Encyclopedia of the Occult*, 129.
9 Wall, *Devils: Their Origin and History*, 9.
10 Ibid., 10.
11 In some versions of the story, the fallen angels themselves become the nephilim, along with with their offspring. The gematria for "nephilim" is 770.

interpreted as "giants" and other times as "the fallen ones" although the precise meaning remains unclear. The singular form *nephil* (נפל), is not found in scripture, but it may be derived from the verb *napal*, "to fall" or "be cast down." These beings appear twice in the *Torah*, at Genesis 6:1-4 and Numbers 13:32-33, reportedly written between the 10th and the 6th centuries B.C.E.[12] There are also references in the *Ethiopic Book of Enoch* which dates to the 2nd century B.C.E to 1st century C.E., and also in *The Book of Jubilees* and *The Book of Giants* found in the Dead Sea Scrolls (2nd century B.C.E.).

According to the legend, a group of antediluvian angels identified as part of the host of the *Beni Elohim* ("Sons of God") and also as *grigori* or "watchers" (from the Greek term *egregoroi*), created the Nephilim. Witnessing God's sorrow over humanity's moral decay, a group of Angels descended to earth to prove that man, being the weak creature they had warned about in the Garden of Eden, was solely to blame for his own immorality. Other stories have the grigori sent to earth to simply watch over humanity's well-being. But upon seeing the daughters of men, the angels themselves became enamored and lusted after them. As a result they sired a race of giants:

> "When men began to increase on earth and daughters were born to them, the divine beings saw how beautiful the daughters of men were and took wives from among those that pleased them. The LORD said, 'My breath shall not abide in man forever, since he too is flesh; let the days allowed him be one hundred and twenty years.' It was then, and later too, that the Nephilim appeared on earth—when the divine beings cohabited with the daughters of men, who bore them offspring. They were the heroes of old, the men of renown." [13]

The *Book of Enoch* paints a broader picture of the angels' fall from heaven:

> "In those days, when the children of man had multiplied, it happened that there were born unto them handsome and

---

12 Some modern scholars argue that these texts may have been written as late as the Hellenistic Period, 4th - 2nd centuries B.C.E.
13 Genesis 6:1-4.

> beautiful daughters. And the angels, the children of heaven, saw them and desired them; and they said to one another, 'Come, let us choose wives for ourselves from among the daughters of man and beget us children.' And Semyaz, being their leader, said unto them, 'I fear that perhaps you will not consent that this deed should be done, and I alone will become (responsible) for this great sin.' But they all responded to him, 'Let us all swear an oath and bind everyone among us by a curse not to abandon this suggestion but to do the deed.' Then they all swore together and bound one another by (the curse). And they were altogether two hundred;"[14]

Examples of the fallen angels include Semyaz (also spelled Samyaz, Semyaza and Shemhazai), formerly a seraph who revealed the secret name of God to the maiden Ishtahar. *Jeqôn* (or Yeqon) whose name means "inciter," was another ringleader of the angelic rebellion, as well as *Kesabel* who gave the angels "evil council" in this regard. *Azza* (Uzza, Azazel, or possibly another version of Samyaz), was an angel whose downfall began when he baulked at Enoch's transformation into the mighty archangel Metatron. *Gadrel* (or Gadreel) created weapons of war.

Upon reaching earth, nineteen of these angels, known as "the Chiefs of Ten":

> "... took wives unto themselves, and everyone (respectively) chose one woman for himself, and they began to go unto them. And they taught them magical medicine, incantations, the cutting of roots, and taught them (about) plants. And the women became pregnant and gave birth to great giants whose heights were three hundred cubits. These (giants) consumed the produce of all the people until the people detested feeding them. So the giants turned against (the people) in order to eat them."[15]

The angels taught women magic and herbal medicine, and taught men the sciences and the arts. But they also taught mankind how to

---
14 1 Enoch 6:1-7.
15 1 Enoch 7:1-5.

kill and commit violence. Both acts caused a rise in crime, bloodshed and warfare. Meanwhile the nephilim were devouring everything in their path; they destroyed people, animals, forests, and crops. They spared nothing. Eventually humans cried out for relief.

Moved by man's suffering, the four mighty archangels (Michael, Gabriel, Raphael and Uriel), appealed to God and were given the order to punish the fallen angels and wipe their hybrid offspring from the face of the earth. The Great Flood in the story of Noah soon followed, along with the legendary battle between the archangels and the fallen angels.

Evil Spirits in the Book of Enoch

The nephilim were destroyed, however their disembodied spirits became evil spirits who plagued humanity because *they are descended from humanity*:

> "But now the giants who are born from the (union of) the spirits and the flesh shall be called evil spirits upon the earth, because their dwelling shall be upon the earth and inside the earth. Evil spirits have come out of their bodies. Because from the day that they were created from the holy ones they became the Watchers; their first origin is the spiritual foundation. They will become evil upon the earth and shall be called evil spirits. The dwelling of the spiritual beings of heaven is heaven; but the dwelling of the spirits of the earth, which are born upon the earth, is in the earth. The spirits of the giants oppress each other, they will corrupt, fall, be excited, and fall upon the earth, and cause sorrow. They eat no food, nor become thirsty, nor find obstacles. And these spirits shall rise up against the children of the people and against the women, because they have proceeded forth (from them). [16]

The *Book of Enoch* also discusses the origin of demons who were said to derive from the fallen angels themselves:

> "Here shall stand in many different appearances the spirits of

---
[16] 1 Enoch 15

the angels which have united themselves with women. They have defiled the people and will lead them into error so that they will offer sacrifices to the demons as unto gods, until the great day of judgment in which they shall be judged till they are finished."[17]

The main thrust of the mythological narrative behind the nephilim was the legend of the transgression of divine order which ensured the separation of gods and men. This legend was in keeping with similar pre-flood themes in the Book of Genesis. Later traditions historicized the nephilim, morphing them into the precursors of the Canaanites, or elaborating the tradition of fallen angels as being those who actively instigated humanity's rebellion against divine authority. The violations committed by the angels can be summarized in three primary themes: the dangers of sexual impurity, the corrupting potential of knowledge, and the antediluvian proliferation of violence.[18] In this respect, the fallen angels were said to have taught mankind "all sins."

What truths can we discover from this legend? What is "the moral of the story," so to speak, from a Golden Dawn perspective? The angels "fell" because they lost their connection and special identity of being "at One" with the Divine. A reading of the relevant passages from the *Book of Enoch* shows the Fall in terms of the reversal of the natural affiliation, bond, and function between the celestial and the terrestrial. In Golden Dawn terms, it was not unlike inverting the figure of the pentagram—the upright pentagram is symbol of spirit governing matter, but when inverted indicates matter governing spirit. According to author Annette Yoshiko Reed, the dialog attributed to God in the *Book of Enoch*:

> "... interprets angelic descent in terms of the inversion of the ideal relationship between identity and activity that properly delineates the heavenly and earthly realms. [...] God denounces the once-immortal Watchers for "act(ing) like children of the earth" by bearing Giants for sons. This rebuke occasions a contrast between the proper types of action for

---

17 1 Enoch 19:1
18 Reed, *Fallen Angels and the history of Judaism and Christianity*, 30.

> spiritual and earthly beings: sex is an acceptable activity for "those who die and perish" (15:4-5), but it is categorically improper for "spirits that live forever and do not die for all generations forever" (15:6).
>
> Likewise, the birth of the Giants is explored in terms of the mingling of "spirits and flesh" (15:8). Angels properly dwell in heaven, and humans properly dwell on earth (15:10), but the nature of the Giants is mixed. This transgression of categories brings terrible results: after their physical death, the Giants' demonic spirits "come forth from their bodies" to plague humankind (15:9, 11-12; 16:1). According to 1 En. 16, the angelic transmission of heavenly knowledge to earthly humans can also be understood as a contamination of distinct categories within God's orderly Creation. As inhabitants of heaven, the Watchers were privy to all the secrets of heaven; their revelation of this knowledge to the inhabitants of the earth was categorically improper as well as morally destructive."[19]

Once this divine harmony was breached, what had been unified became divided, disjointed. Wholeness fractured into factions. Separation and complexity entered into the equation.

The "corrupting potential of knowledge" is reminiscent of dangers of the Tree of the Knowledge and Good and Evil that the Golden Dawn student first learns of in the Zelator Grade, and which is further elaborated in the Grades of Practicus and Philosophus. Knowledge is of course a double-edged sword. Wielded intelligently, with respect and proper intent, a plant can become a medicine, and atomic fusion can provide a source of energy. Used carelessly or maliciously, a plant can be made into poison and atomic fusion can destroy a city. This is both the promise and the warning of the Tree of Good and Evil. Consequently, the story of the rebellious angels ties in with story of the Garden of Eden Before and After the Fall.

It should be noted that the nephilim were sometimes referred to as the *gibborim* or "warriors," a term that is linked to the fifth Sephirah of Geburah, which is strongly connected to the Fall of the qlippoth.

---

19 Ibid., 45-46.

The mixed nature of the offspring nephilim was also problematic. Before their angelic fathers fell, the spiritual and the material existed in a state of balance. The nephilim were born as hybrid monsters, confused chimeras, part divine and part animal, but in a fashion that was complicated and conflicted. Although they were part angel and part human, they were also *neither*. They were spiritually off-balanced creatures, who acted much like an invasive species of predator in an environment where they do not belong—devouring everything and everyone in their path. Mankind should be familiar with this motif, our predilection for corrupting the earth with poisons and consuming every last resource sounds very familiar in this context.

One could say that the story of the nephilim is a warning to humans, whose nature is also part angel and part animal. This gives new meaning to the Magician's pledge to always "strive to become more than human."

Goetic Spirits

What we know today as goetic magic has its roots in classical Greece, where the term *goeteia* (γοητεία) referred to the art of the *goes*, a ritual mourner who attended funerals. The term *gôos* was an ancient Greek word for a lament for the dead. Later the term *goes* came to mean a necromancer who could bring back the spirits of the dead from Hades. Eventually the term morphed to indicate a "sorcerer" while the topic of magic itself was sometimes described as *goeteia* and other times as *mageia*. Classical magicians often insisted they were not *goetes* due to the negative connotations associated with the word.[20]

Goetic magic found a fertile environment in medieval and Renaissance Europe where a number of spell-books called *grimoires* were circulated. It is important to understand that many of the European grimoires known to western magicians are Christian books. It is undeniable that bits and pieces of archaic pagan magic found their way into these texts in scarcely recognizable form from Egypt and Greece. Sacred pagan deity names were endlessly butchered by the authors, as were Hebrew names. Nevertheless, the grimoires were written *by* Christians *for* Christians who lived in a

---

20 Greer, *The New Encyclopedia of the Occult*, 201.

Christian-centric universe. That is not to say that the grimoires were sanctioned by the church; they certainly were not. Christian clerics were, however, trained the knowledge of Latin prayers and liturgy, as well as in Christian rites of exorcism. Most of the grimoires were written and used by medieval Christian clergymen and others who were ordained to the minor orders, which included the position of exorcist. University students would be ordained to the minor orders as part of their core curriculum. The world of the medieval grimoires was a secretive and guarded underworld of loosely-knit magical practitioners: priests, monks, and clerics. According to author Richard Kieckhefer, "many were ordained to lower orders and continued to claim the privileges of clergy although they had no clerical employment."[21] As a result there was a glut of unemployed and semi-employed clerics who had access to books of exorcism, were expected to command demons if need be, and may have used this knowledge upon occasion to support themselves. It was primarily among these exorcist-clerics that medieval ceremonial magic as set forth in the grimoires flourished.

Some of the grimoires dealt primarily with archangels, angels, planetary intelligences, and spirits of the celestial realms. These included *Clavicula Salomonis* or *"The Key of Solomon the King,"* dating from the 14th or 15th century. Like many grimoires, *Clavicula Salomonis* was attributed to King Solomon and influenced by Jewish Qabalists and Arabic Alchemists. Several of these texts contained sections on working with spirits which were of mixed nature, not unlike human beings. Still other grimoires such as the *Ars Goetia* from the *Lesser Key of Solomon* (also known as the *Lemegeton*), focused squarely on working with demons.

These texts were thoroughly Christian in culture and mythology as evidenced by every magic circle and every invocation contained in them. It is no surprise then that the grimoires reflect a dualistic worldview in which humans and spirits have an adversarial relationship. This is especially true of grimoires like the *Ars Goetia* that dealt with demons, whom the authors saw as fallen angels. From *their* medieval perspective, these fallen angels were inherently liars and deceivers. They are assumed to be hostile witnesses and unwilling participants—present only because they are ordered to

---
21 Kieckhefer, *Magic in the Middle Ages*, 154.

THE LIGHT EXTENDED

be so through the commandment of God. Their punishment by the Judaeo-Christian god included being forced to serve human magicians who know the right rituals, proper words, seals and sigils, which they learned from the revelation given to them by the celestial angels who won the war in heaven; knowledge which was passed down via the *Book of Raziel*, given over to Adam, and the information delivered to Solomon. In other words, the fallen spirits in these texts are being commanded as prisoners, indentured servants, or slaves.

A good is example of this is the evocation of an evil spirit from the *Goetia*:

> "The Thirteenth Spirit is called Beleth (or Bileth, or Bilet). He is a mighty King and terrible. He rideth on a pale horse with trumpets and other kinds of musical instruments playing before him. He is very furious at his first appearance, that is, while the Exorcist layeth his courage; for to do this he must hold a Hazel Wand in his hand, striking it out towards the South and East Quarters, make a triangle, without the Circle, and then command him into it by the Bonds and Charges of Spirits as hereafter followeth. And if he doth not enter into the triangle at your threats, rehearse the Bonds and Charms before him, and then he will yield Obedience and come into it, and do what he is commanded by the Exorcist."[22]

Liber Juratis Honorii or "The Sworn Book of Honorius," a grimoire dating from the 13th or 14th century, refers to the spirits being evoked as "the enemy":

> "First you must prepare the place thus, for the earth should be flat and level, and free from stones or vegetation, and when it has been drawn, mark in the air above .... saying: "I put the Seal of Solomon upon me for salvation and defence, in order that it protect me in the face of the enemy. In the name of the Father and the Son and the Holy Spirit. Amen." Thus with your circle complete, exit and write outside in the earth or on small pieces of parchment, the seven names of the creator..."[23]

---

22 *The Goetia: Lesser Key of Solomon the King,* translated by Mathers, 34.
23 Peterson, Joseph H., "Liber Juratus Honorii," *Twilight Grotto – Esoteric Archives*. http://www.esotericarchives.com/juratus/juratus.htm, Accessed 2/2/17.

HOW THE MIGHTY HAVE FALLEN

A later text, the *Great Grimoire of Pope Honorius,* written during the 18th or 19th century, continues in this vein:

> "RAIMOND, very mighty prince who governs the West, I summon you by all the highest names of God. I command you by the power of the allhighest names to quickly send N.N. here to answer to me and to always do as I command. If you do not then I will burn you and increase your pain."[24]

The medieval goetic magicians believed that there was a vast and clear difference between the holy angels and fallen angels. This is why they armed themselves with Solomonic Seals to protect themselves from the "foul smell" and other weapons of the fallen demonic angels. They did not hesitate to tortment these spirits by cursing them and roasting their seals, such as in the following "General Curse, called the Spirit's Chain against all Spirits that Rebel" found in the *Goetia*:

> "O THOU wicked and disobedient spirit N., because thou hast rebelled, and hast not obeyed nor regarded my words which I have rehearsed; they being all glorious and incomprehensible names of the true GOD, the maker and creator of thee and of me, and of all the world; I DO by the power of these names the which no creature is able to resist, curse thee into the depth of the Bottomless Abyss, there to remain unto the Day of Doom in chains, and in fire and brimstone unquenchable, unless thou forthwith appear here before this Circle, in this triangle to do my will. And, therefore, come thou quickly and peaceably, in and by these names of GOD, ADONAI, ZABAOTH, ADONAI, AMIORAN; come thou! come thou! for it is the King of Kings, even ADONAI, who commandeth thee.
>
> WHEN thou shalt have rehearsed thus far, but still be cometh not, then write thou his seal on parchment and put thou it into a strong black box; with brimstone, assafœtida, and such like things that bear a stinking smell; and then bind the box up round with an iron wire, and bang it upon the point of thy sword, and hold it over the fire of charcoal; and

---

24 *The Great Grimoire of Pope Honorius,* 17.

say as followeth unto the fire first, it being placed toward that quarter whence the Spirit is to come."[25]

Such threats were intended to terrify the rebellious spirit into obedience. If the spirit was still not compliant, the magician followed up with ever more strident volleys of curses, finally dropping the box containing the seal into the fire. This was enough to make the tortured spirit appear and obey.

> "The magicians of the Middle Ages clearly recognized that the practice of evocation had risks as well as benefits, and they set out to deal with dangers efficiently from the start. The method they used, typical for the time, was sheer brute force...the magician readied his arsenal of words of power and consecrated weapons, and then launched his conjurations like assaults, battering the spirit into submission with threats and rhetoric fortified with the Names of God. A spirit who did not show up quickly enough might have its name and sigil, written on a piece of parchment, scorched over hot coals in the hope that this might torture it into obedience! It's little wonder that spirits, faced with this kind of treatment, were seen as dangerous and treacherous, apt to wriggle out of agreements through any loophole they could find. Most human beings put in the same situation would behave similarly."[26]

Fallen angels and goetic spirits are historically and magically known as evil spirits. Some of these spirits were undeniably based on sacred Pagan gods and goddesses, while many others were derived from Persian, Arabic, and Jewish sources. All of them were distorted through the biased lens of the medieval Christian exorcist-cleric, who thought that *all* Pagan gods were fallen spirits. The result was the corruption of sacred Pagan deities into a class of evil spirits who could be enslaved by the magician. Some of the best known of these corrupted forms include *Ashtoreth* (a degenerated form of the Phoenician goddess Astarte), *Flaurus* (from the Egyptian god

---

25 *The Goetia*, 85-86.
26 Greer, *Circles of Power*, 244.

HOW THE MIGHTY HAVE FALLEN

Horus) and *Amon* (derived from the Egyptian god Amun). The *Goetia* describes Amon as:

> "A Marquis great in power & most strong. He at first appeared like a wolf with a serpents tail, vomiting out out of his mouth flames of fire, but at the command of the magician he putteth on the shape of a man, with dogs teeth beset in a head like a raven, or in a raven's head."[27]

Some authors have correctly noted that many Pagan gods and goddesses have a chthonic aspect, especially when they are depicted in the underworld. These ancient deities often appeared in animal form or with harsh attributes that would have boggled the mind of the medieval Christian magician who barely had a grasp of Hebrew traditions and godnames, much less ancient Pagan belief. Garbled descriptions of these divinities were very likely the source material for *some* of the goetic spirits. Nevertheless, it is unwise to equate the darker side of pagan deities with their demonized forms in the *Goetia*, and it would certainly be wrong to subject any sacred Pagan deity to the kind of spirit torture promoted in many of the grimoires.

The fallen spirits, no matter what their source, now have a life of their own in the unseen worlds. Their existence was divorced from whatever scattered fragments of divinity they may have once had eons ago. Unknown numbers of magicians working from these books for hundreds of years have made it so. And yet there have been numerous attempts to try and whitewash the nature of these spirits, whose primary mythos and narrative is that of fallen, deceptive and hostile entities. They are not misunderstood nature spirits who simply need to be treated with a little love and respect. They will bite. It is their nature to bite.

It is extremely unlikely that medieval grimoires can be retrofit in such a way that the fallen spirits can be reverse-engineered back into being beneficent Pagan deities. The names, characteristics, and even the sigils of these entities have been skryed or otherwise created through the cracked lens of a broken looking-glass.

"If they are pagan gods, then treat them as pagan gods, not

---
27 *The Goetia*, 30.

as underlings to be commanded and coerced through the Christian hierarchy. So the attempt to redefine the various goetic spirits fails because one is still using the Judeo-Christian spiritual hierarchy, and in that hierarchy, the opinions of the theologians holds sway, not the musings of neoplatonists. If you were going to make use of the definition of demons (as the Greek "daimones"), then you would also need to discard the Christian spiritual hierarchy and replace it with one that is uniquely neoplatonic."[28]

Modern Golden Dawn magicians come from a wide variety of religious backgrounds and spiritual paths: Neopagan, Christian, Jewish, Gnostic, Sufi, Buddhist, Hindu, etc., Outside of privacy concerns, contemporary practitioners do not live in fear for their beliefs; they do not have to hide what they do nor cloak their words in the doctrine of an all-powerful church. Golden Dawn magicians *do not* believe that sacred Pagan gods and goddesses are fallen spirits. We have no need to call upon corrupted demonic forms and their associated and often harmful baggage. We work with deities from various pantheons—angels, archangels, planetary intelligences, and spirits—in their pure and original forms and even their chthonic forms with respect, without the need to force, threaten, or torture a hostile or unwilling entity to do our bidding. The antagonistic medieval worldview of human versus spirit interaction is not one we share.

There is another important point to be made here. Evil is real. There IS evil in the universe. If the spiritual reality reflects reality, there should be evil spirits, too. There are great evils like rape, murder, torture, child abuse, genocide, and less monstrous but still truly selfish evils like defrauding elders and other investors, poisoning resources, etc. Therefore, the attempt to recast the evil spirits as "misunderstood" or simply neutral is in fact an attempt (consciously or unconsciously) to remake a universe without real good and real evil. In such a universe, the magician could operate in a purely selfish and amoral fashion without feeling guilty

---

[28] Frater Barrabbas. "Problems with Goetic Magick and the Black Grimoires." *Talking About Ritual Magick*. November 10, 2009. http://fraterbarrabbas.blogspot.com/2009/11/problems-with-goetic-magick-and-black.html. Accessed 2/1/2017.

about it. All of the grimoires stressed that the would-be magician be extremely virtuous—an exceptionally good person—before becoming a magician and attempting to utilize these texts. Anyone who disregards this fundamental directive is simply ignoring one of the key safeguards that the grimoires set in place.

> "Finally, many of the older grimoires, and a few more recent books, discuss the evocation of demons. Here the best advice is a single word: dont. There's nothing of value to be gained by summoning what the Cabala calls the inhabitants of Gehenna, the Kingdom of Shells, and whatever is done with their aid will turn against the doer, sooner or later. They have a place in the universe and a right to exist, but they are as alien and destructive to the fabric of human life as a black hole or the heart of a Star. The only time a magician should have any dealings them is when, as sometimes happens, they intrude on the human world and must be sent back to their own realm through ritual exorcism."[29]

This brings us to our final species of the "fallen" and the one that is the most familiar to Golden Dawn students: the qlippoth.

The Qlippoth

The *qlippoth* (קליפות - singular *qlippah*) is Hebrew for "shells," "peels," or "husks." Of all the fallen ones referenced in this article, the qlippoth have received the most attention in the teachings of the Golden Dawn. This is due in no small measure to their overtly Qabalistic origins, for these demonic entities are the surviving remnants of a failed universe that existed prior to the current one. In the Golden Dawn's Zelator ritual, they are described as "Evil Demons who inhabit the plane contiguous to and below the Material Universe." They are also referred to as the "Adverse Sephiroth" and "Lords of Unbalanced Force."

Although there are qlippoth attributed to the twelve signs of the zodiac and the elements, the best known of these demons are the ten types of qlippoth that correspond to the ten Sephiroth on the

---
29 Greer, *Circles of Power*, 251.

Tree of Life. These are the chaotic, imbalanced, polar opposites of the harmonious Sephiroth of the Qabalah, said to form a second tree which is called evil. The qlippotic tree is usually represented as a mirror image of the Tree of Life, reflected from the base of Malkuth. Formed from an excess of unstable energy, the power of the qlippoth is based upon all forms of overindulgence and excess; imbalance in general. They are the destructive and un-equilibrated aspects of the holy Sephiroth, and just as every Sephirah is said to have a virtue, there is a corresponding "vice" that is embodied in the associated qlippah.

The qlippah of Kether, for example, is *Thaumiel* which has been interpreted as "the Twins of God" or "the Contending Forces." This reflects a dualism that is the exact opposite of the ultimate unity of the holy Sephirah Kether. *Samael,* the qlippah of Hod, is translated as the "Liar of God" or "the Poison of God," which indicates an imbalance of the intellectual, communicative aspects of the eighth Sphere. The fourth Sephirah is opposed by the qlippah *Gasheklah* which means "the Smiters," or "the Breakers" which evinces a disintegrating force, the opposite of the form-building, manifesting energy of Chesed.

Whereas as the Sephiroth symbolize progressive evolution and spiritual reunion with the Divine, the qlippoth represent de-evolution and spiritual disintegration.

The ten adverse qlippoth are also collected into the Seven Evil Palaces, often symbolized by a great red dragon with seven heads and ten horns. The infernal order of the qlippoth correspond somewhat to the various angelic orders. Samael is said to surround the whole of the Evil Sephiroth, thus making eleven instead of ten. This is why eleven is seen as a number which especially refers to the qlippoth.

Origin of the Qlippoth

Whereas the holy emanations of the Sephiroth are described as "vessels," the qlippoth are called the "broken vessels." In one aspect of the tradition, each Sephirah is a container for the one that preceded it, for everything is a husk when viewed from a higher perspective and a seed when viewed from a lower one. Vessels, containers, and outer coverings are common themes in the Qabalistic theory of creation, as is the interplay of boundaries between the container and that which it contains.

The *Zohar* or the "Book of Splendor," an important text penned between 1270 and 1300 by Moses de Leon, states that the root cause of evil is the act of separation. What had been whole became disjointed. The Qabalists referred to the act of separation as the "cutting of the shoots." The domain of evil demons was known as the *sitr ahra*, the "other place" opposite the Holy Place of the Divine. Qabalists often suggested that evil was inherently an overabundance of Geburah force (severity) separated from its vital polar balance of Chesed (mercy).

The Zohar contains a number of different ideas and even conflicting views regarding the qlippoth. They are sometimes understood in a Neoplatonic fashion as "the last links of the chain of emanation where all turns to darkness."[30] Elsewhere the realm of evil is described as "the natural waste product of an organic process and is compared to bad blood. A bitter branch on the tree of emanation, foul waters (*Zohar* 2:167b), the dross which remains after the gold has been refined (*hittukhei ha-zahav*), or the dregs from good wine."[31]

The nature of the qlippoth was further explored by Isaac Luria (1534 - 1572) whose works were influenced by a somewhat more Gnostic perspective. Adherents of the Lurianic School presented the Creation as a process that was disrupted by imbalance. This event was the destruction of the initial, failed worlds of a previous Qabalah; the Universe of Chaos (*tohu*). According to the tradition, there were two aspects of the emanation of the Divine Light. One was linear, in the form of the body of *Adam Kadmon*, the archetypal man who was created in a process of *tsimtsum* or "contraction." This was an act whereby the Divine contracted his infinite light (*Ain Soph*) into a vacant place—removing aspects of limitlessness from this space so that Creation could occur there:

> "Adam Kadmon is nothing but a first configuration of the divine light which flows from the essence of *En-Sof* into the primeval space of the *Tsimtsum* .... He therefore is the first and highest form in which the divinity begins to manifest

---

30 Scholem, *Kabbalah*, 125.
31 Ibid.

THE LIGHT EXTENDED

itself after the Tsimtsum. From his eye, mouth, ears and nose, the Lights of the Sefiroth burst forth."[32]

The second aspect of emanation was circular: the Sephiroth took form within Adam Kadmon in a series of concentric circles. The outermost circle was Kether, which was in close proximity to the encompassing circle of Ain Soph. At this early stage the Sephiroth were not yet separate, but bound together as a series of Lights or Points. These Sephirotic Lights were then given "vessels" or fields of containment, in which to organize their substance and operate.

What occurred next was what is called the "breaking of the vessels" (*shevirath ha-kelim*). The vessels of containment belonging to the three Supernal Sephiroth were sturdy enough to receive the Divine Light issuing into them, but the sheer force of the Light was unstable and lacked direction. When the Light struck the next six spheres from Chesed to Yesod it did so with such potency that the vessels shattered one by one, sending fragments falling. The vessel of Malkuth also cracked but did not shatter. The tenth Sephirah is said to be "fallen" because after the Fall when the Vessels were broken, Malkuth descended and came to rest upon the Kingdom of Shells, which is why their influence is so potent in the world of humanity.

Why did the vessels shatter? In the universe of *tohu* the primitive Sephiroth could receive the Light of the Divine as vessels, but being simple points of emanation, they could neither *give back* Light nor interact with each other. In this way, they could not resemble the Divine and were incomplete. Unable to hold the Light of the Divine, they were overwhelmed and shattered. And part of the tradition points to an overabundance of justice and severity, both attributed of the fifth Sephirah of Geburah.

The word *Geburah* is derived from the word *gibor* which means "power," "force," or "strength." One of Geburah's titles is *din*, which means "justice" or "judgment." As a natural extension of these ideas, the Hermetic Qabalah assigned the planet Mars to this sephirah. However, the martial qualities attributed to Geburah also connect it with the negative connotations of excessive force, violence, warfare, and senseless destruction. Because of this Geburah was given the title of "the left hand of the Holy One," alluding to the powers of harsh

[32] Scholem, *Major Trends in Jewish Mysticism*, 265.

judgment. Eventually this aspect of Geburah became an independent attribute, called the *sitra achra*, the "other side" mentioned earlier as an embodiment of the qlippothic realm and the left-hand path. Somehow the aspect of judgment (*din*) became severed from its essential balancing opposite in Chesed (*mercy*). As a result harsh judgments, whether justified or not, became identified with evil if they were not tempered by mercy.

> "According to this idea, evil was the result of unbalanced and aggressive judgment, as that which emerged from the Sephirah Geburah. Since this Sephirah [...] ruled the left side of pillar of the Tree underneath the supernal triad, it became the seed of the left, giving sustenance to all that was unbalanced and destructive (evil) in manifestation. The flow from this current went down and away from the divine qualities of Geburah, following its true nature, and collected in the lower realms, where it became a counter-force to the forces of creation and good. From this dark current and counter-force was born a negative hierarchy, resulting in the demons and evil forces that plaque all those who reside in the material world." [33]

In Lurianic Tradition the Breaking of the Vessels is also called "the death of the Kings." Luria equated the shattered pieces with the Kings of Edom described in Genesis 36:31: "These are the kings who reigned in the land of Edom before any king ruled over the Israelites." In the *Zohar* the seven kings of Edom represented the forces of strict judgment (*din*), completely untempered by the mercy of Chesed. They died because "the world is maintained only through the balance and harmony of these two principles. These 'kings,' that is, structures of the untempered forces of *din*, are identical, according to the *Zohar*, with the primordial worlds which an ancient midrash said were created and destroyed before the creation of our present cosmos. The death of the kings of Edom, that is, of the sphere of untempered *din*, thus proceeded the establishment of a balanced and harmonious cosmos ..."[34]

---

[33] Frater Barabbas, *Magical Qabalah for Beginners*, 165-166.
[34] Scholem, *Sabbatai Sevi: The Mystical Messiah*, 34.

THE LIGHT EXTENDED

Regardless of the exact cause, every level of world below the Supernal Triad dropped from its previous location.[35] Nothing was to remain in its proper position. The World of Assiah, the Active World, plunged into and intermingled with the lowest abodes of the qlippoth. Some of the Divine Light returned to its source, resulting a new, sturdier formation of the vessels into five *partzufim* or "faces."

The *partzufim* included *Arik Anpin*, the "Vast Countenance" a title of Kether; *Abba*, "Father" (equivalent to Chokmah); *Aima*, "Mother" (equal to Binah); *Zauir Anpin*, the "Lesser Countenance" (corresponding to the six Sephiroth of Chesed, Geburah, Tiphareth, Netzach, Hod and Yesod); and finally *Nukba de-Zauir*, the "female [counterpart] of Zauir," also known as *Malkah* the "Queen," and *Kalah* "the Bride" (all titles of the Sephirah Malkuth).

Light not contained in the reformed *partzufim* was propelled down along with the broken vessels. The shattered pieces of the vessels still contained sparks of the Divine Light trapped within them, consequently they were brought to life and became the qlippoth. The Light which was trapped by the qlippoth, supplied the life-force and substance for the demonic realm, which effected all but the Supernal Sephiroth after the breaking of the vessels. The opaque shards of the broken vessels snared within them a portion of the Supernal Light and concealed it from its source in Kether. The obscured Light relates to "the Light shining in the Darkness," described in the Gospel of St. John.

According to Lurianic tradition, the reason these unstable vessels were created in the first place was so that evil should come into being. This would supply humanity with the freedom to choose; which is prerequisite for the *restoration of the vessels*. And because evil emanated from the first and highest of the vessels, *it can be reconstructed and restored to this level*. Luria's Qabalah placed a heavy emphasis on rescuing the trapped sparks of the Divine Light from their imprisonment in the Kingdom of Shells, a theme that is very similar to Gnostic doctrines.

---

35 The death of the Edomite kings in Genesis refers to the breaking of the vessels and their consequent fall to a lower level.

HOW THE MIGHTY HAVE FALLEN

The Qlippoth in the Golden Dawn

Within the invisible matrix of the Golden Dawn's Magic of Light, the qlippoth are astrally situated at the extreme western limits of the Hall of the Neophytes, sometimes referred to as its mythic Egyptian counterpart, the *Hall of Judgment*. Here the qlippoth are prevented from intruding upon the sacred space by the godform of Horus the Avenger acting through the office of the Hiereus. In keeping with the horizontal blueprint of the Tree of Life as seen from above, the Hiereus is stationed upon the darkest section of Malkuth and he represents "a Terrible and Avenging God at the Confines of Matter, at the borders of the Qlippoth [...] is he placed as a mighty and avenging Guardian to the Sacred Mysteries. The Symbols and Insignia of Hiereus are: The Throne of the West in the Black of Malkuth, where it borders on the Kingdom of Shells..."[36] Acting under the holy warrior godform of Horus, the Hiereus defends the temple and protects the entering candidate from the coils of the qlippoth.

The blueprint of the Tree of Life also exists *vertically* within the Hall, therefore the Kingdom of Shells is also situated astrally in the center of the hall, under the floor. This is the invisible Station of Omoo-Sathan, a synthesis of Typhon, Apophis and Set, also called the Evil Triad. "The Evil Persona is a composite figure of the powers arising from the qlippoth. It rises from the eastern base of the Altar facing west, in the Sign of Typhon."[37] In the Ceremony of the Neophyte, Omoo-Sathan is the Accuser who would bind the candidate's soul in darkness with the energies of the qlippoth.

> "At this moment, as the Candidate stands before the Altar, as the simulacrum of the Higher Self is attracted, so also arises the form of the Accuser in the place of the Evil Triad. [...] For seeing that at this time, the simulacrum of the Higher Soul is attracting the Neschamah of the Candidate, the human will is not as powerful in the Ruach for the moment, because the Aspirant of the Mysteries is now, as it were, divided. That is, his Neschamah is directed to the contemplation of his Higher Self [...] his Ruach threatened by simulacrum of

---

36 Regardie, "Z-1: The Enterer of the Threshold," *The Golden Dawn*, 337.
37 Ibid., 357.

the Evil Triad attracted by Omoo-Szathan, and a species of shadow of himself thrown forward to the place of the Pillars, where the scales of Judgment are set. [...] Rarely in his life has he (the Candidate) been nearer death, seeing that he is, as it were, disintegrated into his component parts. The process of symbolic judgment takes place during the speech of the Hierophant to the Candidate, the answer of the Hegemon and his consent to take the Obligation."[38]

Once again, the temple, and specifically the candidate, are protected from the qlippoth forces, this time by Horus the Elder, acting through the Hierophant who treads upon the head of the Evil Triad as the candidate is readied to take the Obligation: "The moment the Candidate thus consents, the Hierophant advances between the Pillars as if to assert that the Judgment is concluded. He advances by the invisible station of Harpocrates to that of the Evil Triad, which he symbolically treads down, so that as Aroueris he stands upon the Opposer."[39] Once again, the warrior godform of Horus acts to defend the temple from the uprising of the qlippoth, and once again protects the candidate from the forces of evil. The psychic crisis is averted. None of the astral work of this ritual is described to the Neophyte undergoing initiation; he does not learn of it until much later in the Second Order. (The act of stomping down evil is later repeated after a fashion by the Chief Adept in the 5=6 Ritual stamping thrice on the head of the Qlippothic Red Dragon with ten heads and seven horns.)

The qlippoth are next found in the Zelator Ritual where they are mentioned in conjunction with the courtyard of the Hebrew Tabernacle "whereon was offered the Sacrifices of animals, which symbolized the Qlippoth or Evil Demons who inhabit the plane contiguous to and below the Material Universe." The aspirant is met by "the Great Angel Samael" played by the Hiereus, who prevents the aspirant from venturing on the Path of Evil, the left-hand side of the Tree and the Black Pillar of Severity. In Judaism, the name of Samael is synonymous with Satan. Samael is one of the best known of the qlippoth, and is often cited as one of the rebel angels in the grimoires.

---

[38] Regardie, "Z-3, The Symbolism of the Admission of the Candidate," *The Golden Dawn*, 365.

[39] Ibid., 366.

His presence in the Zelator Ritual serves as a stern warning from one who has traversed the Path of Evil. "And the Great Angel Samael answered, and said: I am the Prince of Darkness and of Night. The foolish and *rebellious*[40] gaze upon the face of the Created World and find therein nothing but terror and obscurity. It is to them the terror of Darkness and they are as drunken men stumbling. Return, for thou canst not pass by."[41]

The Admission Badge for the Grade of Zelator is the Fylfot Cross, also called the Swastika. This cross is constructed from the qamea of Mars; formed from seventeen of the qamea's twenty-five units. The martial association of this qamea aligns it with Geburah on the Pillar of Severity. Here again is a reference to *din* (judgment) as the aspirant takes his first step onto the Sephirah Malkuth, whose virtue is discrimination.

In the Theoricus Grade, the qlippoth are described in reference to the 32nd Path of Tau. This path alludes to "the Universe as composed of the Four Elements—to the KERUBIM, the QLIPPOTH and the Astral Plane, and the reflection of the sphere of SATURN."[42] The Path of Tau connects Malkuth to Yesod and is one of the primary paths leading away from the Kingdom of Shells toward the crown of Kether.

Knowledge of the breaking of the vessels and the resulting Fall is explained in two phases: the harmonious, pre-Fall stage is examined in the Water Grade of Practicus, while the harsh second stage, that of the shattering of the Sephirotic Tree and the Fall itself, is explained in the Fire Grade of Philosophus.

In the Practicus Grade the aspirant is shown the diagram of the Garden of Eden Before the Fall and learns that "in the garden was the Tree of Knowledge of Good and Evil, which latter is from Malkuth, which is the lowest Sephirah between the rest of the Sephiroth and the kingdom of shells, which latter is represented by the great red dragon coiled beneath, having seven heads (the seven infernal palaces) and ten horns - (the ten averse Sephiroth of evil, contained in the seven palaces)."[43]

---

40 Italics are ours.
41 Regardie, "Ceremony of the 1=10 Grade of Zelator," *The Golden Dawn*, 146.
42 Regardie, "Ceremony of the 2=9 Grade of Theoricus," *The Golden Dawn*, 155.
43 Regardie, "Ceremony of the 3=8 Grade of Practicus," *The Golden Dawn*, 177.

THE LIGHT EXTENDED

The qlippoth are not the only demonic forces mentioned in the Practicus Ritual. This ceremony incorporates elements of the Samothracian Mysteries as well as the Chaldean Oracles, a combination of Neoplatonic philosophy and Persian elements. Here the Hierophant tells the aspirant to hold fast to the path of Divine Theurgy, and warns him to guard against evil spirits that are the primary source of temptation for human souls, leading them off the spiritual path. "Then when no longer are visible to thee the Vault of the Heavens, and the Mass of the Earth; when to Thee, the Stars have lost their light and the Lamp of the Moon is veiled; when the Earth abideth not and around thee is the Lightning Flame—then call not before thyself the Visible Image of the Soul of Nature, for thou must not behold it ere thy body is purged by the Sacred Rites—since, ever dragging down the Soul and leading it from the Sacred Things, from the confines of Matter, arise the terrible Dog-faced Demons, never showing true image unto mortal gaze."[44] Banishing these forces and liberating the soul from their influence was a major part of the work of the ancient Theurgist.

The Fire Grade is where the Golden Dawn student learns much more information concerning the qlippoth. Whereas the Practicus first learned of the great red dragon in its latent form sleeping beneath Malkuth in the diagram of the Garden of Eden, the Philosophus is shown the aftermath of the breaking of the vessels in the Garden of Eden After the Fall, a diagram that is explained to the aspirant with a combination of biblical lore and Lurianic philosophy:

> "For, the Great Goddess, Eve, who in the 3 = 8 Grade was supporting the Columns of the Sephiroth, in the Sign of the 2 = 9 Grade, being tempted by the Tree of Knowledge (whose branches indeed tend upward into the Seven Lower Sephiroth, but also tend downward unto the Kingdom of Shells) reached

---

44 Ibid., 171. The dog-faced demons are also mentioned in Z-3: "The Candidate is waiting without the Portal under the care of the Sentinel —'The Watcher Without'—that is, under the care of the form of Anubis of the West symbolically that he may keep off the 'Dog-Faced Demons,' the opposers of Anubis, who rise from the confines where matter ends, to deceive and drag down the Soul. The Ritual of the 31st Path says: 'Since ever dragging down the Soul and leading it from sacred things, from the confines of matter arise the terrible Dog-Faced Demons never showing a true image unto mortal gaze.'" 363.

HOW THE MIGHTY HAVE FALLEN

downward unto the Qlippoth, and immediately the Columns were unsupported and the Sephirotic system was shattered, and with it fell ADAM, the MICROPROSOPUS.

Then arose the Great Dragon with Seven Heads and Ten Horns, and the Garden was made desolate, and MALKUTH was cut off from the Sephiroth by his intersecting folds, and linked unto the Kingdom of Shells. And the Seven Lower Sephiroth were cut off from the Three Supernals in DAATH, at the feet of AIMA ELOHIM.

And on the Heads of the Dragon are the Names and Crowns of the Edomite Kings. And because in DAATH was the greatest rise of the Great Serpent of Evil, therefore is there, as it were, another Sephiroth, making for the Infernal or Averse Sephiroth, Eleven instead of Ten.

And hence were the Rivers of Eden desecrated, and from the Mouth of the Dragon rushed the Infernal Waters in DAATH. And this is LEVIATHAN, the Crooked Serpent.

But between the Devastated Garden and the Supernal Eden, YHVH ELOHIM placed the Letters of the NAME and the FLASHING SWORD that the uppermost part of the Tree of Life might not be involved in the Fall of Adam. And thence it was necessary that the SECOND ADAM should come *to restore all things*[45] and that, as the First Adam had been extended on the Cross of the Celestial Rivers, so the SON should be crucified on the Cross of the Infernal Rivers of DAATH. Yet, to do this, he must descend unto the lowest first, even unto Malkuth and be born of her."[46]

Tikkun: The Mending

How is the process of rescuing the divine sparks trapped within the fallen shells accomplished? According to the Qabalists, it is through the action of *tikkun* or "redemption":

"Later Kabbalists have lavished a great deal of further

---

45 Italics are ours.
46 Regardie, "Ceremony of the 4=7 Grade of Philosophus," *The Golden Dawn*, 194.

speculative thought on this point. According to some of them, the Breaking of the Vessels is connected, like so many other things, with the law of organic life in the theosophical universe. Just as the seed must burst in order to sprout and blossom, so too the first bowls had to be shattered in order that the divine light, the cosmic seed so to speak, might fulfill its function. At any rate the Breaking of the Bowls, of which we find exhaustive descriptions in the literature of Lurianic Kabbalism, is the decisive turning point in the cosmological process. Taken as a whole, it is the cause of that inner deficiency which is inherent in everything that exists and which persists as long as the damage is not mended. For when the bowls were broken the light either diffused or flowed back to its source, or flowed downwards. The fiendish nether-worlds of evil, the influence of which crept into all stages of the cosmological process, emerged from the fragments which still retained a few sparks of the holy light—Luria speaks of just 288. In this way the good elements of the divine order came to be mixed with the vicious ones. Conversely the restoration of the ideal order, which forms the original aim of creation, is also the secret purpose of existence. Salvation means actually nothing but restitution, re-integration of the original whole, or *Tikkun,* to use the Hebrew term. Naturally enough the mysteries of *Tikkun* are the chief concern of Luria's theosophical system, theoretical and practical."[47]

Tikkun is the restoration of the divine universe to its primal purity and design; the reversal of the confusion and chaos caused by the Breaking of the Vessels. With the creation of the partzufim, a new pattern of dynamics was introduced to the Tree of Life as part of the process of tikkun, to cleanse and reconstruct the Tree. The Divine Light from the Atzluthic World of the partzufim passes down into the other Qabalistic worlds. The full potency of the Light is filtered and modified on its descent, but the complete process of tikkun can only be completed by mankind. The human task is to restore the system of the Tree of Life by restoring the World of Assiah, the

---

47 Scholem, *Major Trends in Jewish Mysticism*, 268.

Physical World, to its original state of spirituality; to remove it from the realm of the qlippoth and permit a state of ultimate unity to exist between every being and the Divine, uninterrupted by the qlippoth. This task is an inner spiritual cleansing which is to be undertaken by each individual.

The perennial question of why the Divine allowed evil to come into existence is a topic that reaches far beyond the scope of this article. But according to the Qabalah, when the Vessels shattered, some of the shards fell away from the partzufim and became the essence of evil:

> "Evil, then, was created from fallen good. The primary reason for this was so that it could be elevated back again to the good. If evil had existed as an entity unto itself, there may have been no way to make evil other than what it was. But if evil were was really broken shards of good, then it would certainly be possible to take them and bring them back to their original source. At that point, they would become good again. This is indeed what Jewish mystics see as the task of humanity as a whole and of every individual. Man's role on earth is to take these broken pieces and, through our actions and way of life, to elevate them back to the source of good. When this cosmic process is completed, all evil as we understand it today will cease to exist. From God's point of view, therefore, first there was good and then there was evil. But on our level, evil came before good; that is why we have darkness preceding light."[48]

Restoring the Vessels

The Golden Dawn teachings regarding the qlippoth, demons, and fallen spirits runs parallel to the Qabalistic idea of tikkun. All of these broken vessels contain a spark of the Divine Light. Our goal is not to condemn, destroy, torture, or enslave such entities. Neither do we mistake them for misunderstood nature spirits. We do not need their help in obtaining spiritual gifts or otherwise manifesting our goals. Instead, we work unhesitatingly in fellowship with the archangels and angels in such matters for they are our companions in

---
48 Sheinkin, 91.

"the Great Chain of Being." We are connected to the spiritual entities by virtue of belonging to the same ultimate Macrocosmic Tree of Life: "All the Shining Ones (whom we call Angels) are microcosms of the Macrocosm Yetzirah, even as Man is the microcosm of the Macrocosm of Assiah. All Archangelic forms are microcosms of the Macrocosm of Briah, and the Gods of the Sephiroth are consequently the Microcosms of the Macrocosm of Atziluth. Therefore apply this perfecting of the Spiritual Nature as the preparation of the Pathway for the Shining Light, the Light Divine."[49] The higher angels and archangels stand ready to assist the magician who reaches out to them in friendship, with respect. "For the True Order of the Rose Cross descendeth into the depths, and ascendeth into the heights—even unto the Throne of God himself, and includeth even Archangels, Angels and Spirits."[50]

At various points in the rituals, we are given hints concerning the restoration of the shards. In the Practicus Ritual we are told:

> "Nature persuadeth us that there are pure daemons and that even the evil germs of matter may alike become useful and good. But these are Mysteries which are evolved in the profound abyss of the Mind."[51]

And in the Adeptus Minor Ceremony:

> "The Floor has upon it also the Symbol of a Triangle enclosed within a Heptagram, bearing the titles of the Averse and Evil Sephiroth of the Qlippoth, the Great Red Dragon of Seven Heads, and the inverted and evil triangle. And thus in the tomb of the Adepti do we tread down the Evil Powers of the Red Dragon and so tread thou upon the evil powers of thy nature. For there is traced within the evil Triangle the rescuing Symbol of the Golden Cross united to the Red Rose of Seven times Seven Petals. As it is written 'He descendeth into Hell.' But the whiteness above shines the brighter for the Blackness

---

49 Regardie, "The Microcosm - Man," *The Golden Dawn*, 106.
50 Regardie, "Ceremony of the 5=6 Grade of Adeptus Minor," *The Golden Dawn*, 231.
51 Regardie, "Ceremony of the 3=8 Grade of Practicus," *The Golden Dawn*, 171.

which is beneath, and thus mayest thou comprehend that the evil helpeth forward the Good."[52]

On its face, this passage states that, by emphasizing the perceived difference between Light and Darkness, the Light seems brighter, and therefore "the evil helpeth forward the good." But this does not appear to be the only meaning. The previous quotation from the Practicus Ritual states that even evil "can become useful and good." This does not mean that it can be *used* for good, it can be *transformed* into good. The "rescuing symbol" of the Golden Cross and the Red Rose, is not simply placed on the floor of the Vault for the benefit of the aspirant, it is placed *within* the evil to rescue *it* as well.

In his paper on "The Devil, and Evil Spirits," Westcott tells us: "Like all other forms of being Samael proceeded from the One Infinite Source, and must in the end return to Light and purity and to the One Fount; at which time Samael, SMAL, will lose his Poison SM and remain AL, an angel of God: Hell will disappear, and with them all sin, and there will be one eternal Sabbath of Peace."[53] How can this be achieved?

It is important to remember the Hermetic Axiom "As Above, So Below." While some will argue that the gods, angels and spirits we work with as magicians are completely separate beings that exist outside of man, others will insist that all spiritual beings are merely archetypes that have no real existence outside of human psychology. The truth embraces the middle path: these are merely two sides of the same coin. Angels and demons exist both within and without of our psyches—they dwell in the Great Macrocosm beyond as well as within the mind of the Microcosm in man. What is the lynch pin that connects the two? WE are. We have the opportunity to become reconcilers and redeemers, forged in the image of the Christos. For this task we need only turn to the ideas expressed in Qabalah and alchemy. Both systems hold that humanity alone has the ability to form a connecting link between the heights and the depths, between Kether and Malkuth. "Humanity is the alchemical retort whereby the two can be made one, and the Tree of Life restored to balance

---

[52] Regardie, "Ceremony of the 5=6 Grade of Adeptus Minor," *The Golden Dawn*, 243.
[53] Gilbert, *The Magical Mason*, 135.

and harmony."[54]

There are numerous references to the alchemical process of separation in the Lurianic Qabalah with regard to the breaking of the vessels. There are also frequent references to purification. In similar fashion, the breaking apart of a material in the alchemical process of separation is a vital step in obtaining the Philosopher's stone. In terms of Jungian psychology, the Light trapped within the darkness of the "shells" is akin to autonomous complexes and shadow aspects of the subconscious. Rituals of purification and consecration act as outer expressions of a psychological process of confronting the shadow aspects with the human psyche. As these shadow fragments are brought into the awareness of the conscious mind, Darkness becomes Light, the shattered pieces of the vessels are collected and the Restoration is complete. According to author Steven Marshall:

> "The goal is to produce a complete and perfect separation of the Light from the Darkness. Lurianic Qabalah, like many Gnostic schools, ignores the redemption of the darkness of matter in this process. The symbolism of alchemy supplies a missing key in describing the redemption and transmutation of matter itself as an essential part of restoring the unity of the Tree of Life. The key that is provided by alchemical symbolism is its emphasis on the transformation of the dregs left behind. The separation and release of the spirit are but the beginning of the alchemical process. After the separation, the gross matter must be clarified and transformed through the processes of purification and conjunction."[55]

He goes on to say:

> "Purification is the second basic process in the practice of the spagyric method of alchemy. In this process, purification does not refer merely to the separation of the spirit from the dregs of matter but a purification of the dregs or body of the

---

[54] Marshall, Steven, "The Restoration and Alchemy, *The Golden Dawn Journal: Book Two: Qabalah: Theory and Magic*, (St. Paul, MN: Llewellyn Publications, 1994), 105.
[55] Ibid., 108.

material in order to re-unite it with its spirit upon a higher level of manifestation."[56]

"The alchemist purifies the Salt or dregs of the matter through leaching with water, evaporation and calcination to an ash. Again, the elements of fire and water play a key role in the process of purification. Often, in the final stages of purifying the Salt, the ashes fuse into a translucent glass-like material. From this phenomenon, the term vitriol occurs repeatedly in the alchemical literature, which means "a glass-like substance." This suggests that the "shells" or "qliphoth" of the Tree of Life, must also be purified, so that they lose their opacity and resistance to the Light, and become clear, pellucid mirrors of the Divine Effulgence of Kether."[57]

In closing: just as the alchemical process requires a careful blending of the purified principles of Mercury, Sulphur, and Salt to result in the successful creation of the Stone, Qabalah requires that a proper balance be struck between the two Sephiroth of Geburah and Chesed, between severity and mercy. The same is also a fundamental part of tikkun and the Restoration. This essential truth is stressed continuously again and again, and is clearly emphasized to the Neophyte in a phrase that lies unequivocally at the core of the Golden Dawn's teaching:

Unbalanced Power is the ebbing away of Life.
Unbalanced Mercy is weakness and the fading of the Will.
Unbalanced Severity is cruelty and the barrenness of Mind.

"When the times are ended,
He will call the Kerubim
from the East of the Garden,
and all shall be consumed
and become Infinite and Holy."

---

56 Ibid.
57 Ibid., 109.

Sources

Agrippa, Cornelius. *Three Books of Occult Philosophy*. Edited and annotated by Donald Tyson. St. Paul, MN: Llewellyn Publications, 1993.

Davidson, Gustav. *A Dictionary of Angels including the Fallen Angels*. New York: The Free Press, 1971.

Frater Barrabbas, *Magical Qabalah for Beginners: A Comprehensive Guide to Occult Knowledge,* Woodbury, MN: Llewellyn Publications, 2013.

Finkelstein, Israel and Neil Asher Silberman. *The Bible Unearthed: Archeology's New Vision of Ancient Israel and the Origin of Its Sacred Texts*. New York: The Free Press, 2001.

Forrest, Adam P., "This Holy Invisible Companionship," *The Golden Dawn Journal: Book II: Qabalah: Theory and Magic,* St. Paul, MN: Llewellyn Publications, 1994.

Frater Barrabbas. "Problems with Goetic Magick and the Black Grimoires." *Talking About Ritual Magick*. November 10, 2009. http://fraterbarrabbas.blogspot.com/2009/11/problems-with-goetic-magick-and-black.html. Accessed 2/1/2017.

Gilbert, R.A., *The Magical Mason: Forgotten Hermetic Writings of William Wynn Westcott, Physician and Magus*. Great Britain: The Aquarian Press, 1983.

_____, *The Sorcerer and His Apprentice: Unknown Hermetic Writings of S.L. MacGregor Mathers and Brodie-Innes*. Great Britain: The Aquarian Press, 1983.

Ginzberg, Louis. *Legends of the Bible*. Old Saybrook, CT: Konecky & Konecky, 2001.

Godwin, David, *Godwin's Cabalistic Encyclopedia*. ST. Paul, MN: 1994.

Great Grimoire of Pope Honorius, Seattle, WA: Trident Books, 1999.

Greer, John Michael. *Circles of Power*. St. Paul, MN: Llewellyn Publications, 1997.

_____, *The New Encyclopedia of the Occult*. St. Paul, MN: Llewellyn Publications, 2003.

Kieckhefer, Richard. *Magic in the Middle Ages*. United Kingdom: Cambridge University Press, 2000.

Laurence, Richard. *The Book of Enoch the Prophet*. San Diego, CA: Wizards Bookshelf, 1983.

Marshall, Steven, "The Restoration and Alchemy, *The Golden Dawn Journal: Book Two: Qabalah: Theory and Magic*, St. Paul, MN: Llewellyn Publications, 1994.

Mathers, Samuel Liddell MacGregor. *The Goetia: Lesser Key of Solomon the King*. Boston, MA: Red Wheel/Weiser, 1995.

Peterson, Joseph, "Liber Juratus Honorii," *Twilight Grotto — Esoteric Archives*. http://www.esotericarchives.com/juratus/juratus.htm, Accessed 2/2/17.

Reed, Annette Yoshiko. *Fallen Angels and the History of Judaism and Christianity: The Reception of Enochic Literature*. New York: Cambridge University Press, 2005.

Regardie, Israel. *The Golden Dawn: The Original Account of the Teachings, Rites, and Ceremonies of the Hermetic Order*. St. Paul, MN: Llewellyn Publications, 1989

Scholem, Gershom. *Kabbalah*. New York: Dorset Press, 1974.

_____, *Major Trends in Jewish Mysticism*. New York: Schoken Books 1967.

_____, *Sabbatai Sevi: The Mystical Messiah*, Princeton, NJ: Princeton University Press, 1973.

Skeinkin, David. *Path of the Kabbalah*. New York: Paragon House, 1986.

Van Der Toorn, Karel, Bob Becking and Van Der Horst. (ed.) *Dictionary of Deities and Demons in the Bible*, Grand Rapids, MI: Brill Academic Publishers and William B. Eerdmans Publishing Co., 1999.

Vermes, Geza. "The Book Enoch and the Book of Giants," *The Complete Dead Sea Scrolls in English*. New York: The Penguin Press, 1997.

Wall, J. Charles. *Devils: Their Origins and History*. London: Studio Editions, 1992.

About the Authors

Charles "Chic" Cicero was born in Buffalo, New York. An early love of music, particularly of the saxophone, resulted in Chic's many years of experience as a lead musician in several jazz, blues and rock ensembles, working with many famous performers in the music industry. His interest in Freemasonry and the Western Esoteric Tradition resulted in research articles on Rosicrucianism and the Knights Templar, printed in such publications as *Ars Quatuor Coronatorum and the 1996-2000 Transactions of the Metropolitan College of the SRIA*. Chic is a member of several Masonic, Martinist, and Rosicrucian organizations. He is a Past Grand Commander of the Grand Commandery of Knights Templar in Florida (2010–2011) and is the current Chief Adept of the Florida College of the Societas Rosicruciana in Civitatibus Foederatis. A close personal friend and confidant of Dr. Israel Regardie, Chic established a Golden Dawn temple in 1977 and was one of the key people who helped Regardie resurrect a legitimate branch of the Hermetic Order of the Golden Dawn in the United States in the early 1980s, with initiatory lineage that dates back to the original Order of 1888. He met his wife and co-author, Sandra Tabatha Cicero, shortly thereafter. Chic served as the G.H. Cancellarius of the Hermetic Order of the Golden Dawn from 1985 to 1994, and as G.H. Imperator of the Order from 1994 to the present day.

Sandra "Tabatha" Cicero was born in rural Wisconsin. A lifelong fascination with the creative arts has served to inspire her work in the magical world. After graduating from the University of Wisconsin-Milwaukee with a Bachelor's Degree in Fine Arts in 1982, Tabatha worked as an entertainer, typesetter, editor, commercial artist, and computer graphics illustrator. In 2009 she obtained a degree in Paralegal Studies. She met Chic Cicero in in 1983 and the Golden Dawn system of magic has been her primary spiritual focus ever since. Tabatha spent five years working on the paintings for *The Golden Dawn Magical Tarot* which she began at the encouragement of Israel Regardie. Tabatha is a member of several Martinist and Rosicrucian organizations, and is the current Imperatrix of the Societas Rosicruciana in America (www.sria.org). She has served as the G.H. Cancellaria of the Hermetic Order of the Golden Dawn from 1994 to the present day.

Both Chic and Tabatha are Chief Adepts of the Hermetic Order of the Golden Dawn as re-established by Israel Regardie (www.hermeticgoldendawn.org), the oldest continuously operating Golden Dawn Order in the United States, as well as an international Order with temples in several other countries.

The Lesser Ritual of the Pentagram

The Foundational Ritual of the Golden Dawn Tradition

by Samuel Scarborough

The Lesser Ritual of the Pentagram, the very first ritual that any Neophyte of the Golden Dawn is supposed to learn and practice on a regular basis, and has over the ensuing 120 plus years since the founding of the Golden Dawn in 1888, has become one of the most widely used and even misunderstood rituals in Ceremonial Magic. In fact, this foundational ritual of the Golden Dawn has even found its way into other magical traditions which have incorporated it into their work and understanding. With the proliferation of information via the Internet and through nearly all beginner's books on Ceremonial (and other forms of) Magic more has been written on this ritual with each author placing their own spin on it.

In the Outer Order we are given two aspects of the Lesser Pentagram Ritual to use for our growth and protection. These are the Lesser *Banishing* Ritual of the Pentagram and the Lesser *Invoking* Ritual of the Pentagram. These aspects of the same ritual can be seen as the quintessential Golden Dawn Ritual, though there is often some confusion among the students in the Outer Order as to just what these particular Pentagram Rituals do and represent.

If you will notice, I refer to the ritual as the *Lesser Ritual of the Pentagram*. In many modern books, and even websites, referencing this ritual generally concentrate merely on one of the two aspects mentioned above; the *Lesser Banishing Ritual of the Pentagram* also called the LBRP, while neglecting the Invoking aspect altogether for the Neophyte to learn, practice, and use.

The traditional name of this ritual is the Lesser Ritual of the Pentagram, and when you look at the early published versions from Aleister Crowley and later Israel Regardie, you will see this name used. In fact, the verbiage given in Regardie's seminal work, *The Golden Dawn*[1], originally published by Aries Press and later by Llewellyn, gives a great example of how this first ritual was viewed by the members of the Stella Matutina and the previous Hermetic Order of the Golden Dawn.

Over the ensuing years there have been many misconceptions that have been built up surrounding this ritual, many of which will be discussed in this article.

General Symbolism of the Pentagram

Looking at the Pentagram as a symbol and what that symbol represents is a good way to understand how this symbol is used as a glyph within Golden Dawn rituals. First, we must have a good definition of what a pentagram is and where it derives its name.

The word itself is derived from the Greek Πεντάγραμμον (Pentagrammon), meaning a figure of five lines (Penta = five and Gram = lines). It is a mathematical figure formed by extending the sides of a regular pentagon to meet at five points. The figure or lineal figure is sometimes referred to as a pentalpha or pentangle, and sometimes as a pentacle. This figure can be seen in Fig. 1 below.

Fig. 1. A regular pentagram

---

1 While Regardie titled his work *The Golden Dawn*, the material in it was drawn from the Stella Matutina, of which he was a member in the mid 1930s. The Stella Matutina was one of the three offshoot Orders that came about after the collapse of the original Golden Dawn Order in 1903.

THE LESSER RITUAL OF THE PENTAGRAM

The pentagram is also recognized as a form of a star. Juan Eduardo Cirlot in his *A Dictionary of Symbols* gives the following information on stars, of which the pentagram is a five-pointed example:

> "As a light shining in the darkness, the star is a symbol of the spirit. Bayley has pointed out, however, that the star very rarely carries a single meaning – it nearly always alludes to multiplicity. In which case it stands for the forces of the spirit struggling against the forces of darkness. This is a meaning which has been incorporated into emblematic art all over the world. For this reason, 'identification with the star' is possible only to the chosen few. Jung recalls the Mithraic saying: 'I am a star which goes with thee and shines out of the depths'. Now, individual stars are often seen in graphic symbolism. Their meaning frequently depends upon their shape, the number of points, the manner of their arrangement and their colour (if any). The 'flaming star' is a symbol of the mystic Centre – of the force of the universe in expansion. The five pointed star is the most common. As far back as in the days of Egyptian hieroglyphics, it signified 'rising upwards towards the point of origin' and formed part of such words as 'to bring up', 'to educate', 'the teacher', etc. The inverted five-pointed star is a symbol of the infernal used in black magic."[2]

To further illustrate the above concepts which relate to star shapes, especially the five-pointed star or pentagram, particularly when used as a magickal symbol, Eliphas Lévi in his seminal work *Transcendental Magic* has the following to say concerning the pentagram in this form:

> "The Pentagram, which in Gnostic schools is called the Blazing Star, is the sign of intellectual omnipotence and autocracy. It is the Star of the Magi; it is the sign of the Word made flesh; and, according

---

2   Cirlot, *A Dictionary of Symbols*, pp. 309-310.

to the direction of its points, this absolute magical symbol represents order or confusion, the Divine Lamb of Ormuz and St John, or the accursed goat of Mendes. It is initiation or profanation; it is Lucifer or Vesper, the star of morning or evening. It is Mary or Lilith, victory or death, day or night. The Pentagram with two points in the ascendant represents Satan as the goat of the Sabbath; when one point is in the ascendant, it is the sign of the Saviour."[3]

Lévi also goes on to say about the pentagram:

"The Pentagram signifies the domination of the mind over the elements, and the demons of air, the spirits of fire, the phantoms of water and ghosts of earth enchained by this sign. Equipped therewith, and suitably disposed, you may behold the infinite through the medium of that faculty which is like the soul's eye, and you will be ministered unto by legions of angels and hosts of fiends."[4]

The symbolism of the pentagram continues on in Western religion and esoteric thought as well. In Neoplatonic thought, the pentagram was said to have been used by the Pythagorean Brotherhood, called by them hugieia ὑγιεία "health", as a sign or symbol of recognition.[5]

---

[3] Lévi. *Transcendental Magic*, p. 237.
[4] Ibid, p. 63.
[5] Allman, G.J. *Greek Geometry From Thales to Euclid*, pp. 183, 197. citing Iamblichus and the Scholiast on Aristophanes. The pentagram was said to have been so called from Pythagoras himself having written the letters Υ, Γ, Ι, Θ (= / ei/), A on its vertices.

THE LESSER RITUAL OF THE PENTAGRAM

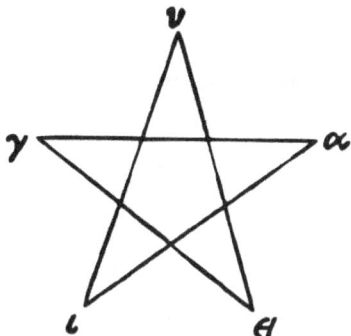

Fig. 2. Pythagorean Hugieia Pentagram

The pentagram as an early Christian symbol was used to represent the Five Holy Wounds or the Five Sacred Wounds of Christ; comprising of one wound each in the hand or wrist, one each in the feet, and one in the side or chest. This symbolism even was transferred to the Arthurian knight Sir Gawain as the heraldric device borne upon his shield.

It is the esoteric symbolism of the pentagram that we are more interested in rather than its mathematical or religious connotations. Henrich Cornelius Agrippa, in his seminal *Three Books of Occult Philosophy*, ascribes the five Neoplatonic Elements to its five points, thus recalling the Pythagorean Hugieia Pentagram.

Fig. 3. Neoplatonic Elements ascribed to the five points of the pentagram as per Agrippa

In this arrangement, as seen in Figure 3, Agrippa attributes the Neoplatonic Element of Fire to the lower right arm of the pentagram while proceeding counter-clockwise in sequence so that Earth is placed at the lower left of the pentagram. At the top arm of the pentagram is placed Spirit or Quintessence (Fifth Essence or Element) which is the highest and most pure element that permeates all of Nature and is the substance comprising the celestial bodies according to ancient and medieval philosophy[6].

This is the arrangement that has become the most popular esoterically since the Renaissance when Agrippa first published it, and is used in many different esoteric traditions in the modern era.

Some Misconceptions Related to the Lesser Ritual of the Pentagram

Due to ubiquiteousness of the Lesser Ritual of the Pentagram, normally just the Banishing aspect, throughout much of the esoteric traditions in the modern era, many believe that the *Banishing* aspect of the Lesser Ritual of the Pentagram is all that there is to this foundational Golden Dawn ritual.

Others have stated that the pentagrams of the Lesser Ritual of the Pentagram are Elemental (in reference to the four basic Elements of Neoplatonic thought) based upon the way that these pentagrams are traced.

The use of Hebrew Divine Names to charge the pentagrams and the use of the four Archangels make this ritual clearly only usable to those of the Judeo-Christian faiths and philosophies, and are antithecal for use by those of a different religion or philosophy.

The color visualized while and after tracing the pentagrams used in the Lesser Ritual of the Pentagram are another sticking point, along with the colors associated with the four Archangels.

There are other arguments and misconceptions relating to the Lesser Ritual of the Pentagram, but the above are the primary ones that come up in discussions relating to this ritual.

First off, let us address the **Banishing** only aspect of the Lesser

---

6 Spirit or Quintessence was derived from the Greek Aether which Aristotle proposed as the "fifth element" over the four physical elements and it is from the Aristotlian Elements that Agrippa draws inspiration for his arrangement.

THE LESSER RITUAL OF THE PENTAGRAM

Ritual of the Pentagram.

When looking at the version of the Lesser Ritual of the Pentagram as given in Regardie's *The Golden Dawn*[7] and comparing it with original copies from the Golden Dawn's Isis-Urania Temple in London from about 1890 there is very little difference between the two versions. The name for the ritual given is The Lesser Ritual of the Pentagram and it begins with the Qabalistical Cross (later called the Qabalistic Cross or abbreivated as QC) followed by the **Invoking** version of the ritual. The Banishing version is nearly relagated to being an afterthought in the original versions as can be seen in the following quote:

> "For Banishing use the same Ritual, but reversing the direction of the lines of the Pentagram."[8]

In Regardie's *The Golden Dawn*, the paper that he is citing from the Hermes Temple of the Stella Matutina then operating in Bristol, England. The Stella Matutina being one of the three offshoot Orders after the collapse of the original Hermetic Order of the Golden Dawn.

While it can be argued that this published version could be seen as something that the "rebels" that broke with Mathers in 1900 could have altered, but if we look at the verbiage from an original version of the Lesser Ritual of the Pentagram from the London Isis-Urania Temple we see:

> "The Ritual is the Same as that of the Invoking save that the Banishing Pentagram is be traced instead of the Invoking."[9]

This sort of verbiage can be found on other exant copies from the original Hermetic Order of the Golden Dawn, and on copies from the later Rosicrucian Order of the Alpha et Omega (the offshoot

---

7 Regardie. *The Golden Dawn*, pp. 53-55.
8 Ibid. p. 54.
9 From an original copy of *The Lesser Ritual of the Pentagram* copied by George T. Pollexfen (Frater F.L.) on 3 February 1893 in the National Library of Ireland, Dublin.

Order headed by and loyal to Samuel L. Mathers) and the Stella Matutina. This leads to the conclusion that the primary version of this Ritual given to the Neophyte was the Invoking one throughout the early Golden Dawn Tradition.

While the names Lesser Banishing Ritual of the Pentagram and Lesser Invoking Ritual of the Pentagram was utilized in all the original Orders (many times simply abbreviated as either LBRP or LIRP respectively), they were called that for specific use, such as Banishing prior to a major working in the overall ritual formualae of the Golden Dawn known as the Z2 Formulae, it is only in the modern era that the name of the Lesser Ritual of the Pentagram became known as the *Lesser Banishing Ritual of the Pentagram.*

This change came about in the last 25-30 years with the proliferation of books published on ceremonial and other forms of magic, and the Internet. As more and more was published, often merely repeating what a previous author had written, the name sort of stuck as the overall name of the ritual amongst modern practitioners, since many of these modern authors also advocated the banishing version for use exclusively.

But since this ritual is a foundational ritual of the Golden Dawn Tradition, the name, in general use within the Golden Dawn, is and should be the *Lesser Ritual of the Pentagram.*

One of the arguments of the name of the ritual also applies to the functionality of the ritual itself. By merely concentrating on one aspect, the Banishing, the overall ritual is left with only half its use by the practitioner.

In true Golden Dawn manner, the use of balance comes into play. Balance here relates to the balance of approach, the equilibrium of force, of good and evil, light and darkness. All of which are addressed within the Neophyte Ceremony itself:

> "Unbalanced Power is the ebbing away of Life.
> Unbalanced Mercy is weakness and the fading out of the Will.
> Unbalanced Severity is cruelty and the barreness of the Mind ..."[10]

---

10 Regardie. *The Golden Dawn*, p.125.

THE LESSER RITUAL OF THE PENTAGRAM

The above taken from the Neophyte Ceremony exortium given by the Hierophant to the thrice consecrated Candidate gives the full meaning of the use of balance and moderation in all things. This also applies to ritual work, particularly that of the Neophyte.

The over use of the banishing aspect of this ritual was known even in the original Golden Dawn in London in the nineteenth century. Contained within an unpublished original Golden Dawn paper written about 1895 which is titled *As to the Invoking and Banishing of Forces by Means of the Rituals of Pentagram and Hexagram* there is a note stating, "The effect of continually using the banishing pentagrams is the weakening of the person who thus uses it."[11] What is meant here by "weakening of the person" is that through the over use of the Banishing Pentagram posed at threat to the physical well-being, as well as the general sphere of sensation of the practitioner.

Having covered the Banishing *only* misconception of this ritual a bit, let us move on to the next misconception; that of the Pentagrams used in the Lesser Ritual of the Pentagram as being Elemental.

This is a persistent misconception based on the symbolism of the Pentagram as given by Agrippa aligning the four Neoplatonic Elements to the arms or points of the Pentagram. While the arms or points of the Pentagram can and are ascribed to these Elements, not all pentagrams are of an Elemental Nature.

Within the Golden Dawn Tradition, the Elemental Pentagrams are part of the Inner Order training derived from *Ritual B - the Pentagram Ritual* wherein not only are the Elemental Pentagrams discussed in detail, but also the Lesser Ritual of the Pentagram is revisited with clarification for the Adeptus Minor.

One of the primary things to grasp here, is that the use of color and that of Enochian was *never* given as part of the Outer Order curriculum of work. This prohibition lasted through the Rosicrucian Order of the Alpha et Omega and the Stella Matutina.

Since the original Orders would not reveal their secrets of color as a magical formula nor the use of the Enochian language, which are

---

11 This paper was clearly written by and for the adepti of the Inner Order, but this particular note highlights how seriously that the overusing of the banishing pentagram was taken, even from nearly the beginning of the Golden Dawn Tradition. This particular copy was written circa 1895 by an unknown or unlisted adept of the original Golden Dawn.

THE LIGHT EXTENDED

used as part of the Supreme Ritual of the Pentagram or the Elemental Pentagrams, to the Outer Order, how are these lesser Pentagrams traced, visualized, and charged?

To see the differences we will discuss in some detail both the Elemental Earth Pentagram and the Pentagram of the Lesser Ritual. Looking at the specific pentagrams drawn when performing these Lesser Rituals of the Pentagram. The comparison with the Earth Invoking and Banishing Pentagrams is appropriate. The Elemental Pentagrams used in the Inner Order are drawn in the following manner:

EARTH

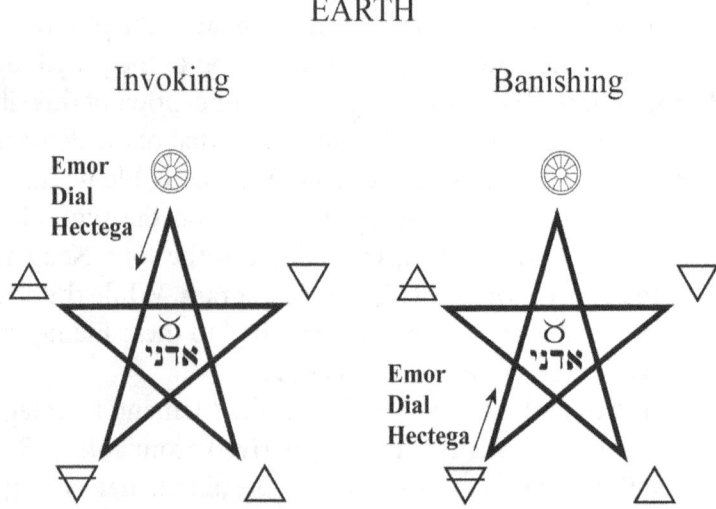

Fig. 4. Elemental Earth Pentagrams

The above illustration of the Earth Elemental Pentagram bears some resemblance to the Lesser Pentagram in that the Pentagrams themselves are only traced in the same manner. This is where the similarities end.

THE LESSER RITUAL OF THE PENTAGRAM

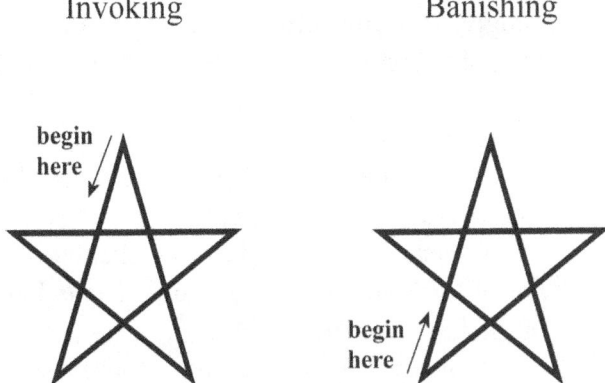

Fig. 5. Lesser Pentagrams

The Lesser Pentagrams are meant to be of use by members of the Outer Order only.[12] They are not traced while visualizing the Pentagrams in the appropriate Elemental color (traditionally this is an oily Black or Russet). Nor does the member vibrate any Enochian Names while doing the tracing of the Pentagram. The Inner Order was jealous of their use of color for magical work, especially in how to visualize such symbols as the Pentagrams. This carried over into the Rosicrucian Order of the Alpha et Omega and to the Stella Matutina.

The color of the Lesser Pentagram was traditionally taught as white (some modern authors have listed this as electric blue-white or bluish) which symbolized purity and balance from the Highest Divine Force.

Additionally, it will be noted that in the center of the Elemental Earth Pentagrams there is an additional figure; the glyph or symbol for the Zodical Sign of Taurus, in this case representing the Kerubic force for Earth. The tracing of this glyph also is accompanied by the vibration of the Divine Name אדני Adonai. Again, something that is not taught in the Outer Order much like the vibration of the Enochian while tracing the pentagram itself.

---

12 In *Ritual B – The Pentagram Ritual*, the Lesser Ritual of the Pentagram is for general use in invocation and banishing so that the Neophyte has protection from opposing forces and may also have some idea as to how to attract and come into contact with spiritual and invisible things. This can also be found worded somewhat oddly in Regardie's *The Golden Dawn*, pp. 281-282.

THE LIGHT EXTENDED

Within the Golden Dawn Tradition paradigm without the use of the Spirit Pentagrams (both Active and Passive) and the vibration of the Enochian Force for the Elements and the charging of the Pentagram with the appropriate Inner Order Divine Name of the Element, and the visualization of the pentagram in its appropriate color, there is no way for the Pentagrams of the Lesser Ritual to be remotely considered as Elemental in nature.

There is a further argument that the Pentagrams of the Lesser Ritual are of an Elemental nature and that is based on the visualizations of the four Archangels.

Originally in Golden Dawn teachings, there were no color attributions given to the Archangels of the Quarters but over time these color attributions crept into the visualizations associated with the four Archangels in the Lesser Rituals of the Pentagram. This led to the confusion as to the nature of the Archangels evoked during the Lesser Rituals of the Pentagram, leading many within the Golden Dawn Orders (the Golden Dawn, Stella Matutina and Alpha et Omega, and especially in the many modern incarnations of the original Golden Dawn), as well as many outside of the Golden Dawn tradition, to assume that these Archangels represented aspects of the Elements. The relationship of these Archangels is rather to the four winds and the four quarters of Earth. According to Agrippa, the four angels ruling over the corners of Earth are Michael מיכאל, Raphael רפאל, Gabriel גבריאל, and Uriel אוריאל.[13] These are further explained in *Three Books of Occult Philosophy* as follows:

> "There are also four princes of the angels, which are set over the four winds, and over the four parts of the world, whereof *Michael* is set over the eastern wind; *Raphael* over the western; *Gabriel* over the northern; *Nariel*, who by some is called *Uriel*, is over the southern."[14]

These archangels are associated with the four corners in the heaven, which relates to the positions of the sun.[15] This would be the East

---
13 Agrippa. *Three Books of Occult Philosophy*, p. 257.
14 Ibid. p. 533.
15 Ibid, p. 260.

THE LESSER RITUAL OF THE PENTAGRAM

for the rising sun; the South for the noontime sun; the West for the setting sun; and finally the North for the sun at midnight.

In addition, Gareth Knight also lists the Archangels as those of the Cardinal Points, but places them in their Golden Dawn arrangement.[16] At which time, and by whom (Mathers or another) within the original Golden Dawn the traditional Archangels of the four winds were moved to their current positions within the Golden Dawn, is unknown. Their placement works in relation to the four quarters as guardians, especially when used in the Lesser Rituals of the Pentagram. To add to the concept of these four archangels as being guardians, there is a legend that it is recounted in the *Revelation of Moses* that Adam was buried by the four angels Uriel, Gabriel, Raphael, and Michael.[17] While we give the Archangels used in the Lesser Rituals the corresponding colors associated with the four.[18] While we give the Archangels used in the Lesser Rituals the corresponding colors associated with the four elements, they themselves are not representatives of the four elemental archangels, Raphael Ruachel (Air), Gabriel Maimel (Water), Michael Aeshel (Fire) and Uriel (Earth).

In the original Orders, these Archangels were not visualized in color at all nor really in any particular form. They were normally seen as giant columns of white light standing at the Quarters.

This leads us naturally into the fact that the Archangels along with the Hebrew Divine Names used to charge the Lesser Pentagrams make this particular rite only suitable for someone whom is a member of one of the Judeo-Christian faiths. This could not be further from the truth. While the Golden Dawn Tradition in general uses a Judeo-Christian cosmology, it being the one most familiar to Western magicians since the Renaissance, the Divine Names and even the Archangels need not be seen as *just* forces from the Bible. They can be seen to represent stations or directions within the Golden Dawn cosmological paradigm, representatives of the Forces of the One Source, the Divine, or however one chooses to define the Highest Divine.

---

16 Knight. *A Practical Guide to Qabalistic Symbolism*, pp. 111-112. Also on p. 199.
17 Davidson. *A Dictionary of Angels*, p. 6.
18 Ibid.

THE LIGHT EXTENDED

The Lesser Ritual of the Pentagram

With the above introduction in mind, let us now consider the Lesser Ritual of the Pentagram itself. This foundational ritual is in truth comprised of two separate rites, the Lesser Ritual of the Pentagram itself and the Qabalistical or Qabalistic Cross which are most often presented as one total ritual in the Golden Dawn Tradition. This is the manner which we will discuss the Lesser Ritual of the Pentagram.

The Qabalistic Cross and Lesser Ritual of the Pentagram[19]

Take a steel dagger[20] in the right hand.[21] Face East.

Invoking.

Touch thy forehead and say **ATEH** *(thou art)*.
Touch thy breast and say **MALKUTH** *(the Kingdom)*.
Touch thy right shoulder and say **VE-GEBURAH** *(and the Power)*.
Touch they left shoulder and say **VE-GEDULAH** *(and the Glory)*.
Clasp thy hands before thee and say **LE-OLAM** *(for ever)*.
Dagger between fingers, point up and say **AMEN**.

Make in the Air towards the East the invoking

---

19 Regardie. *The Golden Dawn*, pp. 53 – 54. This version is what was used in the original Golden Dawn and the Stella Matutina, and with some variance of verbiage in the Rosicrucian Order of the Alpha et Omega based on examination of unpublished versions of this ritual from the Golden Dawn, Rosicrucian Order of the Alpha et Omega, and the Stella Matutina.
20 This dagger is not to be confused with the Air Dagger of the Adeptus Minor. This is just a simple and plain double-edged dagger, often with a black handle similar to what can be found in the Solomonic Tradition, though without any particular symbols drawn upon it.
21 In some extant copies of this ritual, the instruction is a sword or dagger being preferable, but any convenient pointed object can be used. The injunction to use a Sword is in reference to the Magical Sword of the Adeptus Minor. Often the term Wand it used, this is a reference to the Lotus Wand of the Adeptus Minor.

THE LESSER RITUAL OF THE PENTAGRAM

PENTAGRAM as shown and, bringing the point of the dagger to the centre of the Pentagram, vibrate the DEITY NAME – **YOD HEH VAU HE**[22] – imagining that your voice carries forward to the East of the Universe.

Holding the dagger out before you, go to the South, make the Pentagram and vibrate similarly the deity name – **ADONAI**.

Go to the West, make the Pentagram and vibrate **EHEIEH**.

Go to the North, make the Pentagram and vibrate **AGLA**.

Return to the East and complete cour circle by bringing the dagger point to the centre of the first Pentagram.

Stand with arms outstretched in the from of a cross and say: -

Before me	**RAPHAEL**
Behind me	**GABRIEL**
At my right hand	**MICHAEL**
At my left hand	**AURIEL**

Before me Flames the Pentagram –
Behind me shines the Six-Rayed Star.[23]

Again make the Qabalistic Cross as directed above, saying ATEH, etc.

For Banishing use the same Ritual, but reversing the direction of the lines of the Pentagram.

What follows the above ritual description is normally notes on the uses of the Lesser Pentagram Ritual and accompanying visualization

---

22 Generally in the unpublished versions of this paper, regardless of original Order, the Divine Names are written out in Hebrew. This carries over to the Hebrew used in the Qabalistical Cross and those names of the Archangels.
23 Within the original Rosicrucian Order of the Alpha et Omega, there is an additional optional phrase which may follow "Behind me shines the Six-rayed Star", and that phrase is "And above my Head the Glory of God!"

commentary. There are also normally graphics showing the manner in which the two lesser pentagrams are to be traced. These can be seen in Fig. 5 above.

As can be seen from the above description of this ritual, it appears to be rather simple, at least upon first glance. There is much more going on in this basic ritual which we will explore below.

The Qabalisitical or Qabalistic Cross

This is in reality a separate ritual or rite, deserving of its own paper. We will briefly go into the functionality of this other primary rite of the Golden Dawn Tradition.

The function of the Qabalistic or Qabalistical, as it was original named and called within the Golden Dawn and its offshoot Orders, Cross is to draw down the Divine Light or Brilliance[24] into the Sphere of Sensation of the practitioner while at the same time equilibrating that same force.

This force is drawn down into the Kether gilgal[25] located at the top of the head, and from their it is drawn down to the Tiphareth gilgal, located at the solar plexus, but is visualized continuing down to the feet and beyond into the personal Malkuth of the practitioner. This could even be considered to flow down into *actual* Malkuth, the ground beneath the feet of the practitioner.

From Malkuth, the Light is then drawn to the right shoulder, the Geburah gilgal, which is representative of Severity or Strength. Hence for Geburah, it is traced or drawn to the left shoulder, the Gedulah or Chesed gilgal for Mercy.

Finally, the practitioner brings it all together at the center junction of the Cross of Light in the Sphere of Senstion by clasping the hands before their heart or solar plexus, the symbolic Tiphareth within the Sphere of Sensation.

It is at this point that the words vibrated, LE-OLAM and AMEN

---

24 Within the Golden Dawn Tradition, this Divine Light is often called *LVX*, *Divine White Brilliance*, or *Divine Light* depending upon whether in the Outer or Inner Orders, or depending up the particular overall Order using the term.

25 Gilgal is Hebrew for "Circle", "Wheel", or "Sphere" is a singular reference to a singular sphere of the Tree of Life. Gilgalim is the plural which refers to all ten spheres of the Tree of Life.

THE LESSER RITUAL OF THE PENTAGRAM

are performed, thus fully balancing and activating the Divine Light within the Sphere of Sensation.

From this point, the practitioner can move forward with Lesser Ritual of the Pentagram.

The Lesser Ritual of the Pentagram

The meat of the Lesser Ritual of the Pentagram is the tracing of the appropriate pentagrams, either the Invoking or Banishing, in the Quarters and charging them with the appropriate Divine Names, the formulation of the Archangels at the Quarters, and the final statement which helps to seal the Sphere of Sensation of the practitioner.

Each of these will be handled below in detail.

Tracing the Pentagrams

The practitioner starts by taking the basic dagger, pointed object (such as a wand), or merely their hand to do the actual tracing of the pentagrams in the Quarters.

Facing East, which should be determined ahead of time, the Golden Dawn magician traces the appropriate Pentagram, either the Invoking or Banishing version.

One of the things about tracing the Pentagrams is that they should proportionately traced or drawn in the air before the magician. There should be a definite starting and stopping point, which are the exact same place.

The size of the Pentagram is also to be considered. From some practical points it is roughly traced or drawn from the outside of the hips, to just above the head, and slightly outside of the shoulders of the practitioner. It will eventually be approximately the height of the Golden Dawn magician that traced it.

The tracing of the Pentagram, whether with a dagger or not, should be done deliberately. One piece of advice concerning this is given below by the Alpha et Omega's Greatly Honored Soror Vestigia Nulla Retrorsum, "I never retrace my steps", the motto of Mina "Moina" Bergson Mathers:

THE LIGHT EXTENDED

IN DESCRIBING the Symbol with the Steel Point, it should be traced slowly and with fixed attention: and therefore not with a too rapid or slashing movement of the instrument employed.[26]

The form of the Pentagrams for the Lesser Ritual of the Pentagram, as well of those later for the Supreme Ritual of the Pentagram, should be traced so that the figure itself is of a proportional nature. To this end, Very Honored Frater Anima Pura Sit, Dr. Henry Pullen-Burry, wrote *Flying Roll VIII – A Geometrical Way to Draw a Pentagram* for the original Order in the 1890s. This paper is a mathematical scheme to draw a perfect pentagram. While this can be applied to drawing on paper or another objects, it can also be adapted to the tracing of the Pentagrams during ritual work, most importantly to those pentagrams of the Lesser Ritual and the Supreme Ritual of the Pentagram.

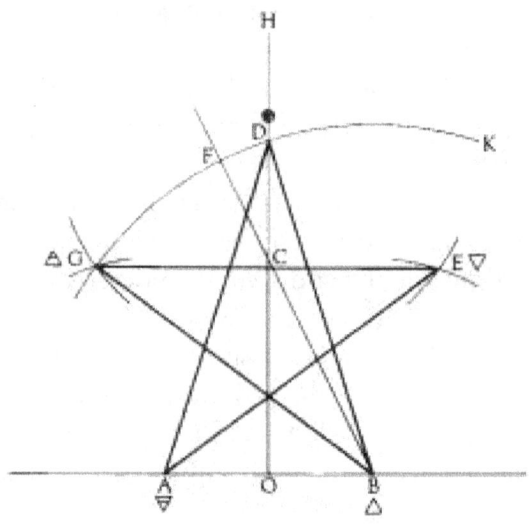

Fig. 6. Perfect Geometric Pentagram.

---

26 From an unpublished *Lesser Pentagram Ritual Paper* for the Neophyte Grade of the Rosicrucian Order of the Alpha et Omega circa 1920. There are a series of Notes given by Moina Mathers on what should be done during the performance of the Lesser Ritual of the Pentagram.

THE LESSER RITUAL OF THE PENTAGRAM

The appearance of the Pentagram being proportional is no accident, but rather an example of sacred geometry. Within the symbol of the Pentagram itself is the Golden Mean or Divine Proportion, also termed the Divine Section (this latter is called *sectio divina* in Latin). This is a mathematical ratio expressed as the Greek letter φ (Phi, normally in lower case), a revered number with the value of 1.6180339887..., or 1.618. This ratio has fascinated various and diverse individuals in the West for the last 2400 years, including Pythagoras and Euclid in the ancient world. The ancient Greeks normally attributed the discovery of this important ratio to Pythagoras and his followers, the Pythagorean Brotherhood. The Pythagoreans used the pentagram as their symbol. Euclid provides the first known documented definition of what is now known as the Golden Ratio, this being "A straight line is said to have been cut in extreme and mean ratio when, as the whole line is to the greater segment, so is the greater to the lesser."[27] This ratio can be used to divide a line or rectangle into two unequal parts, so that the proportion of the two new parts or portions is the same as the proportion of the larger part of the original line or rectangle.

Now φ or the Divine Proportion is expressed entirely in terms of 5, so that "fiveness" is a quality of φ and that φ occurs in proportions of the pentagon and pentagram.[28] This "fiveness" can be calculated and seen in the square root of 5. The answer to the quadratic equation of $x^2 = x + 1$ (the positive quadratic equation) is $(1 + \sqrt{5})/2$ or φ. It is because of the $\sqrt{5}$, φ shows up in nature when there is any "fiveness". Think of something like the seeds of an apple and how when the apple is cut in half the seeds are seen as five in number in an arrangement similar to a pentagram.

The human body can be laid out on a pentagram and be seen to be composed of the Golden Ratio or Divine Proportion. This is best represented in the well-known drawing of the human body by Leonardo da Vinci that is known as the 'Vitruvian Man' which shows the Divine Proportion of the human body.

---

27 Euclid. *Elements*. Book 6, Definition 3.
28 Skinner. Sacred Geometry, p. 36.

THE LIGHT EXTENDED

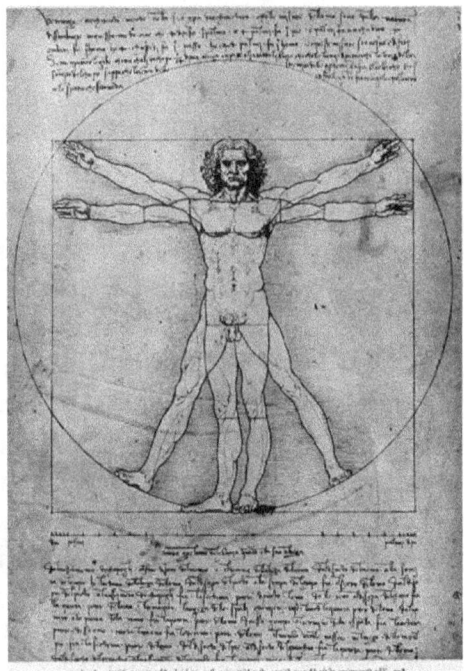

Fig. 7. Vitruvian Man.

Now that something of the proportions and proportionality of the Pentagrams has been discussed, we should move forward to the actual instructions for tracing the Lesser Pentagrams. In the original versions of the Lesser Ritual of the Pentagram paper as distributed by the Hermetic Order of the Golden Dawn, the Rosicrucian Order of the Alpha et Omega, and the Stella Matutina, the primary example for tracing of the Pentagram is the Invoking model.

The Invoking Lesser Pentagram is simply traced by starting slightly above the head of the practitioner, tracing a line to the outside of the left hip. From the outside of the left hip, the next line proceeds to just outside the right shoulder. Next the line continues over to just beyond the left shoulder. From the left shoulder the line continues to the outside of the right hip, and from the outside of the right hip the practitioner traces back to the beginning point above the head.

The Banishing version simply has a different starting point, in this case just outside of the left hip. From there the line is traced to just above the head; down to outside of the right hip; thence

THE LESSER RITUAL OF THE PENTAGRAM

to beyond the left shoulder; then over to just outside of the right shoulder; and finally returning to the starting position of the left hip.

When tracing the pentagrams in ritual or ceremonial work, the magician should endeavor to make the pentagrams as perfect as possible; this is to represent the highest ideal that is being aspired to, or the most perfect force to be invoked. In the case of banishing, this would be using the force of the Divine in the most balanced and proportional manner to illicit the desired effect in the Physical World.

Additionally, when discussing the proportions and proportionality of the Pentagrams there is the case for the force of the pentagram. Since the Pentagram itself is an image of the Divine Proportion or Golden Ratio, there should be a balance to of energies or force involved. If the "arms" of the Pentagram are not in proportion to each other or the figure itself, this leads to an inbalance of energy and force.

Additionally there is a need to "close" the Pentagram. That is to return to the exact starting point so that one of the legs or arms of the pentagram is not left "open" or with a gap in it. The gap or openness allows for a leakage of the particular invoked force or energy to bleed away from the ritual or ceremonial working at a much faster pace than the normal and expected dissipation of the force contained by the Pentagram.

Visualization of the Pentagrams

Visualization is one of the first skills that any practitioner of the Art Magic must learn. It is the ability to "see" things that are not normally seen by the human eye. This practice is utilized in the vast majority of the Golden Dawn Tradition, and begins even in the first ritual work undertaken.

Traditionally, the Pentagrams of the Lesser Ritual of the Pentagram are visualized in White or Golden-White light.

There have been some writers whom have claimed that they should be seen in electric blue-white light, and that this is how the clairvoyant actually see the traced pentagrams. While it may be the color that a clairvoyant sees them, the Initiate should see them as

THE LIGHT EXTENDED

White or Golden-White.

There are several reasons for this White visualization. First of all, the color of the Elemental Pentagrams, were jealously guarded, so Blue, Red, Yellow, Black or Russet would not have been shown to those of the Outer Order.

There is also a certain practical reason for this visualization of the Pentagrams in White. It is that White in one of the easiest colors to visualize, particularly in a flaming manner as these Lesser Pentagrams are meant to be visualized.

The color here is very important, especially when looking at the white of the pentagrams in the Lesser Rituals. White is our concept of the Highest Divine aspirations. To coincide with the white light as being the highest aspiration of the Divine, the symbol or sigil of the pentagram itself can be considered a facet of the highest aspect of the Divine. The exhortation from the *Ritual B Paper* (also known as *The Pentagram Ritual Paper*) in the work of the Adeptus Minor gives the following reference to the Pentagram used generally:

> "Traced as a symbol of good, it should be placed with the single point upward, representing the rule of the Divine Spirit. For if thou shouldst write it with the two points upward, it is an evil symbol, affirming the empire of matter over that Divine Spirit which should govern it. **See that thou doest it not.**"[29]

Further in *Ritual B*, the notes concerning the uses of the *Lesser Ritual of the Pentagram* indicate that the banishing version is used to overcome adverse forces and that the invoking version is to help with attracting and communing with spiritual influences.

> "These two Pentagrams are in general use for invokation or banishing, and their use is given to the Neophyte of the first Order of the Golden Dawn under the title of the Lesser Ritual of the Pentagram. This Lesser Ritual of the Pentagram is only of use in general and unimportant invokations. Its use is permitted to the Outer that Neophytes may have protection against opposing forces,

---
29 Regardie. *The Golden Dawn*, p. 280.

THE LESSER RITUAL OF THE PENTAGRAM

and also that they may form some idea of how to attract and to come into communication with spiritual and invisible things."[30]

In addition to this particular exhortation, there is a paper which lists the various sigils of the Elements in the Four Worlds. The first sigil given is that for Spirit in the King Scale, which corresponds to the Qabalistic World of Atziluth, and is a depicted as pentagram seen in a paper written by S. L. Mathers (G. H. Frater D.D.C.F.) which is included as an appendix in *The Golden Dawn Court Cards*, edited by Darcy Küntz. The color given for this sigil or glyph is "white merging into grey."[31]

Since the pentagram as a sigil relates to the highest aspects or qualities of Spirit, then it can be likened to the symbol best used in all four Qabalistic Worlds and that is exactly how it can be seen in the case of the Lesser Pentagram Ritual. While the pentagrams used in the Lesser Pentagram Ritual have been called a *Pentagram of Assiah*, it would be better to say that it represents the highest Divine force from the Qabalistic World of Atziluth operating in the physical world of Assiah, which the magician brings into manifestation through the act of drawing down the Divine Light, tracing the lesser pentagrams and charging them with the appropriate Divine Names. This further connects the lesser pentagram with attracting and communing with spiritual forces. The uses of the Lesser Pentagram Ritual as a form of prayer also support this.[32]

This visualization of the Pentagram in white would make the Lesser Pentagrams more akin to the Spirit Pentagrams utilized in the Inner Order's Supreme Ritual of the Pentagram, and is reflected in *The Uses of the Pentagram Ritual* notes that normally accompany the traditional *Lesser Ritual of the Pentagram* document. This will be covered more in detail later in this article.

To further connect the Lesser Pentagrams with the force associated with Spirit manifesting into Matter in the Zelator Ceremony the candidate is given further reference to the Pentagram as a symbol that manifests in Malkuth. Along with the associated

---
30 Ibid, pp. 281-282.
31 Küntz. *The Golden Dawn Court Cards*, p. 25.
32 Ibid, p. 54.

speech, the image is firmly implanted into the Sphere of Sensation of the Candidate and this acts to further the understanding of this symbol by the new Zelator. In this instance, the candidate learns that the pentagram has some specific Qabalistic attributions:

> "… Around the great central Lamp, which is an image of the Sun, is the Great Mother of Heaven, symbolized by the letter Heh, the first of the Single letters, and by its number 5, the Pentagram, Malkah the Bride, ruling in her Kingdom Malkuth, crowned with a crown of Twelve Stars. …"[33]

These Qabalistic concepts can be expressed in that the Hebrew letter Heh ה has a numerical value of five, which is the number of points in a pentagram. As the Hebrew letter Heh ה sophith in the Tetragrammaton יהוה, it represents the Daughter manifesting in the World of Assiah in the Sephirah of Malkuth מלכות. Also the titles for Malkuth which are *Malkah* מלכה which means "The Queen", and *Kalah* כלה, meaning "The Bride", especially referring to the Bride of the Microprosopus.[34] These titles are references to the Shekinah hnwkc, the Divine Presence.[35]

To further illustrate the connection of the pentagram as a symbol or glyph of the highest Divine aspects, consider some gematria related to the pentagram itself. Each line of the pentagram is composed of a length that is twenty-one units long. Numerically, twenty-one is the value of the Divine Name EHEIEH אהיה, which is the Atziluthic name used for Kether. This name is one of the Highest associated with the act of Creation. The Twenty-first Key, "the Universe" has the meaning of the completion of creation into manifestation.[36] So, from a gematric point of view looking at the associations of the numerical value of twenty-one, the pentagram used in the Lesser Rituals can be seen as taking the Highest Divine energy (EHEIEH) and manifesting it in Assiah.

---

33 Regardie. *The Golden Dawn*, p. 150.
34 Godwin. *Godwin's Cabalistic Encyclopedia*, p. 158.
35 Ibid, p.185, and also p. 282.
36 Regardie & Cicero. *The Middle Pillar: The Balance Between Mind and Magic*, pp. 189-190.

THE LESSER RITUAL OF THE PENTAGRAM

A summation of this concept is clearly illustrated in a commentary by the Ciceros in Regardie's *The Middle Pillar: The Balance Between Mind and Magic* relating to the pentagram and the Divine Name EHEIEH.

> "So what does all this mean? In tracing a pentagram, the magician invokes the power of Eheieh. This is a glittering, glorious power that pours forth abundantly; pierces and binds all negativity; encloses and separates the pure from the impure; opens and closes gates or doors between different worlds; gives rise to meditation, visions, love, unity and healing; and to the magician who silences the chatter of his mind, sacrifices his lower desires and aligns himself with the divine will, it can be employed with justice as a potent force for transformation, generation, and change (particularly on the material or earth plane), which can be directed by the hand and used to obtain spiritual "gold." Through the number five (the creative Heh and the five elements), Eheieh, as asserted through the tracing of a pentagram, is an expression of the five-fold existence of the power of the divine self and the light (LVX) of Adonai, who is the palace of YHVH. It is that which created the cosmos and which rules over it with justice and strength, permeating every aspect of creation. Everything in the universe is composed of the one true *self* which is both the power that transforms and the object of the transformation."[37]

Charging the Pentagrams and Divine Names

The next thing that the Golden Dawn practitioner does once the Lesser Pentagram is traced is to charge the figure with the appropriate Divine Name.

The method of charging the pentagram traced in the Quarter is to "punch" or strongly place the dagger in the center of the pentagram while vibrating the Divine Name. This is the traditional method, but in some of the modern Golden Dawn Orders the charging is

---
37 Ibid, p. 190.

THE LIGHT EXTENDED

accomplished by performance of the Projection Sign while vibrating or intoning the appropriate Divine Name. This Sign is also called the Neophyte Saluting Sign, the Sign of the Enterer, the Attacking Sign, or the Sign of Horus.[38]

The Divine Names used when charging the Lesser Pentagrams are arranged in a specific manner. As in all Golden Dawn ritual work, the practitioner starts in the East, and thence moves deosil or sunwise to the South, then the West, then the North, and finally returns to the East.

The four Divine Names used for the Lesser Rituals of the Pentagram, YHVH יהוה in the East; ADONAI אדני in the South; EHEIEH אהיה in the West and AGLA אגלא, the notariqon for the Hebrew phrase *Atah Gibor le-Olam Adonai* in the North, are all composed of four letters or a tetragram and relate to the directions they are used by linking the specific Divine name to the four positions of the course of the sun and the concepts associated with those positions, especially since Sol, the Sun, is the visible manifestation of the Divine Light in most of the symbolism of Western Esotericism and in the Golden Dawn in particular.

This makes these Divine Names more postional and directional rather than anything else.

The manner of this linking to the four positions of the sun throughout the day can be seen in that the name used in the East is YHVH יהוי, the highest name of the Divine that represents the powers of the Divine operating in all Four Qabalistic Worlds. Since the Tetragrammaton, the Four-lettered Name, is the highest Divine Name, then its use in the East, the place of the rising Sun is most appropriate as the beginning or first Divine Name to be used.

The Divine name used in the South would seem to be out of place since ADONAI אדני is one of the names used for Malkuth and Elemental Earth. So why is it placed in the South? The word ADONAI

---

[38] While these Signs are traditional and used within the Golden Dawn, they were not used originally in the three original Orders; the Hermetic Order of the Golden Dawn, the Rosicrucian Order of the Alpha et Omega, or the Stella Matutina in this manner for charging the Pentagrams of the Lesser Ritual of the Pentagram. They each have specific uses and functions, which while similar are not necessarily the same depending upon the manner in which they are used and/or named.

THE LESSER RITUAL OF THE PENTAGRAM

means "lord", connoting sovereignty[39] and dominion in general, rather than gender based as a reference to a masculine connotation. Its use in the South, the place where the sun is at its utmost strength is appropriate. According to the Ciceros in *The Middle Pillar: The Balance Between Mind and Magic,* "This is a reminder that here on Malkuth, our immediate symbolic link with the lord of light and strength is through the life-giving rays of the sun."[40]

The name used in the West is EHEIEH אהיה. This is the Divine name associated with the Sephirah Kether, but is also a fitting name to use for the direction of the West. The west is the place of the sunset, a place of completion, especially the completion of the sun's journey daily across the sky. The West is also associated with the completion of the soul's quest for spiritual growth, as well as for the afterlife, especially in Egypt. The name EHEIEH is fitting here as it links the West with the concepts of completion in all esoteric work with our highest eternal self in Kether, thus balancing out the use of YHVH in the East, which is an initial or beginning of the esoteric work.

In the North, the tetragram AGLA אגלא is used when charging the pentagram. This name, as has been previously stated, is derived from the phrase or invocation *Atah Gibor le-Olam Adonai,* meaning "Thou art great forever, my Lord." Its use in the North, "the place of Forgetfulness, Dumbness, and Necessity and of the greatest symbolical Darkness"[41] is a reference to the Divine Name that is used in the South where the strength of the sun is at its greatest, though in the North this same power is hidden or cloaked from us in the great darkness of the quarter. Here the name of Adonai is seen as a guide or aiding force to help get through the darkness. The following quote further expounds this concept:

> "However, all things, manifest or unmanifest (light or dark), exist then, now, and always under the rulership of Adonai. This we affirm by the phrase "Thou are great forever, my Lord!"[42]

---

39 Regardie & Cicearo. *The Middle Pillar: The Balance Between Mind and Magic,* p. 206.
40 Ibid, pp. 191-192.
41 Regardie. The Golden Dawn, p. 124.
42 Ibid, p. 192.

Again is shown a balancing of the force or energy utilized by the practitioner in the opposite side of the ritual space, temple, or personal sanctuary of the magician. In the previous pair of Names, YHVH and EHEIEH which connotate a beginning and completion respectively, here in the North and South we see overt strength of the Divine symbolized in the South while the hidden strength is typified in the North as a place of trial.

Completing the Circle of the Place

Thus far we have looked at the mechanics or tracing the Lesser Pentagrams and charging those selfsame Pentagrams. There is is also additional *Work* used during this phase of the Lesser Ritual of the Pentagram; that being connecting the traced Pentagrams with a band of fiery light, creating as it were a a circle around the place which is studded at the four quarters by flaming pentagrams. This circle of white fiery light is going to be roughly at the level of the practitioner's Tiphareth gilgal.

To accomplish this tracing of white fiery light that connects all the pentagrams is accomplished when the magician punches the center of the Pentagram and charges it. The right arm is left outstretch with the dagger (or other implement) as the practitioner moves deosil or sunwise[43] to the next quarter.

Often in the modern era of the Golden Dawn, the practitioner does this movement with the right arm outstretched while performing the Sign of Silence with the left hand, and is done whether merely turning in place to face the Quarters or while actually circumambulating the ritual space from Quarter to Quarter. This is a complement to the use of the Projection Sign as a means to charge the pentagrams. It does serve as a "shield" to the practitioner to prevent any rebound of the energy expended during the charging portion of this ritual.

---

43 This movement is to the right. There are some in the Southern Hemisphere that proscribe that the movement in those portions of the world should move to the *left*, but that is not the case at all. There is ample evidence from the work of the members of the Smaragdum Thalasses temple in New Zealand in its nearly 70 years of operation that there was no need to make this change to the left at all in any Golden Dawn ritual or ceremony.

THE LESSER RITUAL OF THE PENTAGRAM

This circumambulation can be accomplished in two manners, it can be a full circumambulation from one quarter to the next, or it can be done by merely turning in place with the right arm outstretched. In many modern revival Orders this outstretched hand during the tracing of the circle is often performed with the left hand performing the Sign of Silence at the lips of the practitioner.

Done properly, and in conjunction with the tracing and charging of the Pentagrams, the practitioner will be once again at their exact starting point for this ritual with their right hand in the center of the first Pentagram. This completes around the practitioner a circle.

Invoking the Archangels

Once the circle is completed, the next step for the practitioner is to invoke the Archangels whom act as witnesses and guardians of the quarters.

The visualization here for the Archangels is traditionally just towering columns of white light as has been discussed earlier in this paper. It is acceptable to visualize them in color if that helps and to see them with their traditional implements or weapons, just keep in mind that if the colors are used these Archangels **do not** represent Elemental Forces. The names of the Archangels and their association to the directions or Four Winds has been discussed above, and need not be reiterated here other than to re-emphasize the fact of this association.

A bit of a new paradigm is set up in this invocation. The Archangels are not invoked in a sunwise manner working from East to South to West, etc., back to the East, but rather in a dualistic manner, in pairs as it were. East-West and then South-North are invoked.

This paradigm, while seemingly new is not, but merely a continuation of the lessons of the Neophyte Grade in which there is a balancing of opposites. Two contending Forces and one that continually unites them. In this case two Active Forces, Raphael and Michael, being balanced by two Passive Forces, Gabriel and Auriel respectively. The practitioner is the reconciler between these contending Forces.

The practitioner is standing facing towards the East, with arms outstretched to their side. The palms of the hands are forward, and the head should be erect facing forward. The feet should be together or in a comfortable stance. Essentially the practitioner is standing in the form of a cross. This position can be done in one of two locations within the ritual area. Either the practitioner stands in the East after completing the circle of the ritual place, or more commonly, the magician moves deosil or sunwise to the West of the Altar in the center of the ritual space, and then faces East as described above.

These Archangels, whether visualized as towering colossal columns of white light or as traditional Archangelic figures, are seen behind the Pentagrams in the Quarters; as if standing on the outside of the circle and pentagrams. The Archangels would appear to be holding a flaming Pentagram as if it were a shield.[44]

Declaration

There is a short versicle that follows the Invocation of the Archangels as part of the Lesser Ritual of the Pentagram which marks the end of the ritual proper, and is properly spoken firmly. This versicle is:

> "Before me Flames the Pentagram –
> Behind me Shines the Six-Rayed Star."

This is the traditional phaseology of this section of the Lesser Ritual of the Pentagram, but there are other variants of this section which have crept into usage or are from completely different traditions altogether.

One of these variants, "For about me flames the Pentagram, and in the column shines the Six-Rayed Star." is rather common in many modern texts, and is derived from the work of Aleister Crowley.

We will not be going into detail of these variants, but rather will concentrate on the more traditional verbiage that was used in the original Golden Dawn, Rosicrucian Order of the Alpha et Omega, and the Stella Matutina. There was some alternate verbiage that could be used by practitioner of the Rosicrucian Order of the Alpha et Omega; this being that rather than saying "Behind me Shines the Six-

---

44 Regardie. *The Middle Pillar*, p. 60.

THE LESSER RITUAL OF THE PENTAGRAM

Rayed Star" they could instead say "The HEXAGRAM of LIGHT", and they were also allowed to add "And above my Head the Glory of God!"[45] This alternative verbiage from the Alpha et Omega merely is another way to call the "Six-Rayed Star" and to add the Divine Glory or Light shining down upon the head of the practitioner.

The visualizations associated with this portion of the Lesser Ritual of the Pentagram may lead a person to believe that the in the first portion, "Before me Flames the Pentagram" is a reference to the Pentagram already traced in the East at the formulation of the Pentagrams at the Quarters of the ritual area. This is not the case, but rather the pentagram mentioned here is placed on the chest or just in front of the magician centered around the Tiphareth gilgal of the practitioner.

Likewise with the "Behind me Shines the Six-Rayed Star", Neophyte is to visualize a hexagram centered on the back at the place where the Tiphareth gilgal would be as seen from the backside.

The colors for these visualizations, originally for the Neophyte, and indeed for all members of the original Outer Orders of the early Orders, was in white or golden white light. There was an advanced visualization for these once the person was an Adeptus Minor (or higher). This was to visualize the frontal pentagram as burning fire on the breast[46]. This pentagram on the chest can be seen as flaming white or golden-white light, or as a flaming red. The hexagram on the back was to be visualized in two colors, much like the hexagram on the Banner of the East; one upward pointed triangle as red, while the downward pointed triangle as blue. These triangles are interlaced, just as those of the Banner of the East are.

The effects of this particular visualization along with the associated energies of the symbols employed is to seal the sphere of sensation of the magician, and in essence clothe the practitioner with a "breastplate" that protects the front and back from all negative forces. It also further helps to cleanse and raise the vibrational rate of the sphere of sensation so that the practitioner is thus closer to the Divine, which is one of the goals of the sort of magic represented by

---

45 From an unpublished Lesser Ritual of the Pentagram paper of the Rosicrucian Order of the Alpha et Omega circa 1920 which was made available to Neophytes of this Order.
46 Regardie. *The Middle Pillar*, p. 63.

this particular ritual.

Additionally, the use of the Hexagram of the Banner of the East on the back is another means of sealing the Sphere of Sensation, in the old papers this is sometimes referred to as the aura, and was further developed by the original Orders by "draping" astrally an image of the Banner of the East around the magician or hanging it on the back, sort of like a cape or a shield slung across the back.

Ending the Lesser Ritual of the Pentagram

Just as in the beginning, once the Neophyte magician has completed the declaration portion of the Lesser Ritual of the Pentagram, they then perform the Qabalistical Cross. This is the complete end of the Lesser Ritual.

Some Notes on the Use of the Lesser Ritual of the Pentagram

The Lesser Ritual of the Pentagram is much greater than the sum of its parts. It is, in both forms, a form of prayer as it were to begin to connect the Neophyte to the Divine or Spiritual Forces. This would be the beginning of contact with the Holy Guardian Genius of the budding magician within the Golden Dawn Tradition.

While in *Ritual B - the Pentagram Ritual* given to the Adeptus Minor we are told that, "This Lesser Ritual of the Pentagram is only of use in general and unimportant invocations" is not speaking about its use to connect with Spiritual or Divine Forces. This is part of the ultimate theurgical work undertaken by all whom seek Union or Reunion with the Divine.

As such, the instructions for the use of the Lesser Ritual of the Pentagram tell us to invoke in the morning and banish at night.[47] This in essence makes the morning use of the Lesser Ritual of the Pentagram similar to Lauds, a morning prayer given at sunrise. Lauds is the name in Latin of the office of morning prayer given traditionally at sunrise. It means "to give praise".

While the "banishing at night" can be seen as something akin to a Vespers prayer. Vespers, from the Latin *vesper* meaning "evening",

---

[47] This is seen in many versions of the Lesser Ritual of the Pentagram text, both unpublished and published.

THE LESSER RITUAL OF THE PENTAGRAM

is a prayer traditionally given at sundown. This is a fitting way to end the day, especially since the effects of the Banishing version of the Lesser Ritual of the Pentagram help to remove unwanted obsession, negativity, and to some degree stress which can build up throughout the normal course of the day.

The two periods of sunrise and sunset mark two of the most important times for prayer. The sunrise marks the breaking of the darkness and the visible Light of the Divine as represented by Sol being seen fully once again. Sunset marks the descent of the Sun into twilight and the hiding of the Divine Light behind the wall of Night.

Since the Lesser Ritual of the Pentagram can be seen as a prayer, then it is apropos to see it, and indeed all ritual work from a Jewish or Qabalistic framework. The two most applicable terms for this from traditional Jewish Kabbalah and faith are *Kavannah* כונה meaning "intention" or "direction of the heart." That is that there must be correct intent and reverence in the performance. That the heart is enflamed with prayer and desire to connect to the Divine. This implies that there is an understanding of the words of the prayer or ritual rather than just a bland recitation of the words and sounds. From a Golden Dawn point of view, this is similar as always invoking the Highest first.

Within some forms of Kabbalah and in the Jewish faith as practiced by the Chasidic Jews, kavannah is often a form of meditation, particularly in relation to the names of the Divine.

The, other orthodox Jewish concept is *Keva* כוא meaning a "ritualistic approach," "structure" or "routine." There is a form and formula to the Lesser Ritual of the Pentagram, and indeed all ritual and ceremonial elements within the Golden Dawn Tradition. These should be followed while being filled with kavannah or the highest intention.

While there is a mechanical aspect to ritual work within the Golden Dawn Tradition, and for that matter in all Ceremonial Magic; there is more to the ritual work itself than just tracing pentagrams in the air in the appropriate form, size, and color while breathing correctly and intoning or vibrating the accurate Divine Names during the charging of the pentagram itself. All ritual is greater than the sum of its parts, and the above concepts of kavannah and keva elevate not only the magician, but the theurgical work of that magician.

Having brought up the term *theurgy*, it is likely that it should be defined, and given reference to how it applies to the Lesser Ritual of the Pentagram. Theurgy, from the Greek Θεοργία, meaning "Divine working", describes the practice of rituals, often seen as magical in nature that are performed with the intention of invoking the action or evoking the presence of one or more gods, especially with the goal of uniting with the Divine, thus achieving henosis,[48] and perfecting oneself.

Just from the above definition it should be clear as to how the Lesser Ritual of the Pentagram was conceived as, and is, a theurgical rite. It has the intention of invoking action; manifesting the forces of Atziluth in Assiah through the actions and Will of the magician, and it also evokes the presence of the Divine in a manner to begin the process of perfecting oneself.

The Lesser Ritual of the Pentagram also serves as a *thaumaturgical* rite in that it has some rather practical and immediate affect magically for the practitioner. What is meant by thaumaturgical? In this case, thaumaturigcal is derived from the Greek *Thaumatourgía* Θαυματουργία meaning "Miracle work." This is practical or actual magical work that has the purpose of producing an effect upon the physical world. This is especially true when the Lesser Ritual of the Pentagram is used to remove negative or obsessive forces from the environment of the magician, or when used to counter magical attack, obsessing or disturbing thoughts, or impure magnetism,[49] particularly when the banishing version of the ritual is used.

The invoking version of the Lesser Ritual of the Pentagram also has thaumaturgical applications. One of the early forms was the use of the invoking pentagram for charging holy water for use in Golden Dawn ceremonies or for the personal work of the practitioner. This was to further aid in the charging of the basis of the holy water with the appropriate Divine forces.

---

[48] Henosis from ancient Greek is the word for "oneness", especially mystical oneness. In Neoplatonism it is the union with what which is most fundamental; the One Source or the Monad. In essence, it is the union of the person with the Divine and the ultimate goal of the Magnum Opus.
[49] Regardie. *The Golden Dawn*, p. 54.

THE LESSER RITUAL OF THE PENTAGRAM

The power of the Lesser Ritual of the Pentagram to work both theurgical and thaumaturgical forces simultaneously for the practitioner in not limited to those that are Initiates of the Golden Dawn Tradition, but to anyone that practices ceremonial or ritual magic. For the Golden Dawn Initiate, this foundational ritual takes on new power and a life of its own because the practitioner is now connected to egregore or current of the Golden Dawn which fuels, as it were, the Lesser Ritual of the Pentagram.

Conclusion

The Lesser Ritual of the Pentagram is the first ritual that any Neophyte of the Golden Dawn receives to begin their Work within the Tradition. Thanks to the writings of Aliester Crowley, Israel Regardie, Dion Fortune, Donald Michael Kraig, John Michael Greer, Chic and Tabatha Cicero, and a host of others, the Lesser Ritual of the Pentagram, at least in its banishing form, has now become nearly ubiquiteous thoroughout most of the modern Western Magical Traditions, even being appropriated to some degree or another by the Neo-pagan movement.

The Lesser Ritual of the Pentagram is first and foremost a Golden Dawn ritual. It is the creation of the Golden Dawn founders for use within the Golden Dawn. It partakes in the symbolism and teachings of the Golden Dawn Tradition, and really takes on a life of its own once a practitioner has been initiated into the Golden Dawn Tradition.

The Ritual espouses the most basic tenents of the Golden Dawn, particularly the exortium given to the Neophyte that balance in all things must be maintained. To that end, the modern concentration on the *banishing* aspect of this foundational ritual can go a long way to damaging the practitioner, actually creating an imbalance for them. Performance of the invoking form of this ritual in addition to and in conjunction with the banishing form goes a long way towards creating a balance for the practitioner. Particularly in that the *invoking* form of the Lesser Ritual of the Pentagram begins the process of spiritual contact with one's Holy Guardian Genius and Higher Genius.

THE LIGHT EXTENDED

The ritual is balanced in that it is to be performed at least twice per day, once in the morning as an invoking form, and once in the evening as a banishing form. These twin aspects can be likened to prayer to the Highest to help cause change within and about the practitioner, especially at the times of the rising and setting sun.

They symbolism of the Lesser Ritual of the Pentagram is both simple and complex, like many things in the Golden Dawn Tradition. The simplisity of the Lesser Ritual is part of its charm and ease to both learn and perform. The use of "white light" for the visualization of the Pentagrams, circle, and even the Archangels assures that even those that are challenged by the techniques of visualization can perform this ritual so that its use causes effect for the practitioner.

It is this simplistic looking ritual that is the basis for much of what will be used ritualistically in the Golden Dawn Tradition. The Lesser Ritual begins the theurgical process of connecting to the Higher Guardian Genius (some would call this the Holy Guardian Angel). While the founders of the Golden Dawn wrote that the Neophyte "may form some idea of how to attract and come into communication with spiritual and invisible things."[50] they clearly had in mind that the practitioner was beginning their journey towards better understanding their own Higher Genius through the Guardian Genius. This is a purely theurgical approach which is later used in the Inner Order work of the Adeptus Minor, and in grades higher than Adeptus Minor, through such things as Spiritual Development given in Shin c portion of *Ritual Z2 – The Formulae of the Magic of Light*.

The use of the Lesser Ritual of the Pentagram whether in a banishing or invoking form is something that a member of the Golden Dawn utilizes as part of their ritual Work no matter the grade. A Neophyte whom is new to the Golden Dawn Tradition to the long-practiced Adeptus Exemptus all make use of this foundational ritual. Whereas the Adeptus uses it not only as a stand alone rite, but also as an integral part of more complex ritual work, the benefit is the same as for the Neophyte just beginning the path.

Let the practitioner be enflamed when performing this foundational ritual. Be full of kavannah while performing this and any other ritual work within the Golden Dawn Tradition. Do the

---

50 Regardie. *The Golden Dawn*, pp. 281-282.

THE LESSER RITUAL OF THE PENTAGRAM

Lesser Ritual of the Pentagram often, daily, and note how your ritual work will progress and be enhanced.

Bibliography

Abiyah, Frater. *LBRP: The Genius Child of the Golden Dawn*. Abiyah Books. CreateSpace Independent Publishing Platform, 2012.

Agrippa, Henry Cornelius. *Three Books of Occult Philosophy*. Edited and Annotated by Donald Tyson. St. Paul, Minn.: Llewellyn Publications, 1997.

Allman, George Johnston. *Greek Geometry from Thales to Eculid*. Dublin: Printed at the University Press by Ponsonby and Murphy, 1877.

Cicero, Chic, and Cicero, Sandra Tabatha. *Ritual Use of Magical Tools*. St. Paul, Minn.: Llewellyn Publications, 2000.

_____. *Self-Initiation into the Golden Dawn Tradition*. St. Paul, Minn.: Llewellyn Publications, 1998.

_____. *The Essential Golden Dawn*. St. Paul, Minn.: Llewellyn Publications, 2003.

Cicero, Sandra Tabatha. *The Book of the Concourse of the Watchtowers: An Exploration of Westcott's Enochian Tablets*. Elfers, Fl.: H.O.G.D. Books, 2011.

Cirlot, J. E. *A Dictionary of Symbols*. New York, New York: Barnes & Noble Books, 1995.

Coleman, Wade. *Sepher Sapphires: A Treatise on Gematria: Vol. I*. Fraternity of the Hidden Light, 2008.

_____. *Sepher Sapphires: A Treatise on Gematria: Vol. II*. Fraternity of the Hidden Light, 2008.

Crowley, Aleister. *Magick in Theory and Practice*. Secaucus, NJ: Castle Books, 1991.

THE LESSER RITUAL OF THE PENTAGRAM

Davidson, Gustav. *A Dictionary of Angels*. New York, New York: The Free Press, 1971.

Euclid. *Elements*. Edited by Sir Thomas Heath. Dover, Mineola. 1956.

Farrell, Nick. *Cracking the Lesser Ritual of the Pentagram*. Hermetic Virtues; Autumnal Equinox 2007; Vol. I, Edition 2. Magazine. Published by Hermetic Virtues.

Forrest, Adam P. *This Holy Invisible Companionship*. The Golden Dawn Journal; Book II; Qabalah: Theory and Magic. St. Paul, Minn.: Llewellyn Publications, 1994.

Ginzberg, Louis. *Legends of the Jews: Vol. I*. Philadelphia, Pa.: The Jewish Publication Society, 2003.

Godwin, David. *Godwin's Cabalistic Encyclopedia*. St. Paul, Minn.: Llewellyn Publications, 1997.

Godwin, Joscelyn. *The Mystery of the Seven Vowels: In Theory and Practice*. Grand Rapids, Mi.: Phanes Press, 1991.
Greer, John Michael. *Circles of Power*. St. Paul, Minn.: Llewellyn Publications, 1997.

Henson, Mitch, and Gail. *Shebilim Bahirim (The Bright Paths)*. The Golden Dawn Journal; Book II; Qabalah: Theory and Magic. St. Paul, Minn.: Llewellyn Publications, 1994.

Kaplan, Aryeh (trans.). *Sefer Yetzirah: The Book of Creation*. York Beach, ME: Samuel Weiser, Inc., 1997.

Keck, David. *Angels & Angelology in the Middle Ages*. New York, NY & Oxford, England: Oxford University Press, 1998.

Knight, Gareth. *A Practical Guide to Qabalistic Symbolism*. York Beach, ME: Weiser Books, 2001.

Küntz, Darcy. *The Golden Dawn Court Cards As Drawn by W.W. Westcott & Moina Mathers.* Edmonds, WA: Holmes Publishing Group, 1996.

Lévi, Eliphas. *Transcendental Magic.* A.E. Waite (trans.). York Beach, ME: Samuel Weiser, Inc., 1992.

Regardie, Israel. *The Golden Dawn;* 6th edition. St. Paul, Minn.: Llewellyn Publications, 1992.

_____. *The Middle Pillar: The Balance Between Mind and Magic.* Edited and Annotated by Chic and Sandra Tabatha Cicero. St. Paul, Minn.: Llewellyn Publications, 1998.

_____. *The Tree of Life: An Illustrated Study in Magic.* Edited and Annotated by Chic and Sandra Tabatha Cicero. St. Paul, Minn.: Llewellyn Publications, 2001.

Skinner, Stephen. *Sacred Geometry: Deciphering the Code.* New York, New York, USA: Sterling Publishing Co., Inc., 2006.

About the Author

Samuel Scarborough is a Senior Adept with the Ordo Stella Matutina, a modern Golden Dawn Order following the work of the original Stella Matutina. He has been interested in the occult for the last 30 years and a practitioner of the Golden Dawn system and tradition for over 25 years. His interests include Alchemy (both Practical and Spiritual Alchemy), Tarot, Astrology, Geomancy, Qabalah, and Ceremonial Magic. Historical research, Ritual and Ceremonial work are passions of his, particularly in the Golden Dawn Tradition.

Over the years he has contributed to various publications relating to his occult and esoteric interests, including *The Alchemy Journal*, *The Journal of the Western Mystery Tradition*, *Hermetic Virtues*, and *The Hermetic Tablet*. Scarborough has also contributed material to *Commentaries on the Golden Dawn Flying Rolls* and *The Philosopher's Stone: Spiritual Alchemy, Psychology, and Ritual Magic* by Israel Regardie with additional material edited by Charles "Chic" Cicero and Sandra Tabatha Cicero.

The Lord of the Universe

by Frater YShY

One of the particular features of Freemasonry and Golden Dawn ritual, is that god is always invoked in a prayer during the opening ceremony. This is not dissimilar to many institutions in Western Society, dating back to the beginning of recorded history. Examples are prayers before a Coronation, or before appropriate governmental body meetings, such as the United States Congress. What makes these prayers in Freemasonry and the Golden Dawn different, is that they usually invoke the deity with peculiar ancient titles and attributes of what is now termed the *Meditative Kabbalah*. Sometimes these names are taken from Christian mystical literature, or from bible personages that are relevant to the grade or degree being worked. The particular title of god invoked in the *Opening of the Neophyte Ceremony* is "The Lord of the Universe." In modern magical literature, this prayer is correctly understood to be taken and redacted from *The Divine Pymander of Hermes*, but there are other sources that are just as relevant that will be examined. Other sources are in some ancient Jewish prayers still in use today, and the specific prayers used in Freemasonry to open and close a Lodge. Such are the topics of this paper.

One of the problems facing new Neophytes and those who would promote the tradition through modern Golden Dawn Orders, is that it is confusing as to exactly which deity is being invoked in the Neophyte. A new member hearing our work for the first time usually assumes that this is the exoteric Jehovah, a Christian, male-gendered god. It may come as a surprise to many that while this is a good assumption, this is not the only interpretation possible. The actual god being invoked here is not the exclusively male deity worshipped in mainstream religions, but rather a creator deity that is beyond such ideas of trait and gender. Hopefully this paper will begin to explain in basic terms the different portrayals of deity in the

Golden Dawn tradition. For those true Neophytes amongst us, who may not already be familiar with the gender-fluid approach to deities in *Lurianic Kabbalah* and the Golden Dawn, this could shed some light as to the spiritual nature of the Order they have just joined. The Order has a very clear direction and openness to both masculine and feminine deities, an approach that is progressively revealed as one progresses further in the order grades.

A note on terminology and parenthesis in this paper. In order to make this undertaking the most intelligible to the reader, I have had to give unofficial titles to the various prayers, which I have placed in italics. Thus we have *The Opening Prayer*, which is sometimes informally referred to as "the holy art thous" in modern Orders, *The Neophyte Kneeling Prayer, The Emulation Entered Apprentice Opening Prayer*, etc. Usually these titles are not from any particular source, but rather my own convention. When a title is from a rubric of one of the old Orders, I have noted that and usually used the original title instead. I felt this would add some clarity to the paper, because each of these prayers are constantly cross-referenced throughout. I have used square brackets for my editorial, and boldface to assist the reader find important lines that enter into my investigation of each prayer.

Therefore, here are the scripts or rubrics for *The Opening Prayer of the Neophyte Ceremony* which invokes The Lord of the Universe, followed by the *Neophyte Kneeling Prayer* from *Bristol Temple, Whare Ra, Stella Matutina* and the *Alpha et Omega*.

NEOPHYTE OPENING PRAYER:
ADORATION TO THE LORD OF THE UNIVERSE

Holy art thou, Lord of the Universe, *(salute)*
Holy art thou, whom nature hast not formed, *(salute)*
Holy art thou, the vast and mighty one, *(salute)*
Lord of the light, and of the darkness. *(Sign of silence)*

This *Neophyte Opening Prayer* has not changed from the original 1888 *Golden Dawn*, and is identical in *The Stella Matutina* and *Alpha et Omega* rubrics from the various temples.

The original *Neophyte Kneeling Prayer* has been through very few changes over the years. In most cases these have been relatively minor, the bulk of the short prayer being remarkably consistent compared to other areas of the Neophyte Ceremony which have been adapted based on the working. The Bristol Temple prayer is the same as the Stella Matutina, with only minor punctuation changes, and a word here or there. The exception to this is in the Stella Matutina or Whare Ra *Alternate Invocation*, which is very different, but as we shall see later, it has actually been carefully composed from appropriately selected sources.

GOLDEN DAWN, ISIS URANIA #3
ORIGINAL NEOPHYTE KNEELING PRAYER

Hiero: Let the Candidate kneel while I invoke the LORD OF THE UNIVERSE!
    [Candidate kneels – S.S.].
    LORD OF THE UNIVERSE! The Vast and Mighty One! Ruler of the Light and of the Darkness! We adore Thee and we invoke Thee! Look with favour upon this Neophyte, who now kneeleth before Thee, and grant thine aid unto the higher Aspirations of his Soul, so that he may prove a true and faithful Frater among us, to the glory of thine Ineffable <u>Name</u>! Amen!

The prompt at the beginning "Let the Candidate kneel…" is a commonplace addition in these sort of kneeling prayers throughout masonic ritual. It is interesting that both the rebels in the SM and the Mathers AO Order both have made use of this masonic prompt, while it is dropped out in many of the other versions. We can see here that it is a feature in the original. This is the version of the *Kneeling Prayer* that is in use in the *Hermetic Society of the Golden Dawn* in Canada.

THE LORD OF THE UNIVERSE
STELLA MATUTINA NEOPHYTE KNEELING PRAYER

Hiero: Let the Candidate kneel while I invoke the Lord of the Universe.
(Candidate kneels).
Lord of the Universe, the Vast and Mighty One, Ruler of the Light and of the Darkness, we adore thee and we invoke Thee. Look with favour upon this Neophyte, who now kneeleth before Thee and grant thine aid unto the higher aspirations of his soul, so that he may prove a true and faithful Frater among us unto the Glory of Thy Ineffable Name. Amen.

We can see that in the CGDSM, the punctuation and grammar are slightly different, "unto" for "to," "Thy" for "thine," that sort of thing. In the following few prayers, I note that these are likely just slight drifts due to the nature of the different copyists at work. However, using *The Complete Golden Dawn System of Magic* as a source for any paper is problematic. Regardie published it under the assumption that it was the original Golden Dawn ceremonies, but even a casual read of the rest of the Neophyte Ceremony, and the other rituals and papers will show that it is actually a complete set of Stella Matutina documents. Who knows how so many re-written sections entered the CGDSM that are unsupported by any documented source MSS. We can speculate that there was some efforts and perhaps even subterfuge on the part of Regardie or perhaps the CGDSM publisher Christopher Hyatt, in order to circumvent the fact that another publisher, Llewellyn, had the copyright to Regardies original *The Golden Dawn*. Because there are so many errors and re-written sections in the other papers in the CGDSM, it should be treated as an unreliable source.

THE LIGHT EXTENDED

MORGEN ROTHE NEOPHYTE KNEELING PRAYER (INDEPENDENT AND RECTIFIED RITE)

Hiero: Let the Candidate kneel and pray while I invoke the Lord of the Universe.

The Candidate is assisted accordingly. All officers and members stand. Hierophant (turning to Altar):

O Lord of Heaven and Earth, who didst constitute all things in Wisdom, we adore Thee and we invoke Thee. Look with approval on this Neophyte, here on his knees before Thee, and grant that he may attain the heights. **Accept the pure offering of his soul aspiring unto Thee.** May he prove a faithful brother among us, to the glory of thy Name **and of the Hierarchies.**

This is apparently the *Morgen Rothe* version from 1902, which was the proto-Order that eventually became the *Stella Matutina*. It is taken from Gilbert, where he notes that it may also be an early re-write for A.E. Waite's *Independent and Rectified Rite*.

FELLOWSHIP OF THE ROSY CROSS: NEOPHYTE KNEELING PRAYER

MT: Behold, I wait without Thy door and knock. Open thy heart, O novice of this fellowship. Take in thy spiritual hands the desires and **aspirations** that have brought thee to our holy temple, and **kneeling with bended head**, place them with humility and reverence on our altar of sacrifice.

THE LORD OF THE UNIVERSE

The head of the novice is bowed, and he is directed to cross his hands on the altar.
The Master of the Temple gives a battery of one knock, and all present rise up.

MT: O Thou who sanctifiest the **heart** of man, Who leadest our desires into attainment and our **aspirations** to the steps of Thy house, sanctify, eternal God, this novice of our fellowship. **Lead him to the** perfection that is in Thee, into the splendor of Thy great white throne. May that which I have here and now restored to him in the outward signs of Thy most blessed sacraments and Thine all sacred symbols be ratified above **in Thy presence** and realized essentially within him, **to the glory of Thy name**, world without end, **Amen, and to the joy of Thy redeemed hierarchies**.

The FRC prayer, therefore shows influence of the MR or possibly IRR prayers. It also shows considerable masonic influence, with the expected similarities between the MR and SM or WR *Alternate Invocation,* given below.

BRISTOL TEMPLE
NEOPHYTE KNEELING PRAYER.

Hiero: Lord of the Universe, the Vast and Mighty One! Ruler of the Light and of the Darkness! We adore thee and We invoke thee! Look with favour on this Neophyte who now kneeleth before thee. And grant thine aid unto the higher aspirations of his soul, So that he may prove a true and faithful **Frater Neophyte** among us. To the glory of Thine Ineffable Name. Amen!

This prayer is from the Aries Press and Llewellyn publication of the SM rituals. It has not changed much since the original order.

THE LIGHT EXTENDED

WHARE RA
NEOPHYTE KNEELING PRAYER

Hiero: Lord of the Universe--the Vast and Mighty One; Ruler of the Light and of the Darkness; We adore Thee and we invoke Thee; Look with favour upon this Neophyte who kneeleth before Thee, and grant Thine aid unto the higher aspirations of his Soul, so that he may prove a true and faithful Frater *(Soror)* among us; to the Glory of Thine Ineffable Name. Amen!

Apart from the punctuation changes, and the term "Frater Neophyte," the published Bristol and Whare Ra kneeling prayers are the same.

WHARE RA "ALTERNATE INVOCATION"
(STELLA MATUTINA "ALTERNATE INVOCATION")

Hiero: Oh Thou Whom nature hath not Formed; Oh Thou Who didst in reason Constitute the things that are; **Oh Thou Whom naught but Silence can Express**; Look with favo[u]r upon this Neophyte; **grant that he may labo[u]r in high things.** Accept the pure offering of his reason from **heart** and soul stretched up to Thee. Let him become a faithful Frater among us to Thy glory and to the glory **of Thy Hierarchies.** Amen!

This is a very different prayer, and yet it has the same sentiment as the originals. Here we have "his reason from heart and soul" being offered to the deity, similar to the MR or IRR prayer. It is reminiscent of the sacrifice of passions represented in the occult tradition by the *Altar of Burnt Sacrifice* in King Solomon's Temple. While we are indebted to Zalewski's Commentaries for this prayer, interestingly enough, this prayer may not be unique to Whare Ra. Much of the Whare Ra material came from Amoun Temple in the UK, which was the Mother Temple of the Stella Matutina. The boldface here will be looked at more closely at in the Greek and Masonic portions of this paper.

ALPHA ET OMEGA
NEOPHYTE KNEELING PRAYER

Hiero: Let the Candidate kneel. *(Done.)* Lord of the Universe, The Vast One, The Mighty One, Ruler of the Light and of the Darkness. Thee we adore. Thee we invoke. Look with favour upon this Neophyte who now kneeleth before thee, and grant thine aid unto the Higher Aspirations of his *(her)* soul so that he *(she)* may prove a true and faithful Frater *(Soror)* among us. Unto the Glory of Thy Ineffable Name. Amen.

The A.O. prayer is pretty much the same as the *Stella Matutina*, but with more punctuation changes, different sentence stops, and the later sentences joined into one longer one. The most noticeable adjustment is that the A.O. prayer has actually added in prompts in brackets for both genders in every instance where it would be needed. While the Golden Dawn has always been concerned with equality in its membership, this is the first time it is clearly in the script other then the Whare Ra version, which would also have been copied at a later time period, we could estimate the early 1920's. We can also speculate that by the time this ritual was developed in the early 20_{th} century, S.L. Mathers, Moina Mathers, or the copyist for this script, Frater N.I.S.I. may have been keener to make note of the feminine in writing, a concern that was always addressed in the Order's practices, but that really did not get addressed in mainstream culture until later on in the 20th Century, but it is only my speculation that this may be the case.

THE LIGHT EXTENDED

GREEK SOURCES

The following translation of *The Divine Pymander of Hermes* is by John Everard in 1650. This older translation is not done according to modern standards, but it bears the importance of being the version Mathers, i.e. Frater DDCF would have used to flesh-out our final written rubric for the Neophyte Ceremony. As we can see, many of the lines are similar or identical to *The Neophyte Opening Prayer*. The boldface is my interjection, and is only suggestive as to where our prayer may have been adapted from. While it is not attributed directly as such in any of the papers of the old Order I am familiar with, this link is implicit and in context with the various Adept papers, such as Z3 where Thoth and therefore Hermes are central features. However, the Neophyte can see these gods reflected in the name of the branches of *The Order of the Golden Dawn*, which in the various renditions of the title of this *society*, we frequently find to be styled as *esoteric* or *hermetic,* as in pertaining to one of the most important patrons of learning, education and magic from the Greek world, *Hermes.*

THE DIVINE PYMANDER OF HERMES
By John Everard (1650)

Holy is God, the Father of all things.
   Holy is God, whose will is performed and accomplished by his own powers.
   Holy is God, that determineth to be known, and is known by his own, or those that are his.
   Holy art thou, that by thy Word has established all things.
   Holy art thou, of whom all Nature is the Image.
   Holy art thou, whom Nature hath not formed.
   Holy art thou, that art stronger than all power.
   Holy art thou, that art stronger than all excellency.
   Holy art thou, that art better than all praise.
   Accept these reasonable sacrifices from a pure soul, and a heart that stretched out unto thee.

THE LORD OF THE UNIVERSE

> **O unspeakable, unutterable, to be praised with silence!**
> I beseech thee, that I may never err from the knowledge of thee;
> > look mercifully upon me, and enable me,
> > and enlighten with this Grace those that are in
> **Ignorance,**
> > the brothers of my kind, but thy Sons.
> Therefore I believe thee, and bear witness, and go into the Life **and Light.**
> Blessed art thou, O Father; thy man would be sanctified with thee,
> > as thou hast given him all power.

As we can see at this point, this is clearly the origin of the short, four-lined prayer from the Neophyte. Here is the start of a short line-by-line comparison, which is by no means exhaustive, with the intent to open up further study.

Line one of the Neophyte Opening Prayer is **Holy art thou, Lord of the Universe.** The inference is that the Lord of the Universe is the King, regent or ruler of all. The corresponding line one of *The Divine Pymander* gives **Holy is God, the Father of all things.** The next few lines supplement this regency, stating that **(god's) will is performed and accomplished by his own powers,** and that **...(g)od... (determines) to be known, and is known by his own, or those that are his.** This is a reference to those who worship or revere the creator deity, whom in *The Divine Pymander* is identified as a form of Hermes, acting as the creator. The line **Holy art thou, that by thy Word has established all things...** suggests that by the divine fiat and word, all has been created. So we can see that this older translation lends itself to a ready interpretation of Hermes with the Christian creator deity, Jehovah, or the Jewish YHVH, as evidenced by the date of this translation (1650), and Genesis 1:2 "and the Ruach Elohim moved across the face of the Waters."

Line two of the Neophyte Opening Prayer is **Holy art thou, whom nature hast not formed.** Compare this with lines 5 and 6 of *The Divine Pymander*, which state: **Holy art thou, of whom all**

Nature is the Image... and of course provides the identical **Holy art thou, whom Nature hath not formed.** These again intimate the biblical creator in Genesis, of whom nature is the image, and whom all of nature is therefore a derivative of, and created by this deity. The primary spirit symbols in the Golden Dawn are either the eight-spoked wheel from the *Vision of Ezekiel,* or the hexagram as a symbol of the Ruach Elohim in *Genesis,* where the fire is the deity, and the water is the reflected creation. This interpretation of the hexagram does not originate from our tradition, but as we can see from *The Divine Pymander* is rather a tenet of the preceding Hermetic and Kabbalistic traditions as evidenced by *The Ancient of Days* of Elphias Levi, which in turn draws heavily upon *The Zohar.*

Line three of the Neophyte Opening Prayer is **Holy art thou, the vast and mighty one.** Compare this with lines 7 and 8 of *The Divine Pymander,* which states **Holy art thou, that art stronger than all power...** and **Holy art thou, that art stronger than all excellency.**

Line four of the Neophyte Prayer is **Lord of the light, and of the darkness.** Compare this with lines 14 and 16 of *The Divine Pymander,* which are: **and enlighten with this Grace those that are in Ignorance,** and **Therefore I believe thee, and bear witness, and go into the Life and Light.** Here ignorance is the same as darkness, and light is used as a primary metaphor for personal clarity. The enlightenment described in the Great Work of our Order does not solve all problems, or remove all afflictions, but it is rather the prerequisite state by which one may live their life, and begin to conquer their own ignorance with the clarity that light brings.

The final gesture or sign of silence in *The Neophyte Opening Prayer* is very fitting when compared to line 11 in *The Divine Pymander,* which goes **O unspeakable, unutterable, to be praised with silence!** I have often meditated on the origin of our grade signs, and for the sign of silence, it is not only the secrecy of a fraternity meant, but that of initiatic secrecy. From the quote, we can see that with so many similar terms found, it is likely that this line of *Pymander* is the origin of this particular gesture. Let us dilate upon the concept of a deity that is unspeakable, and unutterable. In this regard, there is a teaching that says all images of deity are really a daemon or spirit of the god, rather than the true reality. Compare this to the emphasis placed on silence in the Hermetic tradition, as the exclusive way to worship the highest divine, teaching that all other names and symbols at best connect only to the demiurge, a lower, wrathful and terrifying creator deity, rather than the ultimate or true god.

When the Neophyte Hall is finally declared open in the original *Golden Dawn* and *Stella Matutina*, the Kerux announces:

> In the Name of the Lord of the Universe, I declare that the sun hast arisen and that the Light shineth in the Darkness.

However, these various influences, particularly from the *Corpus Hermeticum*, are seen clearly summarized in the *Bristol Temple* and *Whare Ra* Neophyte ceremonies, where the Kerux declares the temple open with the variant, boldface mine:

> In the Name of the Lord of the Universe, **Who works in silence and whom nought but silence can express,** I declare that the sun hast arisen and the shadows flee away.

This emphasis on silence is not pure innovation based solely on *Corpus Hermeticum*, but rather has a very specific, quotable source in Mead's translation of *The Divine Pymander*. When reading Whare Ra's *Alternate Invocation* for the *Neophyte Kneeling Prayer*, one is struck by the vast departures compared to the various originals. Some of these changes can be explained by the Mead translation, other portions are from the corresponding masonic prayers we will look at later in this paper.

Here follows Mead's 1906 translation of *The Divine Pymander*, which also influences the extra sections of Whare Ra's *Alternate Invocation,* but is of course came after the original 1888 Neophyte rubric, and so Mead's work is not a factor in the original *Golden Dawn*. We can assume that the *Stella Matutina* re-write committee, or perhaps Neville Meakin, who was instrumental in the S.M. Portal re-write, may have turned to Mead as the most recent and therefore

THE LIGHT EXTENDED

more reliable translation of *The Divine Pymander*. My boldface is set to indicate the exact quote from Mead used in the *Whare Ra* and *Stella Matutina* ceremonies. As has already been mentioned, this is a reference to the *Corpus Hermeticum* teachings on silence as being the only fitting way to worship the true deity. I leave it to the diligence of the reader to compare the Mead translation to Everard, as well as to our *Neophyte Opening Prayer*.

A TRIPLE TRISAGION
[THE DIVINE PYMANDER OF HERMES]
By G.R.S. Mead (1906)

    Holy art Thou, O God, the Universals' Father.
    Holy art Thou, O God, Whose Will perfects itself by means of its own Powers.
    Holy art Thou, O God, Who willest to be known and art known by Thine own.
    Holy art Thou, Who didst by Word make to consist the things that are.
    Holy art Thou, of Whom All-nature hath been made an Image.
    Holy art Thou, Whose Form Nature hath never made.
    Holy art Thou, more powerful than all power.
    Holy art Thou, transcending all preeminence.
    Holy art Thou, Thou better than all praise.
Accept my reason's offerings pure, from soul and heart for aye stretched up to Thee, O Thou unutterable, unspeakable, **Whose Name naught but the Silence can express!**
Give ear to me who pray that I may ne'er of Gnosis fail -- Gnosis which is our common being's nature -- and fill me with Thy Power, and with this Grace of Thine, that I may give the Light to those in ignorance of the Race, my Brethren and Thy Sons!
For this cause I believe, and I bear witness. I go to Life and Light. Blessed art Thou, O Father. Thy Man would holy be as Thou art holy, e'en as Thou gavest him Thy full authority to be.

THE LIGHT EXTENDED

JEWISH SOURCES

Ancient formula or convention in Jewish prayer has many common prayers beginning with "*Barukh ata Adonai Eloheinu, melekh ha'olam...*" which translates as "Blessed are You, Lord our God, King of the Universe..." However, it is possible that there is another more distinct origin for the Golden Dawn redaction, in the form of the ancient Jewish prayer *Adon Olam*. This prayer was once an important feature in Judaism, but nowadays seems relegated to being only a children's prayer, something to be sung at the end of Synagogue services to invite the congregation to stay a little longer, or to symbolize that they do not wish this weekly time together with each other and the deity to come to an end.

To switch from the Jewish context to the Golden Dawn, the two words *Adon Olam* become familiar to the beginning practitioner or Neophyte as they both appear in *The Lesser Ritual of the Pentagram*. *Adon* is the divine name *Adonai*, meaning "The Lord," which is used along with the other divine titles and names in charging the pentagrams. The Hebrew word *olam* is translated as "forever and ever" in the Qabalistic Cross, which is a Hebrew redaction of the important Christian staple of *The Lord's Prayer*.

Below is an older version of Adon Olam that was contemporary with the founding of The Golden Dawn. It should be compared with both The Neophyte Opening Prayer and The Divine Pymander of Hermes. Here follows the prayer or song.

ADON OLAM

The Lord of the Universe who reigned
before anything was created.
When all was made by his will
He was acknowledged as King.

And when all shall end
He still all alone shall reign.
He was, He is,
and He shall be in glory.

And He is one, and there's no other,
to compare or join Him.
Without beginning, without end
and to Him belongs diminion and power.

And He is my G-d, my living G-d.
to Him I flee in time of grief,
and He is my miracle and my refuge,
who answers the day I shall call.

To Him I commit my spirit,
in the time of sleep and awakening,
even if my spirit leaves,
G-d is with me, I shall not fear.

Translations and transliterations from other languages have always been problematic. Older terms can themselves become unclear as language naturally drifts. While the Hebrew *Adon* is indeed translated as "The Lord," it is more a descriptive title used in numerous languages, Semitic or otherwise, than something that is essentially Hebrew. *Adon* is derived from the Greek god *Adonis,* and refers to a youthful male god that is beautiful, handsome, shining, or solar. *Adon* and *Adonis* has a lengthy history, going from being a very specific Greek deity, to a generalized term for "The Lord" in many languages, including but not only in Hebrew, and then today translated as *Adonai,* which is only understood nowadays to be a Jewish word or term for god, or "The Lord." We have to take the time to specify here that the original word is older than Judaism, and was originally not only the Jewish god being referred to, but could be any masculine or lordly Chaldean, Babylonian, Greek or Semitic deity.

The Hebrew *Olam* is translated as "forever," but is also equally means eternity, the endless infinity of reality, the never-ending nature that was assumed of the ancient world and heavens. *Adon Olam* is therefore commonly translated as *Eternal Master,* but a rendering of *Lord of the Universe* as I am asserting may possibly have been done in the Golden Dawn, is also correct.

In the modern day, when we wish to comprehend the right

connotation that the word *olam* would evoke to the mind of one of our ancient ancestors or spiritual antecedents, then we have to use a new, more suitable term, "the universe." In commonplace spiritual speech, we have partially been informed by New Age vernacular which has long-since appropriated scientific or pseudo-scientific terminology. "The universe" does indeed evoke a sense of "eternity" in a way that an English rendering of *olam* as "forever" or "the world" no longer can.

MASONIC SOURCES

The masonic prayers that the founders of the Golden Dawn would have been familiar with are from Emulation Freemasonry, which was the particular mode of working done in Britain at that time. There are several versions of the first three degrees in masonry, and the *Emulation Work* is a type of ceremony that is still performed to the present day in the UK, Scotland, in my homeland of Canada, and elsewhere around the world. We will look at the Opening and Closing prayers of the initial introductory *Emulation First Degree* or *Entered Apprentice* from the Craft or Blue Lodge, as well as the prayer given when the Candidate kneels at the Altar. WM is Worshipful Master, and IPM is Immediate Past Master, equivalent to the Golden Dawn Hierophant and Immediate Past Hierophant. Again, the boldface script is mine to help indicate sections we will look more closely at in the following sections.

ENTERED APPRENTICE OPENING PRAYER

WM: The Lodge being duly formed, before I declare it open, **let us invoke the assistance** of the **Great Architect of the Universe** in all our undertakings; may our labours, thus begun in order, be conducted in peace, and closed in harmony.

IPM: So mote it be.

In some modern lodges, there are a few small changes. For example, the prayer is given by a new Officer named the Chaplain, and in reply, it is the entire lodge that says "So mote it be," but neither of these were part of the original Emulation Ritual.

ENTERED APPRENTICE OPENING HYMN

All: Hail, Eternal by whose aid,
       All created things were made;
       Heav'n and earth Thy vast design;
       Hear us Architect Divine.

       May our work begun in Thee,
       Ever blest with order be;
       And may we, when labors cease,
       Part in harmony and peace.

There is really no equivalent to an opening hymn in the Golden Dawn, but it takes a similar position in the opening ceremonial of the Entered Apprentice to *The Adoration to the Lord of the Universe* in the Neophyte Opening. Comparing the *Entered Apprentice Opening Hymn* to the Jewish *Adon Olam*, one might draw the conclusion that the *opening* masonic hymn is simply a liberal translation of the Jewish hymn or prayer to *close* synagogue services. It is interesting that it both hymns open with creation, proceed through worship and end in death. The masonic prayer has the conventional addition of peace, both in the after life, and the peace of harmony without strife during life.

ENTERED APPRENTICE KNEELING PRAYER

WM: Vouchsafe thine aid, Almighty Father and **Supreme Governor of the Universe,** to our present convention, **and grant that this Candidate** for Freemasonry may so **dedicate and devote his life to Thy service** as to become **a true and faithful brother among us.** Endue him with a competency of Thy divine wisdom, that, if assisted by the secrets of our Masonic art, he may the better be enabled to unfold the beauties of true godliness, **to the honour and glory of Thy Holy Name.**

IPM: So mote it be.

While it is not in the standard *Emulation Entered Apprentice* quote I have included above, it is common practice in many lodges to add the prompt "Let the Candidate kneel while I invoke the assistance of the Great Architect of the Universe. *(done)*."

ENTERED APPRENTICE CLOSING PRAYER

WM: Brethren, before we close the Lodge, let us with all reverence and humility express our gratitude to the **Great Architect of the Universe** for favours already received; may   He continue to preserve the Order by cementing and adorning it with every moral and social virtue.

IPM: So mote it be.

As we can easily see, many of the lines in these prayers, as well as the format, are related to those in to the Golden Dawn. The masonic titles of the deity used in the *Entered Apprentice Degree* is *The Great Architect of the Universe,* and *Supreme Governor of the Universe* (the latter is not used very often in some lodges), are some what analogous to *Adon Olam,* which is often translated as *Eternal Master* or the equally correct *Lord of the Universe.*

While Freemasonry is an important source for Golden Dawn and other types of modern Lodges ceremonial structure, it is important not to conflate the two Orders. The Golden Dawn is very different from what is commonly termed *Regular Freemasonry* primarily in that GD has magical content, while masonry does not. The esoteric components of the Scottish Rite, for example, are actually drawn from Elphias Levi, and do not appear in Regular Freemasonry or Craft Lodge, which is what 99% of Freemasons belong to. Many organizations draw from Freemasonry, for example, some of the rituals of the Mormon Church use adapted masonic degrees. However, there should be no misunderstanding that somehow this would make the Mormons into Freemasons, or that their Church is somehow closely related to occultism, which it is not, such a misunderstanding would be highly offensive to them. Hopefully this example will serve to clarify that similar ceremonial proceedings do not mean the purpose of these organizations are somehow linked.

The first reaction our initiates give when discovering this ceremonial relationship to Freemasonry is often excitement, but more often it is tinged with disappointment. For far too long, the Golden Dawn has been equated with the secret Church, or as some mysterious continental magical Order. It is important to look at the roots of our system, which are magical, but also theosophical and masonic. Experienced magicians tend to welcome new information that can enrich their knowledge, and a study of the masonic and fringe-masonic degrees in relation to the Golden Dawn can be a fruitful one for any occultist to undertake. Those in the latter category who experience disappointment with the masonic connection, seem to initially assume that somehow the Golden Dawn is a mere copy of Freemasonry with magic added in, but nothing could be further from the truth. The fact is that *all* masonic and fringe-masonic ritual bears this same, characteristic structure we are analyzing here. When looking at occultism from a magical perspective, the Golden Dawn is a vehicle for magical tutelage that has switched from one-to-one teaching of practices into a lodge setting with masonic style initiations and advancements through grades and degrees. When looking at the Golden Dawn from a masonic perspective, the Order is then correctly termed *fringe-masonry*, and then it fits under the umbrella of a wider Hermetic, Alchemical, Astrological and Masonic tradition.

Regardless of the above distinctions, in this type of ceremony, there is *always* an Opening ceremony that includes a prayer, then the candidate *always* kneels at the Altar or between the Pillars for the second prayer over the Candidate, and finally a Closing ceremony *always* includes another prayer. It doesn't matter which degree is being worked, what masonic or fringe-masonic order, chapter, lodge or hall, or what the purpose of the various orders are, being masonic, esoteric, mystical, magical or religious, this is the same "lodge" structure, and it is a consistent format. In the higher grades of our order, we study these constant features under the term *formulae*. Hopefully the use of this term *formulae* assists our members in better comprehending how our ritual and ceremonial work nestles into the masonic tradition, but without having been a mainstream part of it, hence the designation *fringe-masonry*.

We see that the masonic line above from the *Entered Apprentice Kneeling Prayer* which goes "and grant that this Candidate for Freemasonry may so dedicate and devote his life to Thy service as to become a true and faithful brother among us" can be compared to the *Alternate Invocation* of the *Neophyte Kneeling Prayer* from Whare Ra already quoted above, the relevant part of which runs: "Look with favo[u]r upon this Neophyte; grant that he may labo[u]r in high things...Let him become a faithful Frater among us..." The "grant that he might **labo[u]r**" in the Whare Ra *Alternate Invocation* shows a definite masonic influence from the *Entered Apprentice Opening Prayer* which says: "may our **labours**, thus begun in order, be conducted in peace, and closed in harmony."

So we have a possible lineage or evolution of these prayers, chronologically: *The Divine Pymander of Hermes, Adon Olam,* then the Masonic Prayers and Hymns used in the *Emulation Entered Apprentice Initiation,* and finally all these elements coming together in *The Neophyte Prayer* or *The Lord of the Universe*. If this is the case, then we have come full circle with the Golden Dawn, where all these elements, Greek, Hebrew, Hermetic and Masonic are unified once again.

GENDER IN THE GOLDEN DAWN PRAYERS

As was briefly mentioned in the introduction, one of the more challenging aspects of the modern Order is how to treat the gender of deities, sepheroth, and our various spiritual concepts. These

THE LORD OF THE UNIVERSE

prayers are all written as if referring to the exoteric male deity worshipped in Christianity and Judaism. Modern orders no longer draw their members from the exclusively Protestant stock of 19th Century Britain, but rather have neo-pagans, Buddhists, Thelemites and atheists joining. Perhaps there was a time and a place where the exclusive male pronoun was correct in regards to deity, or the members joining were culturally used to the male pronoun as a default, but at this time it needs to be addressed; as envisioning god as exclusively male is unsupported in the older documents and teachings of our Order.

Hermes had a common form as both masculine and phallic, but there was also the *Hermaphrodite* or dual-gender Hermes-Aphrodite. The *Elohim* or "gods" in *Zohar* are male and female. In the Lurianic and Sabatean Kabbalah which feeds into modern Hasidim, *Seder Hishtalshelus* or the chain of being, is the first teaching one learns. There, while the deity is still described with male pronouns, the most important initial teaching is that "The King (or regent) delights in himself." This is the creation of the Universe, with no gender implied. This essential principle is above the monad, and can not be given a precise gender. If *En Soph* has a beginning in Kether, but has no end, *Adon Olam*, who has no begining and no end is a higher deity. This type of creation through masturbation or self-pleasure is reflected in various other Egyptian myths, such as that of Ptah, Khnum, or Shu. It is easy to speculate if these Egyptian myths eventually led into the secret Kabbalistic teachings about the Jewish deity "delighting in himself" to create the universe. There is also the teaching that there is a feminine face of god, known as the Shekinah.

While this gender teaching have once been a secret initiatory concept in the Golden Dawn, possibly as a theological and magical subtlety reserved for much higher grades of our order, the current culture of western society makes any obfuscation inherent in this situation intolerable to our new members. The intelligent and well-rounded candidates that the Order attracts these days will immediately question any such concept which appears to be residual from overly Patriarchal or male-dominant society, to the point where their progress in the grades may be self-halted due to conscientious objection to the idea of an exclusively male deity. The cultural diffusion of our once-secret ideas in Thelema, Wicca, and the New Age have all had their influence, and along with the concurrent relative freedom enjoyed by modern academia, feminism, and other political thought, we may easily state that the world has seriously changed since the founding of our Order in 1888. It only makes sense that the expectations of new members would have also changed since then.

Therefore, we can plainly state that the terms *Lord of the Universe* and *Elohim* in the Golden Dawn are to be treated as *The King* in *Zohar*, the import being a genderless regent above the monad, higher than *En Soph* and the *Elohim*, higher than any concept of the union of genders in one god or gods. Thus we have a non-gendered deity or *Adon Olam*, acting as the original creator in a world far above the level of a unified co-creator, which is usually termed the union of *Abba* (father) and *Aima* (mother) as the *Elohim* (gods) in the personage *Arik Anpin* (the vast countenance). While these terms are not going to be familiar at this stage of study for most new members, the descriptions of them are clear enough that the Neophyte should be able to appreciate their relevance. While it is usually deemed inappropriate to quote from higher grade papers in the lower grades, in this case an exception is warranted, as it is our best example of this teaching. Without giving away higher secrets, we may provide a few words from an Adeptus Major paper for the Second Order, where Frater DDCF, or Mathers says:

> The word Elohim, as itself expressing...masculine and feminine, great goddess and great god...(in Genesis) the Elohim created Adam in their own image and likeness, Male and Female (by some said to be Male-Female) created they them...and not merely the "Royal We" as in English.... In the Zohar, there is constant allusion to the nature of male and female in all of creation, even the angels themselves...

Similar sentiments are hinted at but not as expressly stated in Frater DDCF's *Introduction to Kabbalah Unveiled,* an oft-quoted document included in this package for the Neophyte. The esoteric subtitles of the Tarot trumps also show this teaching in application. Later in the same Adept paper, Frater DDCF goes on to say:

> Thus, then, are the Divine Aeons represented both as Gods and Goddesses, though at times the Force may be better symbolized by a Goddess, and at times by a God. But, if thou (wilt) symbolize the Creative Power of the Universe by the one to the exclusion of the other, assuredly thou wilt be led into error.

Hopefully the above quote will confirm my assertions to the satisfaction of our membership as to the true teachings of our tradition, regardless of a member's grade. There will not be any gender teachings that are slanted in the direction of male-dominant orthodox religion in this organization, nor are there any gender exclusions that run contrary to our *Seven Pillars of Golden Dawn* as published on the Thuban Temple website. For later in our Outer Order rituals it is very clear that even *The Elohim* are male and female gods working together in unity. I hope this plain statement will be enough to satisfy any questions the Neophyte may have at this point.

SUMMARY AND CONCLUSION

Adon Olam bears a remarkable resemblance to the prayer from the *Divine Pymander of Hermes*, and it is tempting to wonder if the two prayers were related at some point. We know that at times the Kabbalah was heavily influenced by Neo-Platonism, perhaps this origin has been commemorated by the Neophyte Opening ceremony of our Order. Further scholarship needs to be done in this area.

The Neophyte Opening Prayer, and the further exegesis with *The Divine Pymander of Hermes* and *Adon Olam* is remarkably consistent with the sentiment in our ritual, which is in turn a fringe-masonic rite, with internal consistencies which indicate the Neophyte Prayer was adapted or taken from the prayers and hymn in the *Entered Apprentice Initiation*. I have also shown that Whare Ra was influenced by Mead's newer translation of *The Divine Pymander*, as well as freemasonry. While the masonic prayers are indeed written to the Protestant Jehovah, in later freemasonry, it takes a further nondenominational, non-christian meaning. I believe I have successfully shown that the male gender was not used exclusively in the Golden Dawn, with its use of Gnostic Aeons, gods and goddesses, and other feminine powers in the form of the Shekinah, and the various genders and mailable androgyny of Angels. I will end with a quote from the charge or *Neophyte Address* given by the Hiereus in the Neophyte Ceremony.

> To this end let me first earnestly recommend you never to forget due honour and reverence to the Lord of the Universe, for as the whole is greater than its parts, so is he far greater than we, who are but as sparks derived from that unsupportable light which is in him. It is written that the borders of his garment of flame sweep the ends of the universe and unto him all return. Therefore do we adore him, therefore do we invoke him; therefore in adoration to him sinks even the Banner of the East.

At this point in the ritual, the Hierophant slowly and silently drops the Banner of the East, and then raises it up again. Thus, even our greatest symbol in the Outer Order, *The Banner of the East,* which bears the hexagram of the spirit of the gods, or *Ruach Elohim*, is merely a subservient symbol, and thus, along with all of creation, our holy symbol silently adores the divine reality in the form of its creator.

About the Author

Frater YShY is the Imperator of the Hermetic Society of the G.D. He is a York and Scottish Rite Freemason, and is connected to other lodges of the Western Mystery Tradition and Fringe-masonry. He is the author of *Adept Magic in the Golden Dawn Tradition*.

He has a keen interest in the Golden Dawn, Jewish Kabbalah, Greek and Roman studies and tarot, as well as Talismans, Enochian scrying and Classical Evocation.

Private Ritual for Influencing a Person for Good: or to Correct Evil Habits (Stella Matutina)

Introduction

by Tony Fuller

In the two or three final years of the Golden Dawn many of the senior Adepts began to put the knowledge they had acquired to create their own rituals for a variety of practical purposes. Florence Farr, Annie Horniman, J.W. Brodie Innes, William Butler Yeats, and Dr. R.W. Felkin were all amongst this group although not, curiously, William W. Westcott whose creative output in magical work did not seem to extend beyond the work he had previously carried out in helping to found the Golden Dawn. This tendency to apply the Golden Dawn theory to problems arising in everyday life, as opposed to ceremonies conducted solely for magical purposes, gathered momentum in the short-lived Morgenrothe (M.R.) Order, which was the Golden Dawn renamed in the light of the threat of adverse publicity arising from the Horus scandal, the recent difficulties regarding Macgregor Mathers' allegations about Westcott forging some of the foundational documents, and the emerging problems with Aleister Crowley. But it was Dr. Felkin's Stella Matutina, taking the bulk of the M.R. membership, which appears to have produced the largest number of rituals and papers intended to bring magic into the daily lives of its members, into the lives of their families, and even to those of the unsuspecting public. Indeed, in the latter regard, special rituals were performed in the Stella Matutina during both

World Wars with the purpose of assisting the allied war effort.

The most frequent theme identified in such S.M. material was undoubtedly that of health and healing, and perhaps this is not surprising given that the profession of medicine was well so represented within the ranks of the aspiring magicians. The notion of the 'magician as healer' was given considerable emphasis in the Order and it also blended well with the additional fact that a large proportion of the S.M. membership were priests and clergymen. In Britain at this time the Anglican church, and especially its Anglo-Catholic faction, encouraged the notion of 'spiritual healing' and several 'guilds' were founded under the auspices of the church with the express aim of healing sickness and disease through the power of prayer and meditational exercises. All this was fertile ground for the priests within the S.M. who were especially attracted to the idea of a priest of the church being also an active magician who was able to help the community not merely by means of his spiritual rank and vocation but also through his knowledge and ability as an Adept of the magical arts.

Perhaps the most notable example of the 'magician-priest' was Father Charles Fitzgerald from the Community of the Resurrection (also known as the "Mirfield Fathers"), an Anglican Order of celibate monks which had been created in the late 19th century in the wave of increasing interest in Catholicism within the Anglican church. Like many other Mirfield Fathers, the Rev. Charles Fitzgerald joined Felkin's Stella Matutina and proceeded quickly to the Second Order. Indeed, he rose to the high Grade of Magister Templi 8=3 and became a Chief of the Amoun Temple in charge of instruction. His magical prowess became quite well known even amongst some of church-going members of the public whom he sought to assist. Father Fitzgerald adapted many S.M. rituals to assist distressed people requiring spiritual help, and carried out a number of exorcisms and banishments which employed both Anglican rituals and adaptions of the Lesser Banishing Ritual of the Pentagram. But it was clearly healing work which was the focus of Father Fitzgerald's work and no doubt because of his expertise he was asked by Dr.Felkin to establish the Anglican St. Raphael's Guild of Healing. This Guild grew rapidly in the Church, spread to other countries, and still operates today.

It seems highly unlikely that its origins within the Stella Matutina are known to the present membership. Father Fitzgerald had a brave war record in the First World War and served alongside the troops as chaplain, sharing their horrors in the trenches. Apparently, or so he believed, his magical beliefs and expertise was of considerable assistance to him and, perhaps, to those he helped.

Within the Order of the Alpha et Omega, which was the section of the old Order remaining loyal to Mathers, there is little evidence that A.O. members created the equivalent rituals for everyday purposes. Nevertheless, this may well be because there was at that time a very close relationship between the A.O. and the Cromlech Temple, officially known as the 'Holy Order of the Sun'. The foundation of the Cromlech Temple, or Sun Order, seems to be contemporaneous with that of the Golden Dawn and the two existed alongside one another and shared some membership. It is understood that both Mathers and his wife Moina joined the Cromlech, along with many of the A.O. Adepti. Indeed, J.W. Brodie Innes, who officially succeeded Mathers upon his death in 1918, was the Head of the Cromlech Temple, a position known as "Metatron". While there is some overlap between the activities of the G.D. and Cromlech, there is considerable emphasis in many of the latter's papers and rituals on healing various human ills. Such illness, whether physical, mental or spiritual, is attributed to malfunction within an individual's Aura, or Sphere of Sensation, and several of the papers are devoted to explaining the theory behind this and ritualistic methods of rectifying the situation and bringing health to the individual. All this Cromlech material is consistent with that of the G.D. (or A.O.) and indeed there are numerous references within Cromlech papers to the A.O. With the decline of the A.O. in subsequent decades the same relationship was established between the S.M. and the Cromlech Temple.

Below is a short ritual written by Dr. Felkin to enable an Order member to "influence a person for good". There are several variations of this ritual, some longer, and also within the S.M. corpus there are many other examples of small rituals intended to assist the process of daily living. Some concern the blessing of a home, some exorcising evil spirits, some alleviating depression or suffering, while others give directions for making holy water, particular talismans and so forth. I have replicated the spelling and capitalization of the original.

PRIVATE RITUAL FOR INFLUENCING A PERSON FOR GOOD: OR TO CORRECT EVIL HABITS

Never to be told without Frater F.R.'s permission (F.R. was Dr. R.W. Felkin).

Get a small photograph, full face, of the person to be treated. Draw around the photograph the shape of an egg, then with "Chinese White" paint within the egg-shape so that the face alone stands out from the White Colour. Take a sheet of writing paper which, when folded in half, is the size to fit the photo, then cut out a Pentagram in gold paper with the lines half an inch thick, the size of the photo and paste it on the inside of the left side of the sheet of paper facing the photo. Then cut out a Hexagram in silver paper and paste it on the other side of the paper so that the photo, when the paper is closed and folded over the photo, will have the Pentagram before the face and the Hexagram behind it. Have a stout envelope ready to receive the photo after the following ceremony has been performed.

On a small table in the Centre of the room place the sheet of paper open with the photo upon it, the top of the photo facing East.

Perform the Banishing and then the Invoking Rituals of the Pentagram around the room.

Then stand in the West facing the Photo. Make three Circles around the photo against the Sun.

Then make the Banishing Pentagram over the photo.

Then make 3 circles round the photo with the Sun.

Then make the Invoking Pentagram over the photo, and then the Qabbalist Cross.

Then, after Crossing yourself, point a thin-pointed object (e.g. a hat pin) towards the photo, and say: "I ……….. a Frater (vel Soror) of the S.M. in the Outer, of the …… Grade do propose, if the Lord of the Universe does so will, at this present day and hour to help (or bring relief) to N or M who is in pain (or in trouble or doubt or whatever it is you want to do). Try to realise the person as if in the photo. Then raise the eyes to Heaven and say a short prayer or meditation to the Lord of the Universe stating what you wish done for the person in question. Then, again trying to think that the person is before you, make the 0=0 Sign towards the photograph, concentrating the Will on it, stopping as soon as you feel enough force has gone from you. Then make the Sign of Silence. Do this thrice.

Then cover the Photograph with the paper and say, "N or M by the Power in me I command you to be relieved, if the Lord will, for before you flames the Pentagram and behind you shines the Six Rayed Star.

Put the Photograph in the envelope and then offer a short address or prayer of thanks, and then put it away till you need it again. This same ceremony should be done two or three times a week but NOTE, the Banishing Circle round and the Banishing Pentagram over the photograph are not to be done again.

For a Second Order Member: Say, "I ………. A Frater (vel Soror) of the R.R. et A.C. of the …….. Grade do propose, if the Lord of the Universe etc.

Instead of the 0=0 Signs make the LVX Signs and project them on the photograph or a simulacrum.

About the Author

After a brief period as an academic, Tony Fuller spent a long career in the New Zealand diplomatic service initially and then working for related government agencies.

He first came into contact with members of the last surviving Stella Matutina Temple in 1975 and thereafter became keenly interested in the Order of the Golden Dawn and its offshoots, an interest he has retained ever since.

In 2010 he received his doctorate of philosophy from Exeter University on an aspect of the Golden Dawn, and he has written various articles relating to the Order.

Dr. Fuller is retired and now lives in Scotland.

Theurgy and the Body of Light

by Jayne Gibson

> The Augoeides is the Higher Self's luminous radiation when freed from the flesh. Though during incarnation it is only a shadow. It alone can redeem the soul. It is Divine Spirit, our seventh and highest principle. It is the personal god of every man. It is the Atman, the Self, the Mighty Lord and Protector who shows his full power to those who can recognize the "still small voice." It is the man being released from its gross counterpart bathing in the light of his essence, reflecting the Spirit of Truth.
>
> — Excerpts from *Nous Augoeides of the Neoplatonists*

Due to its incarnation in matter the soul has lost touch with its Divine nature and has forgotten its essential origin and true identity. It was the Neoplatonists who developed theurgical practices in order to restore the contact between the human and the Divine in the self. Theurgy is a spiritual practice designed to return the soul to its Divine origins through certain rites. This is possible due to the fact that although the embodied soul is dominated by matter and physical necessity, it is still Divine in origin.

The Neoplatonic philosopher Porphyry believed that contemplation alone could lead the soul back to its origins, but Iamblichus—his student—disagreed, which led to his writing *On the Egyptian Mysteries*. Iamblichus believed that the transcendence of the Divine could not be grasped by contemplation alone, because it is beyond the rationale of the human being and cannot be understood or expressed by the reasoning mind. Iamblichus posited that theurgy was an imitation of the gods, and he described theurgic observance as "ritualised cosmogony"[51] that endowed embodied souls with

---

51 Cosmogony is the study of the origin and development of the universe.

the Divine responsibility of creating and preserving the cosmos. This is analogous to the ancient Egyptian belief of the necessity in maintaining Ma'at (truth, order and balance). The ancient Egyptians had a deep conviction of an underlying holiness and unity within the universe and cosmic harmony was maintained by correct public, private, and ritual life.

Theurgy is a series of rituals and operations aimed at recovering our transcendent roots by retracing the distinct characteristics of the Divine through the layers of our own being. Theurgic ritual occurs on two levels simultaneously in that the magician works with correspondences, the physical symbols of spiritual forces, and also utilizes the mental and spiritual practices of visualization, vibration and the invocatory recitation of prayer. In the context of ritual, the theurgist starts out with correspondences of the Divine in matter (talismans, candles, incenses, etc.) and then transitions into the purely mental and spiritual aspects of ritual, eventually reaching a level of consciousness where the inner spark of the soul unites with the Divine.

There are only a few ways to achieve a return to Primal Unity, or union with Divinity, i.e., death, certain forms of ritual and meditative work, and the creation of the Body of Light, often called the Augoeides, which means the luminous body. The Body of Light is a spiritual term for the non-physical body associated with enlightenment. It is known by many names in different spiritual traditions such as the Resurrection Body in Christianity, the Immortal Body (soma athanaton) in Hermeticism, and the Luminous Body (Akh) in Ancient Egypt, to name just a few.

There is a misidentification of the Body of Light as the astral body, but the astral body is an etheric form common to all people. The Body of Light is deliberately built by the magician for a specific purpose. In theurgy this purpose is to achieve enlightenment and experience union with the Divine Light.

In Tablet IX of the Emerald Tablets of Thoth, it states:

THE LIGHT EXTENDED

List ye, O man, hear ye my voice,
teaching of Wisdom and Light in this cycle;
teaching ye how to banish the darkness,
teaching ye how to bring Light in thy life.

Seek ye, O man, to find the great pathway
that leads to eternal LIFE as a SUN.
Draw ye away from the veil of the darkness.
Seek to become a Light in the world.
Make of thyself a vessel for Light,
a focus for the Sun of this space.

… Thy LIGHT, O man, is the great LIGHT,
shining through the shadow of flesh.
Free must thou rise from the darkness
before thou art One with the LIGHT.

… Long, long ago, I cast off my body.
Wandered I free
through the vastness of ether,
circled the angles
that hold man in bondage.

Know ye, O man, ye are only a spirit.
The body is nothing.
The Soul is ALL.
Let not your body be a fetter.
Cast off the darkness and travel in Light.
Cast off your body, O man, and be free,
truly a Light that is ONE with the Light.

The Body of Light is that part of consciousness which has the ability to separate from the physical body while maintaining a connection to the material senses and the conscious mind. It is the perfection of a spiritual vehicle for the projection and continuation of consciousness beyond material reality. The substance of the Body of Light is composed of the vital life force of the magician, called in some spiritual traditions Prana[52] or Chi.[53] It is thus an integral part of the self, but also under the command of the self, and it works in the spiritual realms separate from the physical realm.

Mark Stavish, in his paper entitled *The Body of Light in the Western Esoteric Tradition*, a paper written for the online Hermetic Library, states that the stages of the growth of the Body of Light correspond to total realization on the Lunar (or Yetziratic), Solar (or Briatic), and Saturnine (or Daath) planes of consciousness. Above the Solar World, it is the Body of Light or the expression of consciousness used for reintegration with Unity. Stavish says that the three basic ideas around the subtle body are that (1) the Body of Light progresses though the levels of the spheres, (2) it increases in power and purity, and (3) it is made of Light. It is described as (1) the Spirit Body; (2) the Radiant Body and (3) the Resurrection Body, depending on its degree of purity.

In the above-named paper written by Mr. Stavish, a definition of the three phases of the Body of Light is given:

(1) The Spirit Body is the force closely aligned to the physical body. Similar to the nephesch, or vegetative-animal soul, in Jewish Qabalah.
(2) The Radiant Body allows us to experience the Vision of Beauty Triumphant or the realm of Tiphareth.
(3) The Resurrection Body is the reunification with the Divine Light or Unity.

These bodies are not really separate bodies, but are instead increasingly purified expressions of the Body of Light. As one body is purified, another takes its place. Mark Stavish asserts that what makes the Resurrection Body different is that, while it can and does exist within the material world, it is free from material constraints, because this

---

52 Prana is the Sanskrit word for breath or the "life force", the vital principle, which refers to the universal principle of energy or force responsible for the body's life, heat and maintenance.
53 In traditional Chinese culture, also known as Qi, Chi is an active principle forming part of any living thing. The word is frequently translated as "natural energy", "life force", or "energy flow." The literal translation means "breath" or "air." These same concepts can be found in the Hindu religion (prana), in ancient Greece (pneuma), in Hebrew culture (ruach) or in Western philosophy (vital energy).

THE LIGHT EXTENDED

perfected body is essentially a quintessence. It is differentiated into subtle and simple elements whereas the physical body is composed of the grosser elements. The physical body can be understood as the exterior life mirroring the invisible subtle embodiment of the life of the Divine Mind or Nous. The Augoeides can be considered the subtle embodiment beyond the physical vehicle that can be developed by means of magical (theurgic) practices.

According to Dr. Valerie Hunt in her book entitled *Infinite Mind: Science of the Human Vibrations of Consciousness*, consciousness exists outside of the physical body, outside of the constraints of space and time, and is therefore able to dwell anywhere, within the physical vehicle or outside of it, being non-local in the same sense that quantum objects are non-local. This related notion of non-locality, the moving out of consciousness from the physical body, supports the idea of the ability to create and function within the Body of Light.

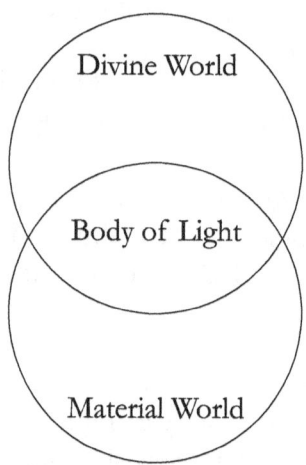

Although many different ideas exist on what the Augoeides exactly comprises, it can be said that the nature of the Body of Light is somewhere in-between the spiritual and material realms. It is both, being a kind of intermediary, a middle sphere which is neither material nor immaterial. Out of this third nature, a spiritual rebirth is possible, that of the alchemical Infans Solaris[54]. This middle sphere,

---

54 The 'Infans Solaris' (Child of the Sun) is also called the 'Filius' Philosophorum' (Son of Philosophers) and is identified in some alchemical treatises as the 'Lapis Philosophorum' (Stone of the Wise).

or intermediate realm, is therefore equated to the Body of Light in the Western esoteric tradition. The Augoeides is conceived as being the result of the union of two states, material and spiritual, with these opposites coming together and representing the sacred marriage, the Hieros Gamos, the goal of the Great Work. The existence of the middle sphere creates an intermediary between psyche and matter, the mortal physical body and the immortal Soul. According to Marsilio Ficino this Body of Light is "not body and almost soul and not soul and almost body."[55] Dr. Jay Johnston[56] provides a very modern perspective on the nature of the Body of Light. She considers this subtle body to be an embodied interface that is 'biometaphysical'—between the physical and the metaphysical—and it is ontologically energetic, nebulous and invisible.[57]

Therefore, the Body of Light is situated in between the physical and spiritual realms, and it functions as an intermediary force uniting these two realms. This Luminous Body is created and controlled by the Adept through a series of spiritual techniques that work through this dual nature, wherein the higher consciousness can be developed and out of which union with the Higher Self can be achieved.

The living universe as a unified whole consists of the human soul and the World Soul, with which the human soul can merge, enabling one to participate in universal wisdom. The human soul and the World Soul become linked by the Body of Light, which is an essential intermediary indispensable for the well-being of the human. According to Paracelsus, the human can control physicality through the life force present in all things and thereby unite with the 'Cosmic Man' (Adam Kadmon) enabling one to acquire original wisdom. According to Ficino, it is necessary to practice natural magic in order to nourish the human spirit and support a healthy state of being.

The Body of Light is worked upon by the Adept through a

---

55 Ficino, Marsilio, *De Vita Coelitus Comparanda*, cap. 3, Venetiis. Aldus. (1516). As paraphrased by Walter Pagel, *Paracelsus and the Neoplatonic and Gnostic Tradition* (October 1960), p. 128.
56 Dr. Jay Johnston (B.A., M.Art Admin., M.Litt(Dist), M.A.Hons, PhD), senior lecturer in the Department of Studies of Religion at the University of Sydney, Australia
57 Ontology is the philosophical study of the nature of being, becoming, existence, or reality, as well as the basic categories of being and their relations.

variety of magical practices in which the trained imagination plays a substantial role. These theurgical practices include the use of sacred images, incense, music and sounds, and the ingestion of wine or foods that influence the soul and stimulate the imagination. Thus, magical practices that work with these stimuli inspire the human imagination and align it with the Divine Imagination.

It is through the imagination that Spirit is transmitted. Celestial influences work directly or indirectly on the imagination with Spirit as the vehicle. As the physical body is nourished by the four elements, so the Spirit must be nourished by subtler elements. In ritual, bread is in the place of Earth, wine is in the place of Water, scent and music are Air, and Light represents Fire. Ficino recommends refreshing the Spirit at least daily by the use of scents that resemble different kinds of spiritual forces. To attract the Cosmic Spirit, he advises the use of the scents of rose and cinnamon. To attract the influences of specific planets, foods, scents and images that are in sympathy with a planet are used. The use of music is based on the Pythagorean and Platonic idea that the microcosmic human and the macrocosmic universe are characterized by the same harmonic proportions, and that the use of something with the same numerical proportions as a certain planet will align the soul to those proportions, thereby invoking the corresponding Cosmic Spirit. Music then can be seen as a living spirit and the celestial realm can be considered as a musical spirit.

Methods for Building the Body of Light

There are several methods for creating the Body of Light. Let us first examine the writings of Aleister Crowley and Israel Regardie. Crowley wrote in Book 4, Appendix III (Notes for an Astral Atlas):

> The technique of Magick is just as important as that of mysticism, but here we have a very much more difficult problem, because the original unit of Magick, the Body of Light, is already something unfamiliar to the ordinary person. Nevertheless, this body must be developed and trained with exactly the same rigid discipline as the brain in the case of mysticism. The essence of the

THEURGY AND THE BODY OF LIGHT

technique of Magick is the development of the Body of Light, which must be extended to include all members of the organism, and indeed of the cosmos.

Crowley explains that the most important practices for developing the Body of Light are:

1. The fortification of the Body of Light by the constant use of rituals, by the assumption of godforms, and by the right use of the Eucharist.
2. The purification, consecration and exaltation of that Body by the use of rituals of invocation.
3. The education of that Body by experience. It must learn to travel on every plane; to break down every obstacle which may confront it.

According to Crowley, the Body of Light is more important than simply for astral travel as it is the storehouse of all experiences. In Magick Without Tears (Ch. 81), he states:

> In Magick, on the contrary, one passes through the veil of the exterior world (which, as in Yoga, but in another sense, becomes "unreal" by comparison as one passes beyond) one creates a subtle body (instrument is a better term) called the Body of Light; this one develops and controls; it gains new powers as one progresses, usually by means of what is called "initiation;" finally, one carries on almost one's whole life in this Body of Light, and achieves in its own way the mastery of the Universe.

Israel Regardie wrote in The Tree of Life that the Augoeides invocation must have precedence above all others. He gave the following method to purify the Body of Light:

1. The assumption of the godform of Harpocrates. The magical assumption of this form is conducive to building the Body of Light, particularly the surrounding of the astral body with

THE LIGHT EXTENDED

the Egg of Indigo, referring to Akasha, the Tatva of Spirit.
2. Developing a new Eucharist, a celestial Eucharist. Regardie states, "The frequent celebration of the Eucharist is also an excellent means of transmuting and exalting the substance of the entire body. That which was formerly terrestrial becomes celestial. In this manner is the transformation of the body of light from a dark lunar body into a solar body accomplished. With this solar body of spiritualized substance, the gorgeous garment of the wedding feast, the theurgist will experience no difficulty in rising on the planes."[58]
3. Rising on the planes. "By means of this does the magician assimilate the highest qualities and characteristics of each Planet and Sephirah."[59]

One method I have found effective for building the Body of Light is through ritual and meditative work with the seven planets of the ancients: Saturn, Jupiter, Mars, Sol, Venus, Mercury and Luna. Biblically, the number seven is a number of Divine perfection and completeness (both spiritual and physical). From the seven days of creation in Genesis to the seven seals of the Book of Revelation, scripture is replete with references to this number. The Egyptians considered it the symbol of life eternal and saw the number seven as humanity's connection to its Divine Source. In the art of numerology, this number is the sum of 4+3, expressing wholeness through the union of earth (4) and the Divine (3). With its ancient connection to the seven planets, it is the number of the universe. This number represents totality, the macrocosm, synthesis, and the merging of spirit and matter. When the magician projects the Body of Light through the seven Planetary Spheres, starting with Luna and working up through Saturn, this Radiant Body is purified, refined, matured, and glorified.

The first step in building the Augoeides is to create this body in a ritualized setting. This is accomplished by invoking the Divine Light in Tiphareth through the Lesser and Supreme Invoking Hexagram Rituals. In this setting, the magician activates the Tiphareth center and begins to breathe in the Divine LVX, seeing the physical body filled

---
58 Israel Regardie, *The Tree of Life*, pgs. 360-366.
59 Ibid.

with bright white Light. The magician breathes in this Tipharethic Light through Kether at the crown of the head, down the Middle Pillar to Malkuth, and then up again into the Tiphareth center. The Body of Light is formed by the exhalation of this Tiphareth-infused breath, which is projected out through the heart center (in a ray of white Light) into the visualized Luminous Body that is formed on the other side of the altar, facing the magician. From this point, the magician connects his or her consciousness with the Luminous Body by visualizing the self as dwelling within it. If the magician wishes, the Body of Light may be consecrated to the Great Work through the 0=0 Z2 Formula.

Utilizing the methods of Crowley and Regardie, the magician will partake of a Repast, blessed by the powers of Tiphareth, and in so doing give form and life to the Augoeides. When eating the Bread and Salt, it is stated that, "Through this Earth of Spirit I form the Luminous Body," and as the Earth of the Repast is consumed, the Body of Light is visualised as becoming more solid.

When inhaling the scent of the Rose or Incense, the magician says, "Through this Air of Spirit I inspire this body with consciousness," and consciousness is perceived as dwelling inside the Augoeides, the magician seeing through its eyes.

For the Wine, the magician recites, "With this Water of Spirit, I connect my innermost self to this body," and the fluid Light of the soul is seen as projecting through the Tiphareth center in a ray of Light and taking up partial residence inside of this subtle body, but always maintaining a connection to the physical body.

When feeling the heat of the Flame, it is stated that, "Through the Fire of Spirit I give this body life." When the Augoeides is fully formed by this method, the magician may then begin to move and act as the Light Body in the spiritual realms. Repeated use of this method will eventually bring about an ability of the magician to unite consciousness with the Luminous Body. When this is accomplished, the magician begins to ascend the Augoeides through the Planetary Realms one at a time, and it is not until each Planetary Body is fully formed that the magician moves on to the next higher sphere.

THE LIGHT EXTENDED

The Lunar Body

When building the Body of Light in the Realm of Luna, the magician regularly will assume (like a Godform assumption) the blue Lunar Body placing the sigil of Luna in the heart center, thereby connecting the consciousness of the magician to this spiritual body. The magician will invoke Luna often over a period of time, along with the evocation and assumption of Lunar Godforms. A Lunar Repast should be included at the conclusion of the rite which should consist of Lunar Elements: (1) a blue candle; (2) a chalice of sweet white wine; (3) a Lunar incense, such as Jasmine and (4) sweet, white bread and Salt. If the magician wants to include ambient music in the background to align the self with Luna, it is recommended that the music be dreamlike and mysterious, possibly the recorded sounds of wind chimes, cymbals, delicate bells, and/or the recorded night sounds of Nature. The magician also should spend some time focusing on magical Lunar activities, such as developing the psychic faculties, divination, dream work, and purification rituals.

The Mercurial Body

When building the Body of Light in the Realm of Mercury, the magician regularly will assume the yellow Mercurial Body placing the sigil of Mercury in the heart center, thereby connecting the consciousness of the magician to this spiritual body. The magician will invoke Mercury often over a period of time, along with the evocation and assumption of Mercurial Godforms. A Mercury Repast should be included at the conclusion of the rite which should consist of Mercurial Elements: (1) a yellow candle; (2) a chalice of a light white wine; (3) a Mercurial incense, such as Mastic or Lavender and (4) a light and airy bread, such as a French bread, and Salt. If the magician wants to include ambient music in the background to align the self with Mercury, it is recommended that the music be well-ordered, graceful, and intellectual ambient music, the recorded sounds of bells and/or the sounds of rushing wind or wind in the trees. The magician also should spend some time focusing on the magical activities of Mercury, such as perfecting the magical journal, invocation and evocation through the vibration of Divine Names, the study of correspondences, and working with Sigils and Qameas. The diligent study of magical texts can produce Mercurial effects in the magician.

The Venusian Body

When building the Body of Light in the Realm of Venus, the magician regularly will assume the green Venusian Body placing the sigil of Venus in the heart center, thereby connecting the consciousness of the magician to this spiritual body. The magician will invoke Venus often over a period of time, along with the evocation and assumption of Venusian Godforms. A Venus Repast should be included at the conclusion of the rite which should consist of Venusian Elements: (1) a green candle; (2) a chalice of a sweet red wine; (3) a Venusian incense, such as Rose or Sandalwood and (4) a decadently sweet dessert such as a blueberry, cherry or sugar-cinnamon cake and Salt. If the magician wants to include ambient music in the background to align the self with Venus, it is recommended that the music be sensuous, passionate, fiery, or playful ambient music, the recorded sound of humming bees, and Nature's voices of the day. Also consider music that utilizes the classical guitar, the violin, zills, or a sitar. The magician also should spend some time focusing on the magical activities of Venus, such as devotional spiritual work, writing rituals, creating beautiful temples, altars and talismans, the making of magical vestments, ritual and meditative work for the achievement of ecstatic states, the use of dance in ritual, writing music, and/or the drawing or painting of beautiful images. A simple walk in nature can produce a Venusian state of being as can the reading of poetry or prose.

The Solar Body

When building the Body of Light in the Realm of Sol, the magician regularly will assume the orange Solar Body placing the sigil of Sol in the heart center, thereby connecting the consciousness of the magician to this spiritual body. The magician will invoke Sol often over a period of time, along with the evocation and assumption of Solar Godforms. A Solar Repast should be included at the conclusion of the rite which should consist of Solar Elements: (1) an orange candle; (2) a chalice of a full-bodied, semi-dry red wine; (3) a Solar incense, such as Frankincense, Copal or Vanilla and (4) a sour-dough bread or sunflower bread and Salt. If the magician wants to include ambient music in the background to align the self with the Sun, it is recommended that the music be noble, generous, and spiritually inspiring ambient music; music that utilizes the lyre or the autoharp, and the recorded sounds of a heartbeat or dawn-song of birds. The magician also should spend some time focusing on the magical activities of Sol, such as obtaining a level of proficiency in visionary work, training the imagination, working for self-knowledge, exploring the nature of consciousness, and rituals of healing for the self and others.

The Martial Body

When building the Body of Light in the Realm of Mars, the magician regularly will assume the red Martial Body placing the sigil of Mars in the heart center, thereby connecting the consciousness of the magician to this spiritual body. The magician will invoke Mars often over a period of time, along with the evocation and assumption of Martial Godforms. A Martial Repast should be included at the conclusion of the rite which should consist of Martial Elements: (1) a red candle; (2) a chalice of a hearty or spicy red wine; (3) a Martial incense, such as Dragon's Blood or a good Tobacco and (4) a spicy or hot bread and Salt. If the magician wants to include ambient music in the background to align the self with Mars, it is recommended that the music be powerful, warlike and dominating ambient music, the sounds of war drums, bagpipes, steel striking upon steel or iron, the recorded sounds of marching feet, a raging fire, a volcanic eruption, or battle. The magician also should spend some time focusing on the magical activities of Mars, such as ritual work with magical weapons, the development of the magical will, and developing a certain discipline in magical work.

The Jovial Body

When building the Body of Light in the Realm of Jupiter, the magician regularly will assume the violet Jovial Body placing the sigil of Jupiter in the heart center, thereby connecting the consciousness of the magician to this spiritual body. The magician will invoke Jupiter often over a period of time, along with the evocation and assumption of Jovial Godforms. A Jupiter Repast should be included at the conclusion of the rite which should consist of Jovial Elements: (1) a violet candle; (2) a chalice of a dry white wine; (3) a Jovial incense, such as Pine or Wood Aloes and (4) a sweetened bread and Salt. If the magician wants to include ambient music in the background to align the self with Jupiter, it is recommended that the music be majestic, joyful and uplifting ambient music, music which utilizes the cello, double bass, the recorded sounds of a conch shell or an electrical storm. The magician also should spend some time focusing on the magical activities of Jupiter, such as oracular work, becoming a priest/ess of a particular Tradition or Deity, and the development of generosity, liberality, tolerance and open-mindedness.

The Saturnine Body

When building the Body of Light in the Realm of Saturn, the magician regularly will assume the indigo Saturnine Body placing the sigil of Saturn in the heart center, thereby connecting the consciousness of the magician to this spiritual body. The magician will invoke Saturn often over a period of time, along with the evocation and assumption of Saturnine Godforms. A Saturn Repast should be included at the conclusion of the rite which should consist of Saturnine Elements: (1) an indigo candle; (2) a chalice of dry red wine; (3) a Saturn incense, such as Myrrh or Patchouli and (4) a dark bread (rye or pumpernickel) or seeded or whole-grain bread and Salt. If the magician wants to include ambient music in the background to align the self with Saturn, it is recommended that the music be brooding, transformative, mystical, and obscure ambient music, Tibetan bowls, a deep-toned gong, a ticking clock, or recorded ocean sounds. The magician also should spend some time focusing on the magical activities of Saturn, such as focused prayer and meditation done in solitude, practicing some form of asceticism, the study of cosmology, and the practice of silence for extended periods of time.

Surpassing the Rainbow Body – The Star Body

If you pass a beam of white light through a prism, you will see the light split into the colors of the rainbow, and this refraction of the White Light of Unity into the colors of the Planets is the initial work on the Body of Light. When the magician has completed the seven planetary levels of consciousness, he or she now has surpassed the attainment of the Rainbow Body to reach a stage of direct and experiential realization of the Self achieved by a fully-awakened individual. At this stage of the work the Luminous Body is composed of pure white light as white light is the combination of the different frequencies of visible light.[60] There is a reason why the color white is known in most cultures as the color of perfection and when the Augoeides is composed solely of white light, it is in its most complete and pure form. It is in this purified Star Body that the magician may experience union with the Higher and Divine Self.

> Remember the clear light, the pure clear white light from which everything in the universe comes, to which everything in the universe returns; the original nature of your own mind. The natural state of the universe unmanifest. Let go into the clear light, trust it, merge with it. It is your own true nature, it is home.
>
> — Tibetan Book of the Dead

In Conclusion

The human being is one thing only, a Divine being, a soul clothed in flesh. We are beings emanating the energy of the Light in multiple colors and sounds. We are creators in every sense of the word and

---

60 In additive color theory the combination of the colors in the light spectrum create white.

THEURGY AND THE BODY OF LIGHT

within us dwells the creative force of the Divine. Therefore, spiritual growth and the creative act are two sides of the same coin. The goal of the formation of the Body of Light is not so much what you will create, but the transformation that will occur in you for creating it.

> There is a principle of the soul, superior to all nature, through which we are capable of surpassing the order and systems of the world. When the soul is elevated to natures better than itself, then it is entirely separated from the subordinate natures, exchanging this for another life, and deserting the order of things with which it was connected, links and mingles itself with another.
>
> — Iamblichus

THE LIGHT EXTENDED
BIBLOGRAPHY

Books:

Crowley, Aleister, *Magick Without Tears*, New Falcon Publications (April 1, 1991)

Crowley, Aleister, *Magick Liber ABA (Book 4)*, Weiser Books; 2 Rev Sub edition (January 1, 1998)

Denning, Melita and Phillips, Osborne, *Planetary Magick: The Heart of Western Magick*, Llewellyn Publications; Reissue edition (November 30, 1988)

Ficino, Marsilio, *Platonic Theology, Volume 1: Books I-IV* (The I Tatti Renaissance Library), James Hankins, Editor, Michael J.B. Allen, Translator, Harvard University Press (April 26, 2001)

Hunt, Valerie, Ph.D., *Infinite Mind: Science of the Human Vibrations of Consciousness*, Malibu Publications; 2 edition (1996)

Kupperman, Jeffrey, *Living Theurgy: A Course in Iamblichus' Philosophy*, Theology and Theurgy, Avalonia (May 7, 2014)

Paracelsus and Waite, Arthur Edward, *The Hermetic and Alchemical Writings of Paracelsus*, Martino Fine Books (September 16, 2009)

Proclus, *The Six Books of Proclus, the Platonic Successor, on the Theology of Plato*, translated by Thomas Taylor, Ulan Press (August 31, 2012)

Regardie, Israel, *The Tree of Life: An Illustrated Study in Magic*, edited and annotated by Chic Cicero and Sandra Tabatha Cicero, Llewellyn Publications; 3rd edition (2001)

Websites:

Bochem, Eline, Homo Lumiens, An Explorative Study on the Body of Light in the Western Esoteric Tradition with a Focus on Two Renaissance Thinkers and their Neoplatonist Sources
http://amsterdam.academia.edu/ElineBochem

The Emerald Tablets of Thoth, translated by Doreal
http://www.crystalinks.com/emerald.html

Nous Augoeides of the Neoplatonists
http://www.philaletheians.co.uk/study-notes/constitution-of-man/nous-augoeides-of-the-neoplatonists.pdf

Pagel, Walter, Paracelsus and the Neoplatonic and Gnostic Tradition from Ambix, The Journal of the Society for the Study of Alchemy and Early Chemistry, (October 1960)
http://ls.poly.edu/~jbain/mms/texts/60Pagel.pdf

Stavish, Mark, MA, The Body of Light in the Western Esoteric Tradition
http://hermetic.com/stavish/essays/bodylight.html

About the Author

Jayne Gibson has been a student of the Western Mystery Tradition for over 20 years, and she is a Senior Adept of the Hermetic Order of the Golden Dawn. She co-authored the book *Astrological Magic, Basic Rituals and Meditations* with Dr. Benjamin Dykes and also contributed to the Golden Dawn community's collaboration project, the *Commentaries on the Golden Dawn Flying Rolls*. She has authored several articles presented in *The Hermetic Tablet* and was a regular contributor to *Hermetic Virtues* magazine.

On the 42 Assessors of the Hall of the Two Truths

A Supplemental Z Libellus on the Enterer of the Threshold for the Study and Practice of the Adepta Major[1]

by Adam P. Forrest

[Exordium to the 125th Formula of the Formulæ of Coming Forth by Day]

To be said when arriving at this Hall of the Two Truths, [for] cleansing [NN] from all wrongs which he hath wrought, and beholding the Faces of All the Gods

Hail, Great God, Lord of the Two Truths. I have come unto Thee, my Lord, that Thou mayest bring me to behold Thy Beauties.[2] I know Thee. I know Thy Name. I know the Name of the 42 Gods Who are with Thee in this Hall of the Two Truths, Who live as Guardians against Evils, Who quaff their blood on that Day of the Reckoning of Natures before Onnofer. Behold: Two-Sons-of-His-

---

1. In the Order in which I study, the default gender of pronouns and Grade names alternate through the Grades and Subgrades to better reflect the true equilibrium of the Magical Universe, and this document falls in a Subgrade with feminine defaults. —APF
2. "Beauties": Egyptian *Noferu*, equivalent to Heb. *Tipharoth*. —APF

THE LIGHT EXTENDED

Two-Singers-of-Truth[3] is Thy Name. Behold: I have come unto Thee. I have brought unto Thee Truth; I have banished from Thee Falsehood[4].[5]

— *Tehuti*[6] *Thōth*,
THE FORMULÆ OF
COMING FORTH BY DAY

[FIRST LINE OF THE TABULA SMARGDINA]

Verum, sine mendacio, certum et verissimum
Truth, without falsehood, certain and most true.[7]

— *Hermēs Trismegistos*,
THE EMERALD TABLET

THE 42 ASSESSORS are Godforms and Divine Theurgic Powers occupying 42 Invisible Stations around the boundary of the

---

3. "Two-Sons-of-His-Two-Singers-of-Truth" is *Sai-Mereti-ef-ent-Maët*. This Secret Name of Osiris shows that He too has an equilibrated, dual nature, as shown in the creative expression of His duality, the generation of His two Sons, Horus the bright celestial Son of His bright Sister Isis and Anubis the dark chthonic Son of His dark Sister Nephthys. "His Two Singers of Truth" are those same Magical Sisters Who, after the death of His body, flew in perfect Circles around Him in the Form of two Kites, singing or vibrating the Formulæ which assured His rebirth in the Otherworld as its King. —APF
4. "Truth" here is of course *Maët* or *Maät*, which is not only Truth but the entire positive principle of the world in balanced, just, and proper order and function, "Right," and the nature of those beings who are in harmony with the proper order of the Cosmos, "Righteous"; "Falsehood" here is *Isfet*, the antonym of Maët, which is not only Falsehood but the entire negative principle of "Evil," imbalance, injustice, dysfunction, and disorder in the world. —APF
5. The first part of the Exordium or Introduction to the 125th Formula (or Spell or Utterance, but not correctly Chapter) of the *Book of the Dead*, my translation from the Latin. Recall that the 125th Formula is that of which the vignette is normally depicted upon the Black Pillar of Nephthys in the Neophyte Hall. —APF
6. Originally Djehuti, by the time of the *Book of the Dead*, the Name had evolved into Tehuti. —APF
7. The first line of the Emerald Tablet of Hermēs Trismegistos, my translation from the Egyptian. —APF

ON THE 42 ASSESSORS

Sanctuary in the Hall of the Two Truths, Whom we first encountered in the Neophyta Adepta Minor Zeds[8] on the Neophyte Hall.

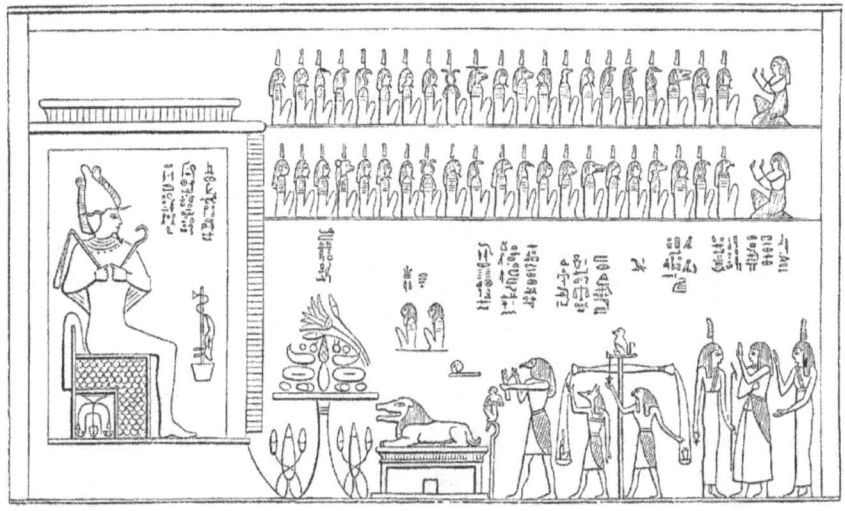

Fig. 1. An illustration of the 42 Assessors as participants in the Judgement in the Hall of Two Truths from George Rawlinson, The Religions of the Ancient World (London, 1880)

As Greater Adepts, let us deepen our Epoptic understanding of the 42 Assessors by exploring Their name and number and the nature of Their Office: that is, first, by considering the term Assessors, and second, by considering the number 42, and learning what that name and number may reveal to us of Their Office, and then undertaking Theurgic Magical Action with the Assessors in support of the Great Work.

I. Assessors

As the Assessors enter into our Z Formulæ from the Egyptian or Kemetic scriptures in the *Book of the Dead*, or the *Formulæ of Coming Forth by Day*, it is important that we understand that the word Assessors does not directly translate any specific term in the original

---

8. "Zeds" is spelled out phonetically here to remind my fellow Americans that the Rosicrucian Z Formulæ and documents should preferably be pronounced thus to honor our British forbearers in this Work. —APF

texts. There, as we read in the excerpt which opens this document, the Assessors are called simply "the 42 Gods Who are with Thee [*i.e.*, Osiris] in this Hall of the Two Truths" (*Nutjeru* XLII *onniu hena-Ek em Usekhet Maëti*), and They are also described as "Guardians against Evils'" (*Saütiu Djutu*), and since They take action on "that Day of the Reckoning of Natures [*i.e.*, natures in the sense of good, evil, just, unjust, true, false] before Onnofer," They might also be rightly called "Reckoners" (*Hasabu*)⁹ or "Reckoners of Natures" (*Hasabu Qedut*), which would be the closest in meaning to Assessors. Later in the 125th Formula, when addressing Osiris, the deceased refers to the Assessors as "Thy Messengers . . . with Their unveiled faces" (*nai-Ek en Opuatiu . . . it tchamut ent horu-Sen*).¹⁰

As Assessors is not a direct translation of any single Egyptian word, it was chosen as a descriptive label by one of the 19th-century Egyptologists,¹¹ and a very excellent choice it is to express Their function. Assessor in English and *assesseur* in French are direct loanwords from Latin *assessor*, where it literally means "one who sits

---

9. *Hasab* has a cognate in Hebrew: חשב (*chasshav*, "reckoner, accountant, calculator"). Recall from your study of Coptic that Egyptian and Hebrew share words not simply because of geographic proximity and cultural interaction, but because both are members of the Afroasiatic or Hamito-Semitic language family. It is also an interesting synchronicity that Ani, whose copy of the *Book of the Dead* we know best due to the work of Budge and the British Museum, actually bore the title *hasab* in life, as amongst his offices was that of Reckoner (*Hasab*) of the Offerings Unto All the Gods, *i.e.*, one might say the Secretary of the Treasuries of the Temples, responsible for keeping track of the vast wealth that was donated to the Temples every year. —APF
10. "Unveiled face" in Egyptian seems to carry a connotation of quickness to anger, rather like *Zeïr Anpin* ("Small Face, or Mikroprosōpos") in the Aramaic of the *Zohar*. —APF
11. I have so far been unable (or, in the interests of full disclosure, unwilling when—as a minor question—it proved somewhat intractable) to pursue the question to its conclusion, but 'Assessors' is clearly already a familiar term by the time of its use by Reginald Stuart Poole in his 1881 series of lectures on *Egypt in Its Comparative Relations* at the Royal Institution of Great Britain. —APF

ON THE 42 ASSESSORS

beside"[12] and referred to legal specialists brought in as assistants to aid a magistrate in the determination of justice. It was in this sense that word first came into the English language (and was still familiar in British law in the 19th century), and was so applied in reference to the 42 Deities assessing the guilt or purity of the enterer into the Hall of the Two Truths. Each is in essence a specialist in that one of the 42 areas which the deceased declares his or her innocence to that Assessor.

Both Latin and English *Assessor* are also regularly used to translate *Parhedros* (Πάρεδρος/ⲡⲁⲣϩⲉⲇⲣⲟⲥ) and *Parhedrōn* (Παρέδρων/ ⲡⲁⲣϩⲉⲇⲣⲱⲛ)[13] in Greek and Græco-Coptic, meaning literally "one who is sitting beside,"[14] with the same use as Latin *Assessor* to refer to specialists or coadjutors assisting judges, and reflecting the image of a tribunal *sitting* in judgement. However, the Greek terms also have an added meaning that you may have encountered in your Theurgic studies. In the Græco-Egyptian Magical Papyri, a *Parhedros* is also a "Familiar Spirit," who attends the Magus to assist in Magical Operations. In the Greek Magical Papyri, the adjective *parhedros* is even used to describe not only persons but also items that are "of Magical assistance," such as lines of verse from Homer[15] in the *Grand Papyrus Magique de Paris*.

---

12. From the classical verb *assidere* (*ad* + *sedere*, "to sit near or beside") through a Mediæval frequentative form (*frequentative* meaning that the "sitting alongside" was an action regularly repeated, as in an office held), *assessare*. From the same root with different prefixes, we get such diverse words as dissident (from *dissidens*, "sitting apart or in opposition," participle of *dissidere*) and president (from *præsidens*, "sitting in front," participle of *præsidere*). —APF
13. Greek doesn't have any way to indicate an *h* sound (the 'rough breathing' in Greek) anywhere other than at the beginning of a word (as in the Greek names of the Greater Officers in the Outer Order, *Hierophantēs*, *Hiereus*, and *Hēgēmōn*), but when a Greek word gets borrowed into Coptic, which does have a letter with an *h* sound (ϩ) that can occur in the middle of words, we can learn about the presence of internal *h*. And so we learn that it is indeed *Parhedros* rather than *Paredros*. —APF
14. *Parhedros* is originally an adjective, here used as a substantive noun; *Parhedrōn* is originally the present participle of a verb, here also used substantively as a noun. —APF
15. A Hellenic equivalent of versicles from the *Psalms* in Judæo-Christian Magic. —APF

THE LIGHT EXTENDED

The most recent use of 'Assessor' to render *Parhedrōn* is in Violet MacDermot's English translation of the Gnostic scripture *Pistis Sophia* from Coptic.[16] In the cosmology of *Pistis Sophia*, there are five Demonic beings in the place known as "the Midst," who may well have a dark correlation to the five Egyptian epagomenal days, and one of them—surely based on Seth or Set, following the *interpretio Græca* in the *De Iside et Osiride* of Plutarch, like Typhon in our Hermetic Sign of Apophis and Typhon—is called in Græco-Coptic *pe-Parhedrōn pe-Typhōn* (ⲡⲡⲁⲣϩⲉⲇⲣⲱⲛ ⲡⲧⲩϥⲱⲛ), and translated by MacDermot as "the Assessor Typhon."[17]

II. The number 42

There is much in the number 42 that will aid our understanding of the Assessors in relation to the Hall of the Two Truths.

---

16. Violet MacDermot (trans.) and Karl Schmidt (text ed.), *Pistis Sophia* (Leiden: E.J. Brill, 1978; Nag Hammadi Studies IX). —APF
17. *Pistis Sophia*, book IV, chapter 140. I had thought that M.G. Schwartze's 1851 Latin translation would have used *Assessor* for Parhedrōn, but found on checking the text that Schwartze chose to translate only the purely Coptic words into Latin, instead rendering many Græco-Coptic loanwords as untranslated Greek in the proper Greek cases, so for example, he translated the manuscript's ⲙⲡⲡⲁⲣϩⲉⲇⲣⲱⲛ ⲡⲧⲩϥⲱⲛ (*em-pe-Parhedrōn pe-Typhōn*) as genitive Greek "Παρεδρωνος Τυφωνος." G.R.S. Mead, the Theosophical scholar, made his 1886 English translation from Schwarze's Latin. Mead's was the first and for nearly a century the only English translation of this important text; and though he was well aware of the limitations of an English translation from a Latin translation of a Coptic text, Mead felt compelled to release a revised second edition 25 years later in 1921 when it continued to be apparent that no Coptic scholar was intending to publish an English translation. Mead followed Schwarze in leaving Parhedrōn untranslated, although he transliterated it and standardized it in the nominative case for the sake of his nonspecialist readership, translating the same phrase as "of Parhedrōn Typhon." MacDermott's text follows the most generous of translation choices, those of the Brill Nag Hammadi Codex series of which her work is a volume: not only is hers a facing-page Coptic–English translation, but she translates all translatable words into English, italicizes her English translations of all words of Greek origin, and occasionally even inserts a transliterated form of the Græco-Coptic word if it is of particular interest. So, in her translation, she gives "of the *Assessor* (Parhedron) Typhon." —APF

ON THE 42 ASSESSORS

42 as a Pronic Number

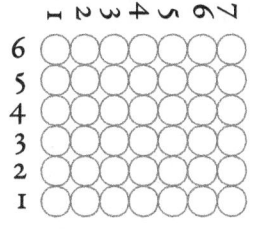

Fig. 2. *The Pronic Number 42*

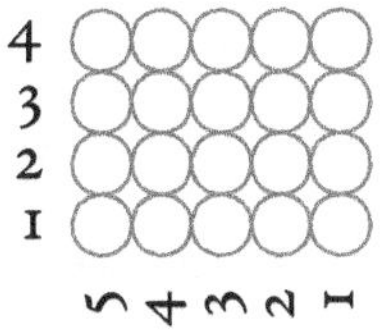

Fig. 3. *The Pronic Number 20*

Fig. 4. *The Pronic Tablet of Union*

First, we must understand that 42 is a Pythagorean number[18] of a type known as Pronic or Heteromecic Numbers. Pronic Numbers are the product of two consecutive integers, and so a formula for their production or identification is $n(n+1)$. 42 is the sixth Pronic Number, and its Formula may be expressed by the equation $6(6+1)=6\times7=42$.[19]

To understand the nature of the Pronic Number as a Formula in Magic, let us examine a Pronic Number which underlies an important Talismanic Table that we have used in our Work since the Degree of Domina Portæ. The Enochian Angelic Tablet of Union follows the Formula of the Pronic Number 20, which is $4(4+1)=4\times5=20$.

---

18. The Ancients (as in the *Metaphysics* of Aristotle) considered Pronic Numbers to be Pythagorean Figurate Numbers, like Triangular, Square, and Pentagonal Numbers, even though they form, by definition, irregular figures, as opposed to the Regular Polygonal Figurate Numbers. You will recall other irregular Figurate Numbers in our curriculum, such as the Temenic or Double Square Numbers studied in Theorica Adepta Minor. In fact, the simplest Temenic or Double Square Number ($1\times2=2$) is the first Pronic Number. See the following note. —APF

19. The zeroth Pronic number is $0\times1=0$; the first is $1\times2=2$, the second is $2\times3=6$, the third is $3\times4=12$, the fourth is $4\times5=20$, the fifth is $5\times6=30$, and the sixth is $6\times7=42$. Another potentially significant characteristic of Pronic Numbers for the Hermetic Qabbalist is that the nth Pronic Number is twice the nth Triangular Number, so that, *e.g.*, the sixth Pronic Number, answering to Tiphereth, is 42, while the sixth Triangular Number (or Mystic Number), also answering to Tiphereth, is 21 ($1+2+3+4+5+6=21$), which is half of 42. See Fig. 5. —APF

THE LIGHT EXTENDED

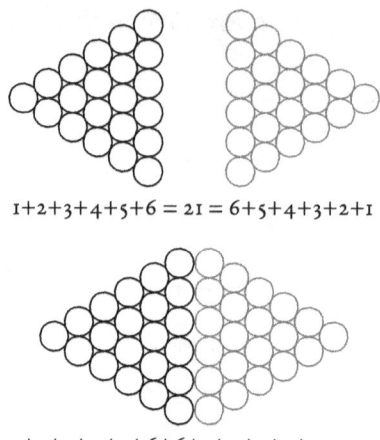

$1+2+3+4+5+6 = 21 = 6+5+4+3+2+1$

$1+2+3+4+5+6+6+5+4+3+2+1 = 42$

Fig. 5. *The Sixth Pronic Number 42 as twice the sixth Triangular Mystic Number*

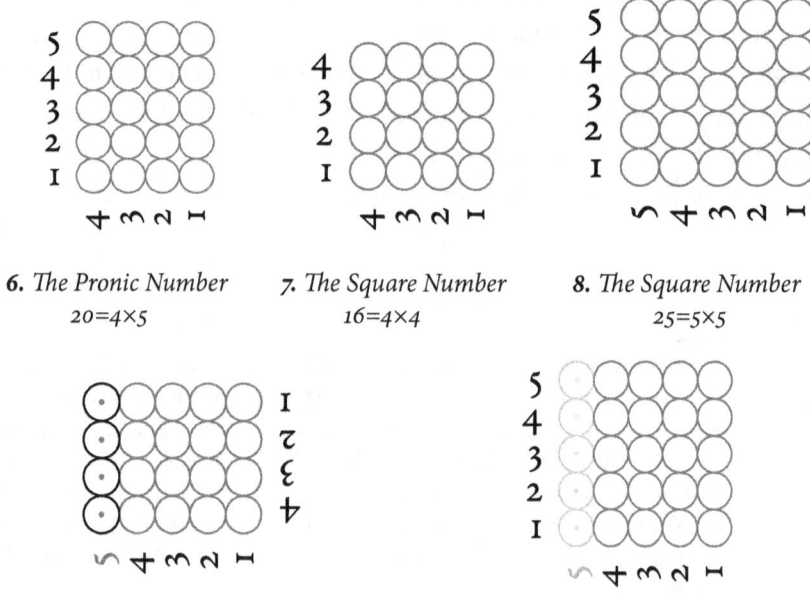

6. *The Pronic Number* $20=4\times5$

7. *The Square Number* $16=4\times4$

8. *The Square Number* $25=5\times5$

9. *The Pronic Number* $20=(4\times4)+4$

10. *The Pronic Number* $20=(5\times5)-5$

Figs. 6–10. *The relationship of the Pronic Number 20 with the Square Numbers 16 and 25*

ON THE 42 ASSESSORS

As the product of 4×5, the Pronic Number 20 may be conceived of as a form of bridge between the Square Numbers 16=4×4 and 25=5×5 (figs. 4–6),[20] or, to formulate it another way, it may be thought of the Square Number of root 4 extended by an additional row or column of 4 (fig. 7), or the Square Number of root 5 diminished by a row or column of 5 set aside or not yet attained (fig. 8), or both. But what does this mean for the Magical application of the Pronic Formula of 20? To understand that, we must identify the symbolic values of 4 and its square and of 5 and its square. Fortunately the principle signification of the number 4 is well known to us as the four Elements under the presidency of Tetragrammaton, and of the number 5 as the five Elements under the presidency of the Pentagrammaton (corresponding to the two midpoints of the Portal Ritual: *viz.*, The Rite of the Cross and the Four Elements, and the Rite of the Pentagram and the Five Paths). Likewise we know that 16 as the Square of the Tetragrammatic 4 corresponds to the 16 Subelements of the four Elements (as in the Geomantic Tetragrams and the Servient Squares of the Lesser Angles of the Enochian Watchtowers), and 25 as the Square of the Pentagrammatic 5 answers to the 25 Subelements of the five Elements (as in the Petals of the Rose Crucifix of Victory upon the Round Altar in the Ritual of the Adepta Minor).[21] And we already know that intersecting these two sets of correspondences (as in the 20 cells of the Tablet of Union) gives us a Pronic matrix (Table 9) yielding five Pentagrammatic Subelements of each of the four Elements.

So now we may apply the same Pronic analysis to the number 42 which we have to the number 20. *Ergo*, as the product of 6×7, the Pronic Number 42 may be conceived of as a form of bridge between the Square Numbers 36=6×6 and 49=7×7 (Figs. 10–12),[22] or, to formulate it in another manner, it may be thought of the Square

---

20. Another mathematical property perhaps worth noting is that $\sqrt{(4^2 \times 5^2)}$ = $\sqrt{(16 \times 25)}$ = $\sqrt{400}$ = the Pronic Number 20. —APF
21. We shall, as Adepts of the Grade of the fifth Sephirah Gevurah, elsewhere be further studying the number five, its square, and the Magic Square Qameya derived from it. —APF
22. And, as with the mediating Pronic square root of the product of the squares of 4 and 5, we note that $\sqrt{(6^2 \times 7^2)} = \sqrt{(36 \times 49)} = \sqrt{1764}$ = the Pronic Number 42. —APF

THE LIGHT EXTENDED

Number of root 6 extended by an additional row or column of 6 (Fig. 13), or the Square Number of root 7 diminished by a row or column of 7 set aside or not yet attained (Fig. 14), or both.

Element	Subelemental Power				
	⊕	△	▽	▽	△
△	⊕ of △ ᛉ (E)	△ of △ Γ (X)	▽ of △ ♃ (A)	▽ of △ ℇ (R)	△ of △ Ω (P)
▽	⊕ of ▽ ᛘ (H)	△ of △ Β (C)	▽ of △ ♄ (O)	▽ of △ Ε (M)	△ of △ ♃ (A)
▽	⊕ of ▽ ♂ (N)	△ of ▽ ♃ (A)	▽ of ▽ ♂ (N)	▽ of ▽ ✓ (T)	△ of ▽ ♃ (A)
△	⊕ of △ ♀ (B)	△ of △ ᛚ (I)	▽ of △ ✓ (T)	▽ of △ ♄ (O)	△ of △ Ε (M)

Table 11. *The Pronic Table of 20 Subelemental Powers corresponding to the Enochian Angelic Tablet of Union*

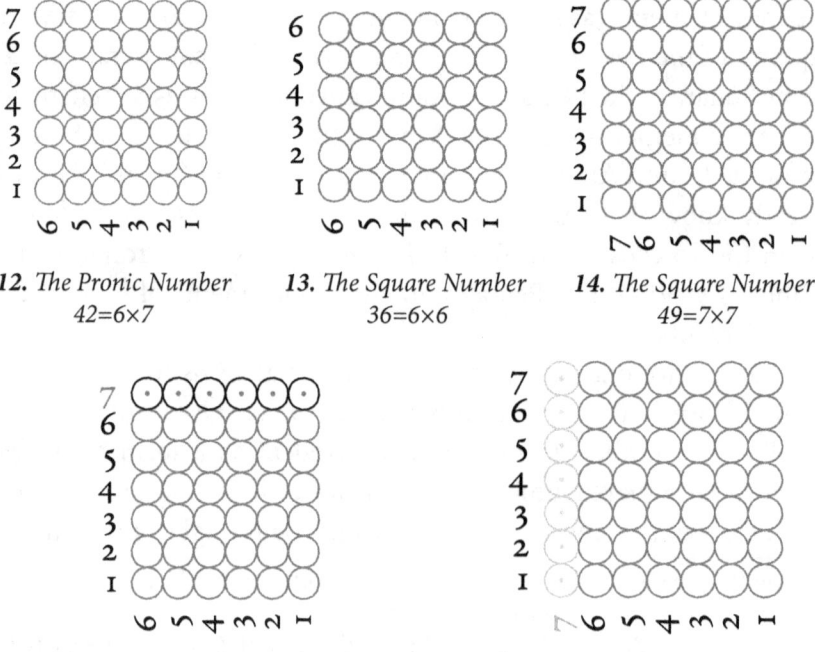

12. The Pronic Number 42=6×7

13. The Square Number 36=6×6

14. The Square Number 49=7×7

15. The Pronic Number 42=(6×6)+6

16. The Pronic Number 42=(7×7)-7

Figs. 12–16. *The relationship of the Pronic Number 42 with the Square Numbers 36 and 49*

ON THE 42 ASSESSORS

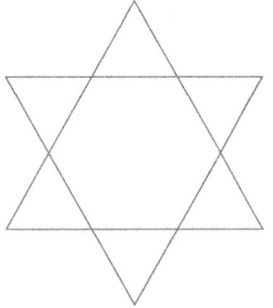 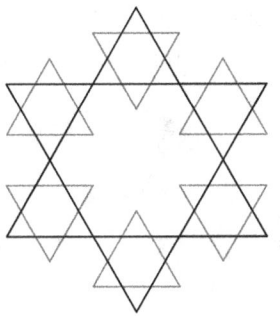 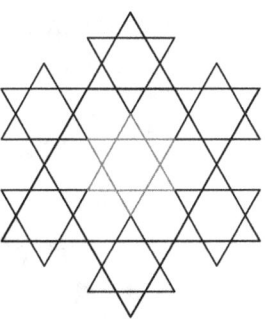

Fig. 17. The Hexagram as the base of the expansion

Fig. 18. The fractal expansion of the triangular arms of the Hexagram into Subhexagrams by mirrored duplication

Fig. 19. The addition of the Centre Subhexagram in accordance with the tiled pattern

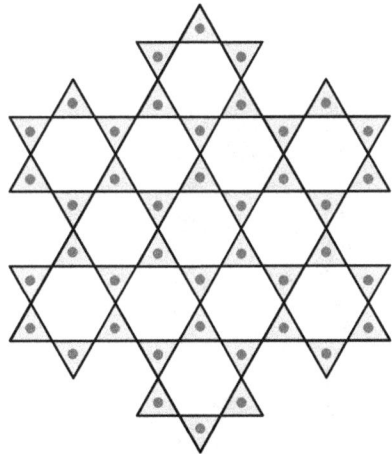 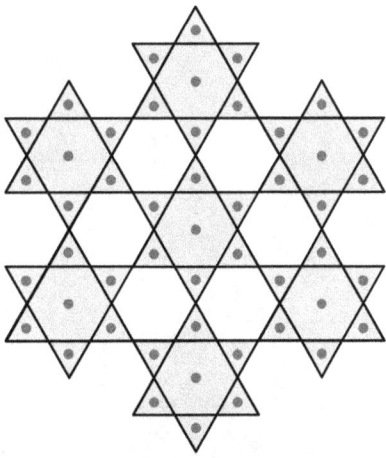

Fig. 20. The 42 Stations in the triangular arms of the seven Subhexagrams

Fig. 21. The 49 Stations completed with the addition of the Central Station in each of the Subhexagrams

Six is equivalent to the Sun and Tiphereth, and manifests polygonally as the Hexagon and the Hexagram.[23] Our system makes much use of a very important correspondence of 36, but the key to the primary Hermetic significance of the Decans is not 6×6, but rather 12×3

---

[23]. Recall that in the Adept approach to *On Polygons and Polygrams*, the Hexagon and Hexagram as a pair may be approached in any particular Action in one of two ways: *viz.*, in a Polygram-centred understanding as the 0th and 1st forms of the Hexagram, or in a Polygon-centred understanding as the Hexagon and the Stellated Hexagon. —APF

THE LIGHT EXTENDED

(three Decans in each Sign). 36 as 6^2 so far in our studies has only corresponded to the Magic Square Qameya of Sol and Tiphereth.

22. *The Heikhaloth as a Form of the Heptad deriving from the Hexagram*

23. *The Heikhaloth as template for seven Hexagrams*

24. *The seven Hexagrams as a Form of the Pronic Number 6×7=42*

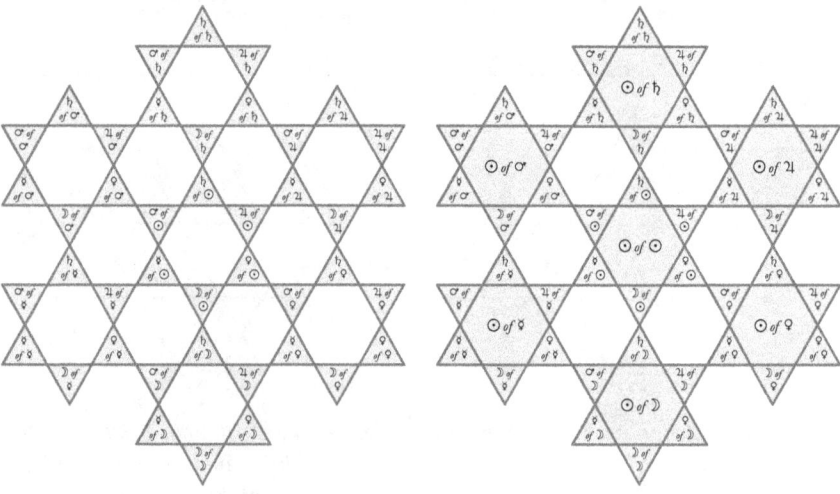

25. *The 42 Subplanetary Powers in the 42 arms of the seven Hexagrams*

26. *The addition of the seven Solar Subplanetary Powers at the hearts of the Hexagrams completes the Formula of 7×7=49 Subplanetary Powers in the seven Hexagrams*

Figs. 22–26. *The 42 Subplanetary Powers in the 42 arms of the seven Hexagrams*

Seven is more dramatically polyvalent, answering not only to Netzach and Venus, but also to the seven Planets, and in Antiquity to the seven Pleiades, as well as to the Heikhaloth and all of the other correspondences of the Heptad cited in the description of the

ON THE 42 ASSESSORS

symbolism of the Heptagonal Vault in the rites of the Inner Order. 49 in our Hermetic system certainly corresponds primarily to the Subplanetary Powers (from ♄ of ♄, then ♃ of ♄, through ☿ of ☽, and finally ☽ of ☽), like the 49 Subplanetary Spirit Vision Cards you crafted in the Subgrade of Neophyta Adepta Major, equivalent to the 25 Subelemental Cards used in Neophyta Adepta Minor. This is also seen in the number of petals of the Rose Jubilant blooming on the Cross on the floor of the Vault and on that on the head of the Pastos (Figs. 28-29). It is also the number of cells in the Qemeyotic Magic Square of Venus and Netzach, and the number of the 49 Subplanetary Good Angels of the Enochian Angelic Heptarchy.

Planet	Subplanetary Power					
	☽	☿	♀	♂	♃	♄
♄	☽ of ♄ *Luna Saturni*	☿ of ♄ *Mercurius Saturni*	♀ of ♄ *Venus Saturni*	♂ of ♄ *Mars Saturni*	♃ of ♄ *Jupiter Saturni*	♄ of ♄ *Saturnus Saturni*
♃	☽ of ♃ *Luna Jovis*	☿ of ♃ *Mercurius Jovis*	♀ of ♃ *Venus Jovis*	♂ of ♃ *Mars Jovis*	♃ of ♃ *Jupiter Jovis*	♄ of ♃ *Saturnus Jovis*
♂	☽ of ♂ *Luna Martis*	☿ of ♂ *Mercurius Martis*	♀ of ♂ *Venus Martis*	♂ of ♂ *Mars Martis*	♃ of ♂ *Jupiter Martis*	♄ of ♂ *Saturnus Martis*
☉	☽ of ☉ *Luna Solis*	☿ of ☉ *Mercurius Solis*	♀ of ☉ *Venus Solis*	♂ of ☉ *Mars Solis*	♃ of ☉ *Jupiter Solis*	♄ of ☉ *Saturnus Solis*
♀	☽ of ♀ *Luna Veneris*	☿ of ♀ *Mercurius Veneris*	♀ of ♀ *Venus Veneris*	♂ of ♀ *Mars Veneris*	♃ of ♀ *Jupiter Veneris*	♄ of ♀ *Saturnus Veneris*
☿	☽ of ☿ *Luna Mercurii*	☿ of ☿ *Mercurius Mercurii*	♀ of ☿ *Venus Mercurii*	♂ of ☿ *Mars Mercurii*	♃ of ☿ *Jupiter Mercurii*	♄ of ☿ *Saturnus Mercurii*
☽	☽ of ☽ *Luna Lunæ*	☿ of ☽ *Mercurius Lunæ*	♀ of ☽ *Venus Lunæ*	♂ of ☽ *Mars Lunæ*	♃ of ☽ *Jupiter Lunæ*	♄ of ☽ *Saturnus Lunæ*

Table 27. The Pronic Table of 42 Subplanetary Powers

III. The Tetracontadigrammaton

The 42-Letter Name[24] has been long known in Qabbalah. There are several variants to be found in the manuscripts, but the principle form—and that employed in the Order—is אבגיתצקרעשטננגדיכשבטרצתגחקבבטנעיגלפזקשקוצית, pronounced— here divided into syllables for easier understanding—*Av-gi-thetz-*

---

24. *Tetracontadigrammaton* is the Anglicized spelling of Greek Τετρακοντα-διγράμματον, meaning "42-Letter Name" just as Tetragrammaton means "Four-Letter Name." However, unless you, like me and more than a few other Hermetists, have the same admittedly unfortunate relationship with polysyllabic words that Dirty Harry had with Magnums, the Name will generally be identified simply as the 42-Letter Name. —APF

qer-ash-tan-nag-di-kash-be-tar-tze-thag-cheq-vet-na-yeg-al-pe-zaq-she-qu-tzith. Its relevance to our current Work is confirmed by the Qabbalistic tradition of subdividing the Name into a Pronic Heptad of Hexads: Avgithetz · Qerashtan · Nagdikash · Betartzethag · Cheqvetna · Yegalpezaq · Shequtzith, each of which corresponds to one of the seven Planets, in the usual Chaldæan order of Saturn through Luna. The six letters of each Hexagrammaton (or each Hexagrammatic portion of the Tetracontadigrammaton) correspond to the six Subplanets marked by the six arms of each Hexagram (Table 30 and Fig. 31), *i.e.*, the Subplanets Saturn though Mars and Venus through Luna, *excluding the central Sun*. The Pronic Divine Name of 42 Letters may be supplemented and crowned by the Heptagrammatic Divine Name of Seven Letters, Ararita, completing and fulfilling the Subplanetary Square of 49, uniting each Subplanetary Hexad into a Heptad under the presidency of the regnal Sun at its Mystic Centre (Fig. 32).

Fig. 28. *The Rose Cross of 49 Petals and Six Squares from the floor of the Tomb*

Fig. 29. *The Rose Cross of 49 Petals and Five Squares from the head of the Pastos*

ON THE 42 ASSESSORS

Planet	Subplanetary Power					
	☽	☿	♀	♂	♃	♄
♄	☽ of ♄ צ	☿ of ♄ ח	♀ of ♄ ,	♂ of ♄ ג	♃ of ♄ ב	♄ of ♄ א
♃	☽ of ♃ ג	☿ of ♃ ט	♀ of ♃ ש	♂ of ♃ ע	♃ of ♃ ר	♄ of ♃ ק
♂	☽ of ♂ ש	☿ of ♂ כ	♀ of ♂ ,	♂ of ♂ ד	♃ of ♂ ג	♄ of ♂ ב
☉	☽ of ☉ ג	☿ of ☉ ח	♀ of ☉ צ	♂ of ☉ ד	♃ of ☉ ט	♄ of ☉ ב
♀	☽ of ♀ ע	☿ of ♀ ג	♀ of ♀ ט	♂ of ♀ ב	♃ of ♀ ק	♄ of ♀ ח
☿	☽ of ☿ ק	☿ of ☿ ז	♀ of ☿ פ	♂ of ☿ ל	♃ of ☿ ג	♄ of ☿ ,
☽	☽ of ☽ ח	☿ of ☽ ,	♀ of ☽ צ	♂ of ☽ ד	♃ of ☽ ק	♄ of ☽ ש

Table 30. The Planetary & Subplanetary Correspondences of the 42 Letters of the Tetracontadigrammaton

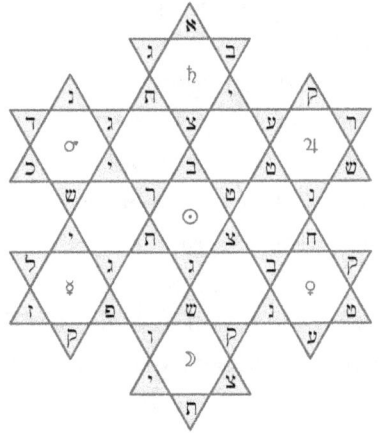
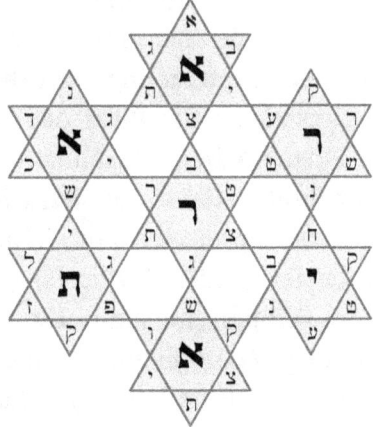

Fig. 31. *The 42 Letters of the Tetracontadigrammaton in the 42 triangular rays of the seven Hexagrams*

Fig. 32. *The 42 Letters of the Tetracontadigrammaton & the seven letters of the Heptagrammaton Ararita in the 49 Stations of the seven Hexagrams*

THE LIGHT EXTENDED

IV. A Mystery Expanding from the Heart of the Tree: Eloah, Elohim, & the Benei Elohim

Our Hermetic and Rosicrucian *Book of the Voice of Thoth* teaches us a further Mystery of the 42 Assessors in relation to the Gods and Angels of the Hermetic Qabbalistic Tree of Life as a Hexagrammatic expansion from Tiphereth through Netzach to Hod (Figs. 33 and 34). The source is in the Solar Heart of the Tree at Tiphereth, where the creative Seed is sown in the Divine Name of Eloah, one of the three conjoined Divine Names in that Sephirah—*i.e.*, YHVH, Eloah, va-Daath ("Tetragrammaton, Eloah, and Gnōsis"). In the Hall of the Neophytes, this Tipheretic Initiator is equivalent to Osiris Onnōphris, the Godform of Hierophant (Fig. 39). From Tiphereth on the Middle Pillar, a Ray (that is a projected Operant or Messenger, *Malakh*, of the creative Divine Life and Light of Eloah is projected into the Sphere of Netzach. There the Divine projection of *Eloah* ("God/Goddess"), interacting with the love and creativity and sevenness of Netzach on the Pillar of Mercy, projects about Himself/Herself six Divine Aspects, formulating the creative Seven *Elohim* ("Gods," the plural of Eloah) of Netzach. In the Hall of the Neophytes, this Heptad of projected Powers answers to the Heptad of Godforms of the seven Ritual Officers, all receiving Their Light in the Ritual Work through the Sun of the Visible Station of Ousiri embodied in the Adept Hierophant, who mediates the Initiatory Current of Light from beyond the Veil in the East. In performing the Initiation of a Candidate into the Order as a Soror or Frater in the Great Work, the Seven Godforms of the Officers enact one Theurgic manifestation of that which is written in *Sepher Bereshith*, the *Book of Genesis*:

ויאמר אלהים אדם נעשה בצלמנו כדמותנו

Va-yomer Elohim, "Naäseh[25] *Adam be-Tzalmenu, ki-Dmuthenu..."*

And the Elohim said, "Let Us make a Human Being in Our Image, according to Our Likeness."

---

25. The verb *naäseh* ("let us make") is from the same root as the noun *Asiyah*, the name of the World of "Making." —APF

ON THE 42 ASSESSORS

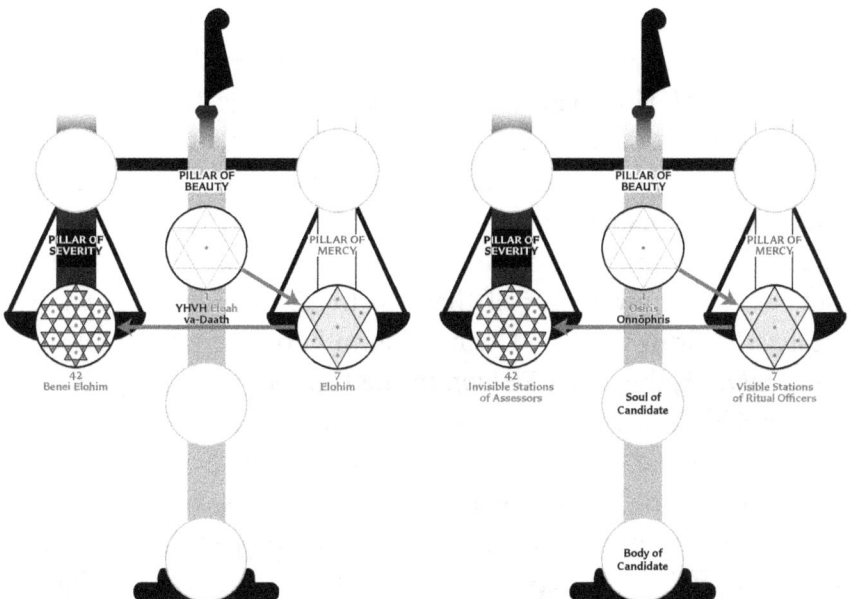

Fig. 33. The Emanation and Multiplication from Eloah of Tiphereth through the Elohim of Netzach to the Benei Elohim of Hod

Fig. 34. The Emanation and Multiplication from Osiris Onnōphris in Tiphereth on the Middle Pillar of Beauty through the Visible Stations in Netzach on the Pillar of Mercy to the Invisible Assessors in Hod on the Pillar of Severity

The *Voice of Thoth* records that this Creative and Loving projection and multiplication of Eloah from Tiphereth is but one of the reasons that the Divine Name in Netzach is *YHVH Tzabaoth*, for Eloah is another Divine Name for YHVH in Tiphereth (in *YHVH Eloah va-Daath*), and reflects that identity well as it is itself a Tetragrammaton (יהוה), and by multiplying Himself/Herself into a plural Heptad of Elohim, Eloah in Netzach is generating one of the Sephirotic Heavenly Hosts (*Tzabaoth*). This interaction of the Hexad of Tiphereth and Sol with the Heptad of Netzach and Venus is yet another aspect of the Pronic Formula of 6×7=42.

Then the seven Elohim in Netzach, in emulation of the Work of Eloah from Tiphereth, project Rays of Their own sevenfold manifestation of Divinity into Hod on the Pillar of Severity, and there each of the seven projected Elohim multiplies into a Heptad by generating six Aspects of Himself/Herself, and these 42 generated Aspects of the seven Elohim are 42 *Benei Elohim* ("Children of the Elohim")[26] of Hod. However, whereas the projected simulacrum or messenger of Eloah is included among the Elohim of Netzach due to the expansive and inclusive nature of the Pillar of Mercy, the restrictive nature of the Pillar of Severity does not provide for the inclusion of the projected Elohim among the Benei Elohim, but retains an awareness of them in the Divine Name of *Elohim Tzabaoth*, for in Hod the Divine Elohim have generated another of the *Tzabaoth*, the *Benei Elohim*. In the Hall of the Neophytes, these 42 Benei Elohim are six Godforms of the Pillar of Severity generated from each of the Godforms of the seven Ritual Officers to comprise the 42 Assessors. When operating in this rôle, this company of 42 of the Benei Elohim may be described as *Chashvei Emeth* ("Assessors of Truth").[27] Rabbi Joseph Gikatilla, in his *Shaarei Orah* ("Gates of

---

26. Elohim is the plural ("Gods") of Eloah, although it also peculiarly serves as a singular ("God") in Hebrew. Whether the singular use of Elohim originates as a grammatical contrivance to explain away originally plural references to the Gods in Hebrew sacred texts, or as a development to express the multiplicity of aspects inherent in an ultimate One Deity is open to debate. However, there is no question that uses of the word as a true plural survive in the Hebrew Bible. Also, the plural *Benei Elohim* ("Children of the Gods" or "Children of God") serves as a general name for Divine Beings just as *Benei Adam* ("Children of the Human") serves as a name for mortal human beings. Apparently even such militantly monotheistic editors and revisers of the Bible as the Elijan school of Prophets and the Deuteronomist generation of priests did not dare to remove all references to such polytheistic groups of Celestial Beings as the *Elohim* and the *Benei Elohim*, doubtless beloved by the populace, and so allusions to polytheistic Hebrew religion survive even in the final forms of the Hebrew and Christian Bibles considered canonical by the dominant monotheistic sects of the two religions. —APF
27. Gematria affirms the truth of this Assessorial title, as *Chashvei Emeth* ("Assessors of Truth") and *Chashvei ha-Nephesh* ("Assessors of the Soul") share the Gematria of 761. Also, *cheshvon ha-Nephesh* ("Assessment or Reckoning of the Soul") is a familiar Hebrew idiom for introspection and self-analysis. —APF

ON THE 42 ASSESSORS

Light"), says that the "harsh Masters of Judgement" are of the *Benei Elohim*.[28]

The *Book of the Voice of Thoth* teaches us that this Formula is inherent in the Divine Tetragrammaton Eloah in Tiphereth, for the Gematric value of אלוה is 1+30+6+5=42. There it is also observed that when Eloah is spelled as a Trigrammaton (אלה), its value is 36, the Square of Tiphereth and Sol, but when as a Tetragrammaton (אלוה), the explicit expression of the Vav[29] (ו bearing itself the number of Tiphereth and Sol) extends the Gematria of that Divine Name to the Pronic 42.

It may be seen that the seven Ritual Officers, in the place of Divine and Angelic Elohim in Netzach on the Pillar of Mercy and Lovingkindness, the Sphere corresponding to the only Grade of the Outer Order on that Pillar and the highest Grade in the Outer Order, are performing one of the most merciful and loving acts, that of Initiation, which also answers to Netzach Elementally as Consecration by Fire. Likewise the 42 Assessors, in the place of discerning and analytical Hod, the Sphere corresponding to the only Grade of the Outer Order on the Pillar of Severity and Judgement, are performing the judgemental act of purgation, which also answers to Hod Elementally as Purification by Water. All of this, however, is initiated by a Current emanating from the Inner Order at Tiphereth, the Osiriac and Maëtic Heart of the Tree.

For those Adeptæ who wish to explore the nature and Work of the Assessors more deeply in a specific context of Hebrew Qabbalah, the names of the 42 Chashvei Emeth of the Subplanets may be revealed

---

28. I currently do not have access to a Hebrew text of *Shaarei Orah*, relying on Avi Weinstein's translation in Joseph ben Abraham Gikatilla and Avi Weinstein, *Gates of Light: Sha'are Orah* (London & San Francisco: HarperCollins Publishers, 1994), but I assume that the phrase "Masters of Judgement" there translates Hebrew *Baalei Din*. The phrase is also employed in the *Zohar* (*e.g.*, in 251a, *Parashath be-Shallach*), where it is rendered in Aramaic as *Marei di-Dina*. — APF

29. That is, technically, the difference between when Eloah is spelled as a Tetragrammaton by the expression of the Name's *o* vowel *cholam* by *cholam male* ("full cholam," with the Vav having the vowel point over it) and as a Trigrammaton by the use of *cholam chaser* ("diminished cholam," without the Vav, but with the vowel point over the following letter). —APF

THE LIGHT EXTENDED

by the 42-Letter Divine Name much as the names of the 72 Angels of the Zodiacal Quinaries may be generated from the 72-fold Divine Name.[30] The Greater Adept should by now in her Magical progress be developing her skills with Hebrew letter manipulation to generate specialized Divine and Angelic Names that will invoke particular manifestations of Supernal energy. This and related Theurgic Work with Divine Names may well lead to the evolution of the Greater Adept into a *Baalath ha-Shemoth* or *Baal ha-Shemoth* ("Mistress of the Names" or "Master of the Names"), who develops great skill in discerning, meditating upon, developing, and employing the formulæ contained within sacred Names, which renders each Divine Name a *Shem ha-Mephorash* (an "Explicated or Analyzed Name"). In the case of the Tetracontadigrammaton, the Angelic names are based on the formulaic analysis[31] which renders this Divine Name as a Heptad of Hexads (*i.e.*, of the mathematical Formula 7×6=42).[32] The resulting names of the 42 Subplanetary Angelic Chasshavim are given in Table 35, along with the letter to which each corresponds and with which it begins. The individual names of the six Chasshavim of each Planet are found by taking the six letters of that portion of the 42-Letter Name which refers to that Planet, and performing a Wheel Permutation upon them, and adding the suffix *-el* to the result. The example in Fig. 36 shows the six letters of Avgithetz, the Saturnine

---

30. The Shem ha-Mephorash is sometimes called the 72-Letter Name, but this is simply not true. The Name has 216 (72×3) letters which may be gathered into 72 Trigrammatic Names, derived from the three consecutive 72-letter verses of Exodus 14:19, 20, and 21. It is in fact the Name of 72 Names. —APF
31. Analysis: *perush*, "explication, analysis, commentary," from the same root (√פרש) as *mephorash*, "explicated, analyzed." —APF
32. Note well, she who would be a *Baalath ha-Shemoth*: The term *Shem ha-Mephorash*, "Explicated or Analyzed Name," is to Hermetic Qabbalists most familiarly the title of the 72-fold Name, but in the longer history of Jewish Qabbalah it has been applied most often (from the Tannaim through Maimonides to today) to the most studied and explicated of all Hebrew Divine Names, יהוה; however, in relation to the Tetragrammaton, the explication was originally meant to be the true and secret pronunciation of the Name. In the more generalized sense in which we use the term in relation to the 72-fold Name, אראריתא is also certainly a Shem ha-Mephorash, familiarly analyzed both in terms of its Notariqonic generation and the Planetary correspondences of its seven letters. Of course to a *Baalath ha-Shemoth*, every Divine Name may be revealed as a *Shem ha-Mephorash* capable of imparting mysteries. —APF

first Hexad of the Name, arranged in a Permutation Wheel. The name of the Angelic Chasshav of ♄ of ♄ is found by reading around the wheel in the counterclockwise direction normal for Hebrew, beginning with the first letter א, and appending אל־. The resulting name is אבגיתצאל (*Avgithetzel*), which you will find in the ♄ of ♄ cell in Table 35. The second name, that of ♃ of ♄, is discovered by following the same procedure with the same Saturn wheel, but starting with the second letter ב, and as with each of these 42 names, adding the אל־ ending. In this case, the resulting name is בגיתצאל (*Begithetzael*), which you will find in the ♃ of ♄ cell in Table 35. The names for the remaining Saturnine Chasshavim of ♂ of ♄, ♀ of ♄, ☿ of ♄, and ☽ of ♄ are all derived from the Saturn Permutation Wheel in Fig. 36, and may be found in the remaining cells on the Saturn row of Table 35. To find the names of the six Chasshavim of ♃ in the second row of Table 35, the Adept must make a Jovial Permutation Wheel (which may easily be made mentally rather than physically once the principle is understood) with the second six Letters of the Tetracontadigrammaton (קרעשטנ[33]), and so on through the final Planetary Wheel of Luna bearing the final six letters (שקוצית) which produces the six names in the last row of Table 35.

Planet	Subplanetary Assessing Angels					
	☽	☿	♀	♂	♃	♄
♄	Tzavgithel ☽ of ♄ צ	Thetzavgiel ☿ of ♄ ת	Yethtzavagel ♀ of ♄ י	Geithetzavel ♂ of ♄ ג	Begithetzael ♃ of ♄ ב	Avgithetzel ♄ of ♄ א
♃	Neqrashtael ☽ of ♃ נ	Tanqrashel ☿ of ♃ ט	Shatneqrael ♀ of ♃ ש	Ashtanqarel ♂ of ♃ ע	Raashtaneqel ♃ of ♃ ר	Qerashtanel ♄ of ♃ ק
♂	Shangadikhel ☽ of ♂ ש	Kashnagadiel ☿ of ♂ כ	Yekashnagdel ♀ of ♂ י	Dikashnagel ♂ of ♂ ד	Gadikashnael ♃ of ♂ ג	Nagdikashel ♄ of ♂ נ
☉	Gevtaretzathel ☽ of ☉ ג	Tagbetratzel ☿ of ☉ ת	Tzathgavtarel ♀ of ☉ צ	Retztagbatel ♂ of ☉ ר	Tartzathgavel ♃ of ☉ ט	Betartzethagel ♄ of ☉ ב
♀	Achqavtanel ☽ of ♀ ע	Naachqavetel ☿ of ♀ נ	Tenachqavel ♀ of ♀ ט	Betenachaqel ♂ of ♀ ב	Qavtenachel ♃ of ♀ ק	Cheqbetnael ♄ of ♀ ח
☿	Qigalphazel ☽ of ☿ ק	Zeqiglaphel ☿ of ☿ ז	Pazqiglael ♀ of ☿ פ	Lephazqigel ♂ of ☿ ל	Galephzaqiel ♃ of ☿ ג	Yegalpezaqel ♄ of ☿ י
☽	Tashqotziel ☽ of ☽ ת	Yethshaqozel ☿ of ☽ י	Tzithshaqoel ♀ of ☽ צ	Vatzithshaqel ♂ of ☽ ו	Qotzithshael ♃ of ☽ ק	Sheqotzithel ♄ of ☽ ש

Table 35. *The 42 Subplanetary Chashvei Emeth of the 42 Letters of the Tetracontadigrammaton*

33. Note that you don't use Nun Final because there is not a fixed end for the letters in a wheeling Permutation. —APF

THE LIGHT EXTENDED

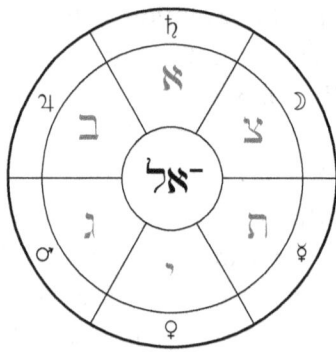
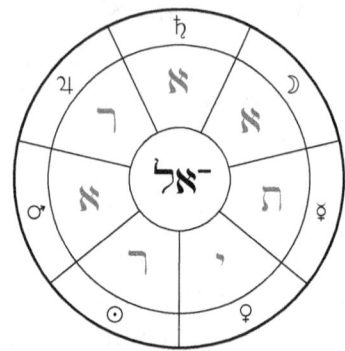

Table 36. The Avgithetz Permutation Wheel for the revelation of the names of the six Subplanetary Angelic Assessors of Truth of the Saturnine Hexad deriving from the 3 Hexagrammaton of the 42-Letter Name

Table 37. The Permutation Wheel for the revelation of the names of the Subplanetary Solar Archangels of the seven Planets from the seven Letters of the Heptagrammaton Ararita

SUBPLANET	ARCHANGELIC NAMES OF THE SUBPLANETARY SUN OF EACH PLANET						
	☽	☿	♀	☉	♂	♃	♄
☉	Aärarithel ☉ of ☽ א	Thaärariel ☉ of ☿ ה	Yithaärarel ☉ of ♀ ׳	Rithaäraël ☉ of ☉ ר	Arithaärel ☉ of ♂ א	Rarithaäel ☉ of ♃ ר	Ararithael ☉ of ♄ א

Table 38. The seven Subplanetary Solar Archangels of the seven Letters of the Heptagrammaton Ararita

The whole formula is completed by the addition of the Heptagrammaton to the Tetracontadigrammaton, and so the 42 Subplanetary Angels whose names derive from the 42-Letter Name are governed by the Archangels of the seven letters of the Heptagrammmaton Ararita,[34] serving in the functional rôle of

---

34. Although the formula is completed for now, there is one further step available, adding the Archangel of Tiphereth as the pinnacle of this Angelic structure, that 42+7+1=50, the number in Hebrew Tradition of the Festival of Weeks and the Counting of the Omer, and in Christian Tradition of the Day of Pentecost, and is the number of Yovel, the Jubilee, in which the completed and perfected Heptad is transcended (as foreshadowed in the name of the 49-petaled Rose of Jubilation). This, however, is a Mystery to be explored fully only in the Grade of Adepta Exempta. —APF

ON THE 42 ASSESSORS

Elohim of Netzach on the Pillar of Mercy.³⁵ To avoid confusion, it is important that the Adept understand that this Ararita Wheel yields in some ways almost the opposite of what the Avgithetz Saturn Wheel (Fig. 36) and the other Planetary Wheels reveal. Whereas each of those seven Wheels provides the names of six of the Assessorial Chasshavim that are Subplanetary Powers of the particular Planet of the Wheel, there is but a single Ararita Permutation Wheel, and it presents the seven central Subplanetary Solar Powers, one for each of the Planets. Table 38 shows those seven names, beginning at the right with 6 of 3, *Ararithael* (אראריתאל), and ending at the left with 6 of 9, *Aärarithel* (אארריתאל).

The esoteric language of Gematria provides further important confirmation of the Formula of the generation of the Assessors of Truth, connecting the Tetracontadiagrammaton with the Hierophantic Godform of Osiris Onnōphris. The numerological value of the 42-Letter Name is 3701, which is the Gematria of Φαπρω Ὀσοροννωφρις (*Phaprō Osoronnōphris*, "Pharaoh Osiris Onnōphris"), the Name of Osiris as the Bornless One, Who clearly proclaims His alignment with Maët and His opposition to Isfet in His great aretalogy in the Magical Papyri, "I am the Truth, the One Who hateth that injustices come to pass in the world."³⁶ Also, the Theurgist in invoking Osoronnōphris proclaims that "Thou hast separated the just and the unjust," the Work of Osiris as the Judge of Souls supported by all the Gods of the Hall of the Two Truths,

---

35. By saying that these Angelic Beings are serving as *functional* Elohim, in that they are seven Angels who are emanated into Netzach from Eloah of Tiphereth and from there produce the 42 Chasshavim who serve as Children of the Elohim in Hod, we mean that they are not *inherent* members of the Netzach Angelic Host. This is the same manner in which Sandalphon and Metatron, the great polar Dyad of Gatekeepers and Equilibrators in Kether and Malkhuth, in Boaz and Yakhin, and in the Holy of Holies of the Temple of Solomon, are *functionally* Kerubim, though that does not mean that they are *inherently* simply members of the Host of Yesod, as they are two of the three Archangels of the Host of the Ishim of Malkhuth, and Sandalphon is the Archangel of the Host of the Chayoth ha-Qodesh of Kether. —APF
36. This and all subsequent excerpts from the *Stēlē of Jeou the Zōgraphos* (the source of the "Invocation of the Bornless One") in British Library MS Papyrus Londinensis 46 (*PGM* v), lines 96–172, are my translations from the Greek. —APF

including the Assessors. Further, the formula of the generation from Tiphereth of the seven Officers as Elohim and the 42 Children of the Elohim may be seen as one esoteric reading of the declaration, "I am the One Who Begetteth and Sendeth Forth Offspring."

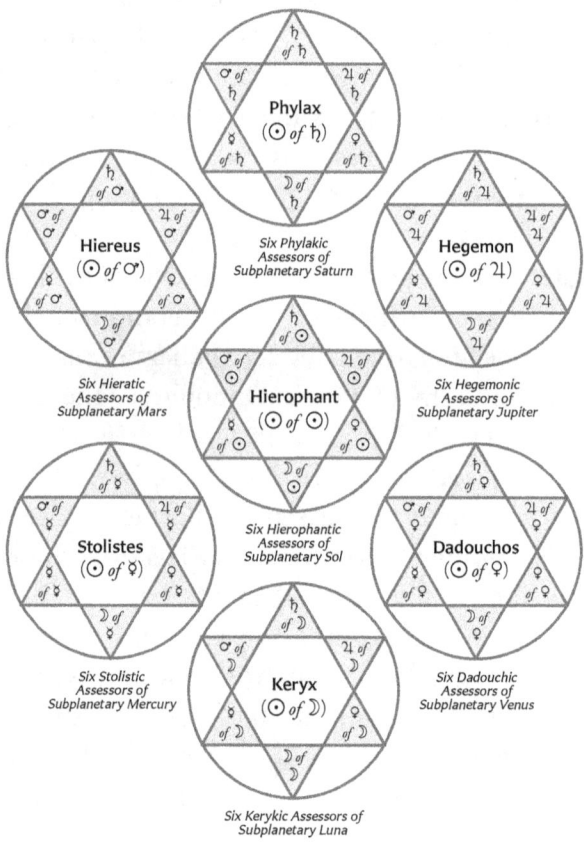

Fig. 39. The Subplanetary Correspondences of the Seven Ritual Officers & the 42 Assessors

This formula presents us with the means to explore the 42 Assessors as consisting of seven Subplanetary Hexads, one deriving from each of the seven Ritual Officers in the Hall of the Neophytes. There is more than one method for ascribing the seven Officers to the Planets, but we will make use of this form (Fig. 39)—the most generally instructive—for our Work here. The Hierophant is ascribed to the Hexagram of the Sun in Tiphereth, the Ruler of and Bringer of

ON THE 42 ASSESSORS

Light and Life to the ancient sevenfold Solar system of Officers. The Hiereus commands the Hexagram of Mars, answering to Gevurah on the Pillar of Severity. The Hegemon is in the Hexagram of Jupiter, corresponding to Chesed on the Pillar of Mercy. The Keryx is found moving, changing, and reflecting the Light of Hierophant through the Hexagram of Luna, attributed to Yesod on the Middle Pillar. The Dadouchos consecrates on the Pillar of Mercy in the midst of the Hexagram of Venus, answering to Netzach, the Sphere of the Fire Grade in the Outer. The Stolistes purifies on the Pillar of Severity in the Hexagram of Mercury, answering to Hod, the Sphere of the Water Grade in the Outer. Finally, the Phylax stands watch in the Outer Darkness of the Pronaos in the Hexagram of Saturn, corresponding to Daath in the Abyss on the Tree.[37] So we see in the primary Solar and Tipheretic Heptad that the Hierophantic Godform of Osiris is surrounded by a constellation of a Hexad of supporting Deities—the Hieratic Horus, the Hegemonic Maët, the Kerykic Anubis of the East, the Dadouchic Thaum-Ēsh-Nēith, the Stolistic Auramoouth, and the Phylakic Anubis (or Ophois) of the West. By a process of fractal multiplication and emanation, each of these seven Gods of the Ritual Offices is in turn supported by a Hexad of six Assessor Gods Who partake of the Planetary nature of the Ritual Officers manifested through a Subplanetary Force.

Please attend to a word of caution here: The Greater Adept must not misinterpret this formula and limit her understanding by believing that this is the only explanation of the Sephirotic Divine Names YHVH Tzabaoth and Elohim Tzabaoth, or that the Chorus of the Elohim of Netzach can only appear as seven and only in this function, or that the Benei Elohim of Hod may only manifest as 42, and only as Assessing Godforms of the Pillar of Severity. Nor is she to blind herself to the fact that there are many other formulæ

---

37. The Adepta Major should here also recall—both from her study of the Stegan Decagrams and Enneagrams (sometimes also called Stegan Hexagrams and Heptagrams) in ThAMinor, and from her new studies of the Z libelli on the Vault here in NAMajor—that when the Sephiroth of the Supernal Triad are excluded from the attributions of the Sephiroth to the Planets, as they are on the ceiling and floor of the Vault, that Saturn may then correspond to Malkhuth among the seven lower Sephiroth. —APF

THE LIGHT EXTENDED

of Osiris to be discerned in the Stele of Jeou the Zōgraphos. This Tetracontadyadic Formula is a powerful formula of Magic, yet it is but one formula among many pertaining to these Gods, Angels, and Sephiroth.

Another formulation of the 42-fold Name (Fig. 40) is also relevant and revelatory. In our Hermetic Qabbalah, one mode of representing the Name is as the letters of the Tetragrammaton bearing 42 Shields (Heb. *Maginnim*, and in a Latin translation *Clipei*, "Round Shields," each with a Circled Hexagram upon it). The letter Shin, which unites the Four Elemental letters into Five under the presidency of Spirit, bears a further seven Shields which raise the 42 Shields of the Tetragrammaton to the completed, perfect Square of the Planets at 49 Shields, uniting the six Planets into seven under the presidency of the mystic Sun.[38]

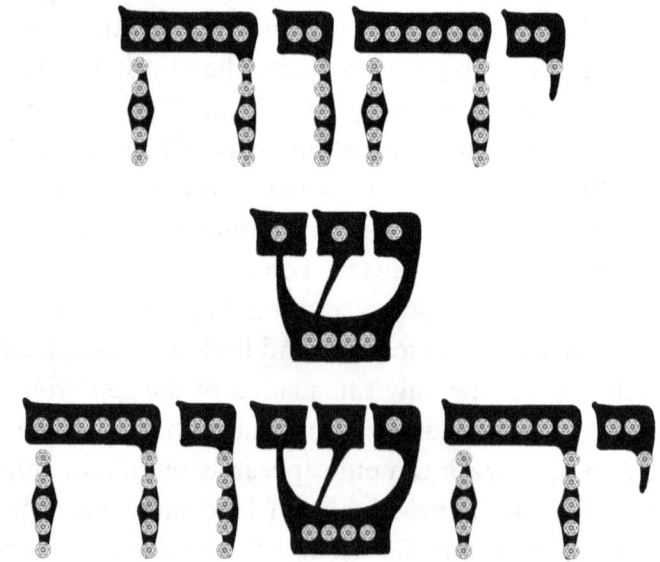

Fig. 40. 42 Hexagrammatic Shields (Heb. Maginnim, Lat. Clipei) on the Letters of the Tetragrammaton plus seven Shields on the Letter Shin yielding 49 Shields on the Letters of the Pentagrammaton

---

38. This symbolic diagram is clearly related to that associated with the 72-fold Shem ha-Mephorash, which depicts the letters of Tetragrammaton bearing 24 Crowns, each Crown having three tines for a total of 72. The division of the 72 into three sets of 24 relates to the mysteries of *Sepher Bahir*. —APF

Fig. 41. *The Calvary Cross of Ten Sephirotic Cubes, having upon its surface 42 squares*

Fig. 42. *The Calvary Cross of Seven Planetary Cubes, each cube having six squares, totaling 42*

V. The Assessors and the Fundamental Adepta Major Formula of the Testing or Assessing Tokens

Since your first studies as an Adepta Minor, you have made regular and important use in your Work—and particularly in Spirit Vision—of the Testing Tokens associated with the seven Hebrew Double letters of *Sepher Yetzirah* and the seven chromatic bands of the Phœnix Wand of the Adepta Major.

The 42 Assessors, like the Testing Tokens, test not for multiple things, but for multiple aspects of one thing, which is Truth, Emeth, Thmē, Maët. In fact, the 42 Assessors may be accurately considered as Yetziratic Divine Personifications of the Testing Tokens; they are the Testing Intelligences. For example, the six Assessors Who are *Parhedroi* of the Hegemon are six Intelligences Who test with the Jovial Token of Probation. When the Major Adept is applying the Token (usually by tracing it while holding the Phœnix Wand by the violet band) to prove or disprove some figure beheld in Spirit Vision, she may visualize the six Jovial Assessors standing or sitting in a

Hexagram (and thus also in a Circle) around the tested figure (as six Officers do about the Candidate in the Hall of the Neophytes), tracing simultaneously with the Adept towards the figure the Jovial Token ⊃ (or ♃, or ♃, as the case may be).

VI. The Work of the 42 Assessors in Relation to the Dead, to the Candidate for Initiation, and to the Senior Adept

For the ancient Kemetic dead, the Assessors were encountered after death as a preliminary stage of the Judgement of the Heart in the Hall of the Two Truths, during which They were to assess the deceased in relation to Their 42 respective areas of right (or wrong) behaviour and nature, and convey Their evaluations to Thoth, Who would add these assessments to the True Record of the state of the Heart which He transmitted to Osiris, regarding the justification (or, more accurately, verification) of the dead. For the unprepared, brought willy-nilly, ready or not, to the Judgement by unexpected death, the result was likely to be devouring by the inescapable chimæra Ammut. For those who were prepared and tutored for their entry into the Afterlife (*i.e.*, those privileged and in many cases initiated pharaohs, priests, sacred artists and scribes, and other *cognoscenti* for whom copies of the *Book of the Dead* were prepared, and who were instructed in the use of the papyrus, at once as an apotropaic Talisman and a practical guidebook to the Otherworld), the function of the Assessors was more nuanced and potentially more supportive. For such aspirants to justification/verification, if they sincerely aspired to rectitude, sincerely regarded their death as a new beginning and a new opportunity to live a life of Maët—in other words, if they sincerely choose to die to the old life and be reborn to the new—the Assessors could, rather than simply reporting factually on the now-ended incarnate lives of the aspirants, perform the purgatorial rôle described in the Exordium to the 125th Formula, assisting in "cleansing [NN] from all wrongs which he hath wrought, and beholding the Faces of All the Gods." On the other hand, for the newly dead Soul who clung to the vices, neuroses, and other negative attachments or bondages

ON THE 42 ASSESSORS

of her Earthly life, the encounter with the Assessors could be more hellish than purgatorial, culminating in her being surrendered to the voracious Ammut. However, we have evidence from Late Antique Egypt suggesting that even devouring by Ammut was not final annihilation. In Sethian texts from Egypt, Gnostic teachers describe celestial Beings who seem to perform a function analogous to that of the Assessors, descending to the liminal levels of reality that occupy the borderlands between the physical and the spiritual, where They appraise the natures of ascending Souls, whether of the newly dead or of Seers and Prophets, like the Gnostic Zōstrianos, ascending in Spirit Vision: *viz.*, ⲈⲚ ⲆⲨⲚⲀⲘⲒⲤ ⲚⲢⲈϤⲆⲒⲀⲔⲢⲒⲚⲈ (Græco-Coptic *hen Dynamis en-Refdiakrine*, "Judging Powers")[39] and ⲈϨⲢⲀⲒ ⲚⲦⲈ ⲚⲒⲚⲞϬ ⲚⲔⲢⲒⲦⲎⲤ (Græco-Coptic *ehraï en-te ni-Notch en-Kritēs*, "the descent of the Great Judges").[40] The Græco-Coptic Refdiakrine and Kritēs come from the same root as the Greek term used in the *Stele of Jeou the Zōgraphos* to express the judgement of Osoronnophris in the Hall of Two Truths: *diakrinas*, "You judge/separate/distinguish" between the just and the unjust.

A Greek text of *The Oracles of Truth of Zōstrianos* was among the scriptures brought to Proclus by Gnostic students in his classes at Rome, and one of those against which he spoke, as recorded in the *Enneads*. Plotinus, engaging in a rare polemic, charges the author of Zōstrianos with both innovation (always true of Gnostic sages in Antiquity, communicating their newly inspired perception of truth, just as—we may observe—did Plotinus) and with plagiarism from Plato. A more sympathetic seeker might say that the Gnostic teachers were incorporating the insights of the master Plato into their evolving worldview just as was Plotinus. Plotinus's comments make it clear that reincarnation was the punishment meeted out by the Judging Powers to the dead unqualified to continue their

---

39. From the *Untitled Treatise* in the Codex Brucianus, one of the very few Gnostic scriptures known directly (rather than through unreliable quotations and paraphrases in anti-Gnostic polemics) before the 1945 discovery of the Nag Hammadi library. The Codex was purchased by the extraordinary Scottish explorer James Bruce at Luxor in 1769, acquired by the Britsh Museum in 1842, and transferred to the Bodleian Library at Oxford in 1848, where it is catalogued as MS Bruce 96. —APF
40. From *The Oracles of Truth of Zostrianos* (NHC VIII, 1). —APF

ascent into the Higher Spiritual realms. While reincarnation is not specifically described in the Coptic version of the text found at Nag Hammadi, one of the liminal Æons to which the Judging/Assessing/Discerning Powers descend to execute Their office is named ⲧⲡⲁⲣⲟⲓⲕⲏⲥⲓⲥ (Græco-Coptic *te-Paroikēsis*, "the Reincarnation/Metempsychosis/Transmigration"). Also, the Platonic text from which Plotinos believes the Gnostics to have borrowed concepts is surely the famous "Myth of Ēr," the near-death experience which is recounted at length by Socrates in Plato's *Republic*, and which clearly depicts a process of reincarnation.[41] And it is very likely that Plotinus was correct, and the influence of Plato was tacitly acknowledged by the Gnostic authot of *Zōstrianos*, as a set of names found in both texts (Pamphylios, Armenios, etc.) make it likely that Zōstrianos was meant to be thought of as an ancestor of Ēr.[42] Therefore, given the testimony of Zōstrianos, it may be that the devouring of an unjust soul by Ammut depicted in the symbolic but experiential (as one does not simply contemplate but *experience* symbols in Yetzirah) language of Yetzirah represents the consumption and reclamation of a soul by its unresolved bonds to the material world.

The Candidate for Initiation into the Order, who has chosen to set forth on the Path of Initiation and has been evaluated (indeed, assessed) by the Chiefs and Members of a Temple as an appropriate Candidate, and is undergoing initiation into the Grade of Neophyte and into the Order of the Golden Dawn, has a similar status to the ancient Kemetic Honoured Dead who had been endowed by the priests with their consecrated *Book of the Dead* and other talismans

---

41. Plato, *Republic* 10.614B–621D. If you have not read the story of Ēr, O Adept, it is recommended that you visit your nearest library and do so. If it interests you, two other surviving Greek accounts of near-death experiences are to be found in the writings of Plutarch. The first is that of Timarchos, a student of Socrates (*De Genio Socratis* 21 ff.=*Moralia* 589F ff.), and the second is that of Thespesios of Soli (*De Sera Numinis Vindicta* 22 ff.=*Moralia* 563B ff.). —APF

42. Zōstrianos was also confused with and assimilated to the Persian prophet and—to the Hellenic and Latin West of Late Antiquity—magus Zoroaster, which the encrypted titles of the Coptic Zōstrianos manuscript make plain had already happened by the time this codex was hidden away at Nag Hammadi in the fourth century CE. Early Christian fathers in Alexandria and its environs (Arnobius and Clement) knew of traditions definitely associating Zōstrianos, Zoroaster, and Ēr. —APF

ON THE 42 ASSESSORS

(amulets, shawabtis, etc.). Indeed, it is the Officers of the Temple holding the Visible Stations, and the Adepts on the Dais along with any witnessing Adepts throughout the Hall who formulate and support the Visible and Invisible Stations and all of the Actions and Patterns of the Zed Formulæ, who serve for the Candidate Initiand[43] as the equivalent of the talismanic *Book of the Dead* for the ancient Honoured Dead. After the first Purification and Consecration, when the Candidate stands in darkness west of the Altar, it is none other than the Goddess of Truth, Maët Herself, who, through the Hegemon, prompts the Initiand in her two key responses to the questions posed by Osiris through the Hierophant. The first response ("My Soul wanders in Darkness seeking the Light of Occult Knowledge, and I believe that in this Order knowledge of that Light may be obtained.") marks her as a chosen Candidate, and the second ("I AM" willing to take the Obligation) proclaims the assent of the free Human Will to Initiation. It is also—unknown to the Human Will, but inspired by Truth Herself—an invocation of the Highest Divine Name EHEIEH in Kether, serving both as a prefiguration of the Kether Clause of the Adepta Minor Obligation and as an invocation by the Human Will of the Higher Self, the Lower Genius, the Supernal Yechidah in Kether, affirming the aspiration of the Ruach to be in accord with and service to the Higher Will. The Lower Genius will at this point be sensed to stir and rise beyond the Veil in the East, and the Simulacrum of the Evil Persona to stir beyond the Pronaos in the West.

It is here that the Judgement of the Initiand as True of Voice is first partially made, after the first Purification and Consecration and *before* the Obligation, for it is the initial verifying Judgement of the Assessors and the Godforms of the Officers that approves the Initiand as capable of truly assuming the Obligation. The six Ritual Officers who are in the Hall (the Phylax being without the Hall in the Pronaos) gather in the form of a Hexagram about the Initiand, though with the Eastern, Saturnine arm of the Hexagram over-extended to the East. In this case, as the Initiand occupies the central, Solar station, the Hierophant fills the distant Saturnine

---

43. Recall that Initiand (from Latin *Initianda/Initiandus*) means "one being initiated," as Initiate (from Latin *Initiata/Initiatus*) does "one who has been initiated." —APF

station corresponding to the Supernals separated by the Abyss from the Lower Sephiroth. The five Officers at the Altar aspire for the Descent of the Hierophant to achieve equilibrium and regularity in the Hexagram, so that it fits a perfect Magic Circle about the Initiand. While Past Hierophant maintains the Enthroned Form of Osiris, the Hierophant as Haroueris, bearing the Sceptre of Power of the Middle Pillar, descends the Middle Pillar to administer the Obligation. As He descends through the Hall, Haroueris passes first through the Station of Maët between the Pillars (where stands the Simulacrum of the Initiand in the Place of Equilibrium and Truth), which He steps through, Entering left foot first. Next He comes to the Station of Harpokratēs which He steps upon with the left foot on the side of Mercy, affirming by that connection with the Innocent Dawning Child the First Purification and Consecration and the Assent of the free Human Will. Next He comes to the Station of the Evil Triad which He treads upon with the right foot on the side of Severity. At this point, the Forms of the Assessors about the upper limits of the Hall may be observed to become clearer and brighter, and that of Their evil and averse antitheses below the outer limits of the Hall to become dimmer. As it is written in the *Book of the Voice of Thoth*, during this period from the entry of the Candidate into the Hall through the Obligation until the Restoration to the Light, were it not for the power of the 42-Lettered Name in the Palaces of יצירה (the Gods of Which are usually called the Great Assessors of Judgement) the actual Evil Persona would at once formulate and be able to obsess the רוח of the Candidate.

Finally Haroueris arrives east of the Altar, stepping with His left foot, then bringing His right to join it. In this position, He interposes Himself between the Initiand and the Evil Triad.

During the Obligation, the three forbidding pressures of the Sword of Justice upon the neck of the Initiand correspond to the threefold bondage represented by the Cord about the waist of the Initiand, to the three Fallen parts of the Human (*i.e.*, the three parts below the Abyss: the physical Guph or Geviyah, the Nephesh, and the Ruach), and to the Evil Triad of Ouammout the Adversary. It should now be understood that the Knives in the Gevuratic right

ON THE 42 ASSESSORS

hands of the Assessors correspond to the Black Pillar of Severity and to the Hiereus and Horus the Avenger in the Hall, while the Feathers in the Chesedic left hands of the Assessors correspond to the White Pillar of Mercy and to the Hegemon and Maët the Preparer of the Way for the Candidate of the Mysteries in the Hall. During the Obligation, the Simulacrum of the Initiand stands between the Black and White Pillars, while the Hiereus and Hegemon stand in the places of the Simulacra of the Black and White Pillars flanking the physical Initiand. Also the threefold warning by the Greater Officers ("They journey as upon the Winds; They strike where no mortal strikes; They slay where no mortal slays.") threatens the Evil Triad and the Simulacrum of the Evil Persona with the Yetziratic Action of the 42-Letter Name and its implementing Gods, the Assessors.

At the conclusion of the Obligation, it is sealed by the Knock of Haroueris (which should be felt to vibrate throughout the cosmos as a Sign to all Spiritual beings of the Becoming of a new Neophyte Initiate). At this point the colossal Godform of Thoth testifies to the Maëkheru Nature of the newly obligated Neophyte by shifting from the Sign of the Enterer to the Sign of Silence of the Divine Child, the Reborn Sun at the Centre of the Reborn Universe, assenting to the Descent of a Projection of the Yechidah to the Station of Harpokratēs in witness of the Assumption of the Obligation. The Descent of the Higher Self to the Harpokratēs Station affirms the renewed innocence of the verified Initiand, identifying the new Member of the ⊙=▣ Grade and the Zero Degree with the infinite potential of the New Divine Child Whose Name is the Grand Word of the Neophyte Grade. However the retention of the hoodwink clearly marks that the Purification, Consecration, and Initiation of the Obligated Neophyte is yet incomplete.

After Osiris Enthroned speaks to the Neophyte on behalf of the Higher Self, the Three sunwise Circumambulations in the Path of Darkness (from the viewpoint of the Hoodwinked Neophyte) take place, with the Invisible Station of Harpokratēs (at which the projected Lower Genius is also still stationed) as the Centre Axis.

Mark well that with each of the three Circumambulations which follow, the Forms of the Assessors above the outer limits of the Hall

THE LIGHT EXTENDED

grow brighter and clearer, while those of the evil antitheses of the Assessors below grow dimmer and less distinct. Also the Simulacra of the Pillars on either side of the Neophyte grow clearer, and the originally barely discernible Light above the head of the Neophyte grows brighter, prefiguring the Dawn, though she is still shrouded in thinning cloud and lessening darkness. Also the Simulacrum of the Neophyte between the Pillars of the Hall at the Station of Maët grows clearer.

The First Circumambulation (which invokes the Supernal Light from the Angle of Binah) formally begins when the Hierophant is first passed in the East, knocking in Mercy as the Neophyte passes. On the Neophyte passing the West halfway through the First Circumambulation, the Hiereus knocks in Severity, and the Assessors all give the Sign of the Enterer, affirming the Neophyte's Right (Maët) to proceed in the First Circumambulation. The First Purification and Consecration which answers to the First Circumambulation preceded it when the Candidate was brought into the Hall.

The First Circumambulation (of Binah) is completed and the Second Circumambulation (invoking the Supernal Light from the Chokhmah Angle) is begun at the same instant, when the East is passed for the second time, the Hierophant knocking in Mercy. The second Circumambulation continues, pausing for the Second Purification and Consecration before coming to the Hiereus in the West. Maët allows the Neophyte a first glimpse of Horus, and the Goddess of Truth, the Interpreter of the Higher Self, answers the Naming Test of the Hiereus on behalf of the Neophyte. The second Circumambulation continues, with the Hiereus knocking in Severity, and the Assessors all give the Sign of the Enterer, affirming the Neophyte's right to proceed in the course of the Second Circumambulation.

The Second Circumambulation (of Chokhmah) is completed and the Third Circumambulation (invoking the Supernal Light from the Kether Angle) is begun at the same instant, when the East is passed for the third time, the Hierophant knocking in Mercy. The Third Circumambulation continues, with the Hiereus at the halfway point in the West knocking in Severity, and the Assessors

ON THE 42 ASSESSORS

all giving the Sign of the Enterer, affirming the Neophyte's Right (Maët) to proceed in the course of the Third Circumambulation. The Circumambulation pauses for the Third Purification and Consecration just before coming to the Hierophant in the East at the completion of the Circumambulation. Maët allows the Neophyte a first glimpse of Osiris, and the Goddess of Truth, the Interpreter of the Higher Self, answers the Naming Test of the Hierophant on behalf of the Neophyte. The third Circumambulation (of Kether) continues, being completed when the Hierophant knocks in Mercy as the Neophyte reaches the East, and the Assessors all give the Sign of Harpokratēs, affirming the Neophyte's completion of the three Circumambulations and the three Purifications and Consecrations invoking the Supernal LVX, and thus her verification to proceed in the remainder of the Initiation. The averse antitheses of the Assessors are now barely perceptible, the Assessors are clear, the Simulacra of the Pillars on either side of the physical Neophyte are much more clearly defined, as is the Simulacrum of the Neophyte between the physical Pillars of the Hall, and though the Neophyte is still wrapped in a thinning nocturnal darkness, the light above her head is much brighter, though still veiled by cloud.

The Neophyte and Officers continue to circumambulate, but the three Circumambulations are complete, and this is simply normal circular movement about the Hall to reach the west side of the Cubic Altar. On reaching the West, Hiereus and Hegemon move into the positions of the Simulacra of the Pillars beside the Neophyte and advance with her between them until she stands against the west side of the Altar. The other Officers come into the same Hexagrammatic positions as before the Obligation. The Past Hierophant, from her own seat, once more maintains the Godform of Osiris Enthroned on the Throne of the East, while the Hierophant as Harouēris with Sceptre and Banner descends the Middle Pillar as before, this time reciting the four beautiful lines of the Aretalogy of the Lightbearer, and consciously bearing the Supernal Light invoked by the Three Circulations. The Hierophant once more descends through the stations of Maët (occupied by the Simulacrum of the Neophyte), Harpokratēs (occupied by both Harpokratēs and the Projection of

THE LIGHT EXTENDED

the Lower Genius), and the Evil Triad to arrive east of the Altar, though this time, considering the energies of each of those Invisible Stations, she may choose to pause in her descent at one of them or not as her intuition suggests in relation to the particular Neophyte, or—if strongly so guided—she may stop at one of these stations for the entire Orison, only proceeding to the East of the Altar afterwards. The Hierophant knocks once, and all in the Hall (including the Chiefs on the dais) rise. Then all except the Hierophant kneel for the Invocation or Orison of the Ruler of the Universe to bless the Neophyte. The Hexagram Formula now shifts, though no Officers change physical position, as it is only the energetic linkages among the vertices of the Hexagram that rearrange, so that from two interlaced equilateral Triangles (Fire Triangle Hierophant · Stolistes · Dadouchos, Water Triangle Keryx · Hegemon · Hiereus) it shifts to two discreet obtuse Isosceles Triangles (Fire Triangle formed by the Greater Officers Hierophant · Hiereus · Hegemon, Water Triangle by the Lesser Officers Keryx · Dadouchos · Stolistes). The Triangle of the Greater Officers represents the active aspiration of the Neophyte for the Divine aid, while the Triangle of the Lesser Officers represents the passive receptivity of the Neophyte to the influx of the Divine favour. All then rise for the climactic Anagōgē or Restoration to the Light. If the Hierophant has stopped at one of the intermediate Stations for the Orison, she now proceeds to the East of the Altar.

When the three Greater Officers raise their Implements over the Neophyte, intersecting at her Middle Pillar above her Kether, they formulate not just a Pyramid or Cone, but—as you have recognized since Theorica Adepta Minor—the Double Cone or Double Pyramid,[44] invoking the Ray of Divine White Brilliance and the Dragon Circulations of the Energies from the World of Yetzirah and the Higher and Divine Genius into the World of Asiyah and the Sphere of the Neophyte through Kether of Asiyah, the natural Abode of the Lower Genius. As the three Greater Officers issue their threefold call of the Neophyte to the Light, the White Triangle appears Astrally in the Aura of the Neophyte before her brow as a Seal of the LVX,

---

44. Observe that even physically the two Sceptres and the Sword do not touch at their tips, but cross and so physically indicate the existence of the Yetziratic inverse Cone touching points with the Asiyatic Cone. —APF

representing both the Supernal Triangle and the Invocatory Cone of Light. As the hoodwink is removed, the Divine White Brilliance flowing into Asiyah from Yetzirah through the Supernals shines forth from the Middle Pillar and dispels all darkness and cloud from the Aura of the Neophyte. The three Greater Officers together affirm the reception of the Neophyte into the Order and together affirm her as a Soror and together speak aloud that personal Magical Formula which is the Motto of the Neophyte. Then the three Greater Officers proclaim the Epiphōnēsis, triply charging the Triangle of Supernal LVX shining in the Aura of the Neophyte, with "Khabs am Pekht" led by Hierophant in charging the Invoking Triangle beginning from the Angle of Kether and Yechidah, then with "Konx om Pax" led by Hiereus in charging the Invoking Triangle beginning from the Angle of Chokhmah and Chayah, and finally with "Light in Extension" led by Hegemon in charging the Invoking Triangle beginning from the Angle of Binah and Neshamah.

Then the Hierophant returns to the East and as Osiris, and before any other event transpires, calls forth the Keryx, the Messenger of the Gods, to hold aloft the Lamp of the Hidden Gnosis to affirm that beyond the Light of the Supernal Self and the Lower Genius, the Divine Light of the Gods Beyond—even if unseen consciously by the Ruach—ultimately and truly guides the Initiate on the Path.

Directed by Osiris through the Hierophant, the Hegemon brings the Neophyte sunwise about the Altar to place her immediately east of the Altar, and then the Goddess of Truth draws the Neophyte forward one stride, so that she stands upon the Evil Triad, just as Harpokratēs is shown in many ancient images, showing that—purified of her past uninitiated life and consecrated to the Magic of Light—she may as an Initiate tread down her own Evil Persona, eventually as a Magus casting it out of the Nephesh into its rightful place below the Tree where it may be of service as a support upon which she stands or even a steed upon which she rides. At this point the false and evil antitheses of the Assessors below the boundaries of the Temple are almost unformulated, being revealed by the Light of Truth to be visually extremely vague and energetically extremely weak to the point of irrelevance.

THE LIGHT EXTENDED

The three Greater Officers now formulate the Triangle east of the Pillars, and the Projected Form of the Lower Genius ascends from the Harpokratic Station to the Hegemonic Station between the Pillars, sharing the Station with the Simulacrum of the Neophyte, though the Form of the Genius faces West between the Pillars (with the Gevurah Pillar on Her/His right, and the Gedulah Pillar on Her/His left) and the Simulacrum of the Neophyte faces the East. Hiereus/Horus entrusts His Insignia to Hegemon/Maët, and descends the Middle Pillar to the Station of Harpokratēs, asserting by His descent unarmed, without the weapon of the Sword and without the shield of the Banner, that the Neophyte in her purified and consecrated state has the full confidence of the Temple and the Order and the Gods. The Hiereus entrusts the Tokens of the Mysteries to the Neophyte, and then—being keenly aware of the Godform of Horus Whose hand grips that of the Neophyte—draws her by the Grip through the Station of Harpokratēs to the Station of Maët, where the Neophyte attains the full symbolic Station of the Enterer of the Threshold, being thus reunited by Hiereus as the Active Agent of the Triad of Light with her Astral Simulacrum projected to the Great Threshold of the Immeasurable Region between the Pillars at the First Purification and Consecration on the outer threshold of the Hall, and also into alignment and direct contact with the projection of the Yechidatic Lower Genius, the Highest Supernal part of the Human. Observe clearly that it is not Maët, Truth Herself, Who brings the Neophyte to Her Station, but the much more exacting Guardian of Truth, Horus, Who thus shows His full assent to the Verification of the Neophyte as True of Voice and Heart. During the uplifting of the Neophyte, as the Hiereus describes the Pillars, the Lower Genius of the Neophyte briefly assumes each Godform and Heroform named ("the Pillars alike of Shu, of Seth, of Hermēs, and of Solomon"), each in the Sign of Osiris Slain. As she is drawn into perfect position between the Pillars, the Lower Genius folds Her/His arms in the Sign of Osiris Risen, and it is as if each of the Forms embraces the Neophyte in that Sign. From this pivotal experience of contact with her Yechidah in the Place of Perfect Equilibrium on the Threshold of the Gate of the Immeasurable Region, within the Astral Triangle of Light above the

ON THE 42 ASSESSORS

brow of the Neophyte there becomes visible to the Spirit Vision of those before the Neophyte on the Dais (and any other Ritual Officers, should they be Adepts) a Vision of that primal moment of *Kheper*, of Becoming, of Birth and Rebirth, which is the Golden Dawn, in the form of the Mystic Sun rising above the primordial Sea.

At the command of the Hiereus (by authority previously delegated by the Hierophant), the Fourth and Final Purification and Consecration begins. This is immediately and conspicuously different from the three prior Purifications and Consecrations. The Chiefs upon the Dais, and any others in the Hall who have attained to the Grade of Adepta Major, should be clearly aware of the multi-aspected Goddesses Whose Forms the Stolistes and Dadouchos bear at this point, reflecting the ability of the Deities—so well known to the Priests and Priestesses of Egypt—to share function and identity in a Compound Form. Stolistes bears not only Auramoöuth of Water, but also that one of the Two Maëti Goddesses of Truth Who is of the Pan of the Scales corresponding to the Pillar of Severity, and particularly at this point is also overshadowed by the Great Form of Nephthys of the Black Pillar, so that She may be truly regarded as ⲁⲩⲣⲁⲙⲟⲟⲩⲫ-ⲫⲙⲏⲉϥ-ⲛⲉⲃⲫⲱ (Auramoöuth–Thmëëph[45]–Nebethō). Likewise Dadouchos acts not only in the Form of Thaum-Ēsh-Nēith of Fire, but also that one of the Two Maëti Goddesses of Truth Who is of the Pan of the Scales corresponding to the Pillar of Mercy, and is also overshadowed by the Great Form of Isis of the White Pillar, so that She may be truly regarded as ⲫⲁⲩⲙⲏⲏⲛⲛⲓⲫ-ⲫⲙⲏⲉⲡ-ⲏⲯⲉ (Thaum-Ēsh-Nēith–Thmëëps[46]–Ēse). This fourth anc final Purification and Consecration is directed to several Theurgic goals: *viz.*,

- Aligning and expanding the Auric Circle and Sphere of Neophyte to be at one with that of the Temple (and symbolically of the dedicatory, tutelary, Egregoric Deity of the Temple) and through it that of the Order.

---

45. Should your memory need refreshing, the Great Goddess Maët or Thmē is omnipresent on the Tree of Life, and the ϥ (*Phi*) suffix indicates that this is Her Manifestation in the Sphere of Gevurah. —APF
46. By the same token, the ⲡ (*Psi*) suffix indicates the Manifestation of the Goddess in Gedulah. —APF

- Affirming and strengthening the presence in the Auric Sphere of the Neophyte of the Four lateral Pillars of the Tree of Five Pillars and of the Station of the Neophyte as the Middle Pillar of the Tree of Five Pillars.
- Affirming and strengthening the Link between the Neophyte and her Lower Genius, and thereby with the Higher and Divine Genius beyond.
- Affirming and strengthening the Initiatory and Probationary Station of the Neophyte in the Gateway between the Pillars as the Enterer of the Threshold.

When the Stolistes completes her Purification of the Four Quarters, returns to the East, and rotates to face the Neophyte (and thus beginning the Purification and Consecration of the Fifth, interior Station within the Circle), the Form of the Genius rotates to face the East and extends Her/His arms in the Sign of Osiris Slain, orienting Herself/Himself for the first time to match the orientation of the Neophyte, affirming that the Ruchanic[47] free will of the Neophyte is in accord with the Higher Will in undertaking the Path of Hermetic Initiation, and once more affirming ritually through both Her/His Eastward Orientation and Osiris Slain Posture that, though the Yechidah in Kether is the Highest in Asiyah, and all perceptions of the Divine come unto the Asiyatic Human through the Yechidah, yet She/He is but the *Lower* Genius, and offers Herself/Himself in sacrifice unto the Higher and Divine Genius Who abides beyond Asiyah in Yetzirah, and beyond Whom rises in Briyah the Archangelic and Divine Genius, and beyond Whom further is the fully and unreservedly Divine One in Atziluth. The *Yetzigah* or Posture of the Genius is also the Sign of the Cross, affirming the revelation of the Four Pillars of the Tree of Five Pillars quartering the Aura of the Neophyte.

With the expansion of the Tree from Three Pillars in two dimensions to Five Pillars in three dimensions, it seems to the Epoptic Spirit Visionary that Nephthys the Goddess of the Truth (in

---

47. Recall that *Ruchanic* is the correct adjectival form of Ruach in English, Anglicized from Hebrew *Ruchanith* (fem.) and *Ruchani* (masc.). —APF

ON THE 42 ASSESSORS

ancient Egyptian *Nebethut Maët*) of the Pillar of Severity expands into two Nephthyes[48] of the Two Truths of the Pillars of Severity (*Nebetihut Maëti*) North and South of the Neophyte (aligned with the two physical Pillars), and that Isis the Goddess of the Truth (*Iset Maët*) of the Pillar of Mercy of the Pillar of Mercy expands into two Isides[49] of the Two Truths (*Iseti Maëti*) of the Pillars of Mercy East and West of the Neophyte.

The Fourth and final Circumambulation is essentially a Triumphal Procession. The three previous Circumabulations invoked the White Triangle of Light from each Supernal Angle, and this fourth Circumabulation invokes the Red Cross. Whereas the Purification and Consecration was essentially passive and receptive on the part of the Ruach of the Neophyte, even though she was in alignment with her Genius, she now actively Circumambulates in alignment with her Genius, processing about the circuit of her Sphere, affirming the Purifications and Consecrations which were administered at the four Quarters of her Circle and Sphere, and passing the East and the West unchallenged. At the completion of the Circumambulation in the East, the Red Cross appears Astrally above the White Triangle in her Aura before her brow, sealing her—for so long as she remains in the Order—with the Seal of the Golden Dawn of Light. When the Hegemon unbinds the Cord from the waist of the Neophyte and replaces it with the Sash of the Dawn of Light, the Assessors have completed in full Their task in regard to the Neophyte, and may pass from the awareness of Adept Spirit Vision.

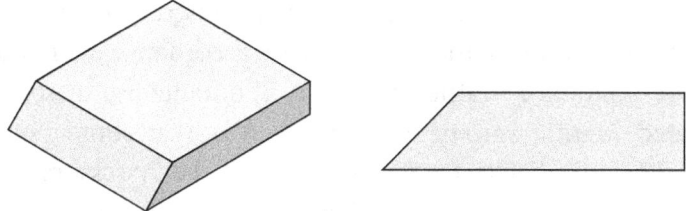

Fig. 43. *The Stone of Truth or Maët Plinth in both isometric and profile views*

---

48. Nephthyes: Gk. Νεφθυες, pl. of Νεφθυς (Nephthys). —APF
49. Isides: Gk. Ἰσιδες, pl. of Ἰσις (Isis). —APF

THE LIGHT EXTENDED

The Formulation of the Assessors by the Adepta Major

The Adepta Major who chooses to engage with the Assessors in relation to the Admission of the Candidate into the Temple and the Order, does so with the intention of enhancing her Epoptic understanding and affirmation of the Assessors' protective and probative functions on behalf of the Egregore of the Temple and the Order. While this is superb Work for any Adepta Major, it is particularly appropriate for the V.H. Imperatrix of the Temple, and (if she be an Adepta Major) the sitting Hierophant of the Temple, as well as any and all Past Hierophants who have attained the ⑥=⑤ grade.

For the Adepta Major who chooses to engage further with the Assessors in relation to her personal Work, the function of the Assessors may also be seen to be purificatory and probatory, and specifically so in relation to the Goetic Theurgic Work of the Adepta Major with the Qlippoth and the Nephilim, further empowering the testing properties of the Magic Circle of the Adept and likewise supporting the attunement of the Sevenfold Body of Light of the Greater Adept. The purifications by the Assessors facilitate the alignment and harmonization with the Higher and Divine Genius, and thus—though as Greater Adepts, you have previously attained to the initial and foundational Knowledge and Conversation of your H∴D∴G∴—to that Union which may, at the climax of the Work of the Exempt Adept, crown the full Attainment of the Great Work.

The Yetziratic Forms assumed by the Assessors should be of the Talismanic variety—that is, consciously constructed by the Adept for the indwelling of the Assessors in accordance with the rules of correspondence—rather than the spontaneous, unconsciously generated Mantic variety. Should the Adept at some point wish to see a Mantic Yetziratic Form of one of the Assessors, after she has successfully established reliable interaction with a particular Assessor or Hexad of Assessors, she may request that an Assessor show her another of Her or His faces and forms.

The generally established Talismanic Yetziratic Forms of the Assessors are of Egyptian Gods having human bodies, some female

ON THE 42 ASSESSORS

and some male, and heads of various forms, some human and some animal. Each bears in Her or His right (Gevuratic) hand a knife, Yetziratic symbol of the Power of Discernment and Judgement, and in Her or His left (Chesedic) a Maët feather, Yetziratic symbol of the light and uplifting Power of Truth which is sought in the Candidate of the Mysteries. Each Assessor wears a white robe (or, if necessary to the particular Godform, a white kilt or white mummy-wrappings), a black-and-white-striped nemyss, and a collar and wristbands with an upper band of white, a lower band of black, and a medial band of the appropriate Planetary colour.[50] Each Assessor stands or sits upon a Stone of Truth[51] (also known as a Maët Plinth) of the form shown in Fig. 40. The stone seen in profile is the hieroglyph ⬛ (Gardiner Sign list Aa 11) representing the triliteral $m3^c$, the root of the Name Maët. The Stone upholding each Assessor should be half black and half white, with the half on the Assessor's right being black and that on the Assessor's left being white, or quartered black and white.

The genders and faces of the Assessors must be assigned by the Adept, as must Their Names (or Epithets), according to her ingenium and experience.

It is difficult to determine the gender of the Assessors from the relatively small images of them to be found in the ancient vignettes, but the determinative hieroglyphs at the end of the Names indicate a great preponderance of male Deities, although the presence of known Goddess Names such as Bast prove the presence of female

---

50. First, note that this is yet another application of the Formula of "Between the Light and the Darkness Vibrate the Colours." Second, note that the relevant Colour is the Planetary, not the Subplanetary, Colour. E.g., the collar of the Assessor Who corresponds to Venus of Luna would be banded black, blue, white, as would the collars of all six of the Lunar, Kerykic Assessors, regardless of the individual Subplanet. Should the Adept wish to apply greater detail in her Assessorial Godforms, she may expand the collars and wristlets to five bands to allow for a Subplanetary band, in which case the ornaments of the Venus of Luna Assessor would be banded white, blue (Planet), green (Subplanet), blue (Planet), black. Also, on a related note, do not allow yourself to make the all-too-common error of using the Queen-Scale Sephirotic Colour when what is called for is the King-Scale Planetary Colour. –APF

51. Stone of Truth: Coptic *Ōne em-Mē* (ⲱⲛⲉ ⲙⲙⲏ), Heb. *Even Emeth* (תמא בא), Gk. *Lithos Alētheias* (Λίθος Ἀληθείας). –APF

Assessors. The Adept may either in her meditations upon the Truths for which the Assessors test assign the gender of a particular Subplanetary Assessor, or—probably a better course—decide upon a formula for the gender of the Assessors. As equilibrium tends to provide the best ground for the manifestation of Truth, a formula such as that of the Ogdoad at Hermopolis balancing the number of Goddesses and Gods naturally recommends itself, perhaps assigning in each Planetary Heaxagram one triangle to Goddesses and one to Gods.

The heads of the Godforms of the Assessors in the papyrus vignettes range across the gamut, including many human-headed Gods, along with others having the heads of hawks, serpents (sometimes even one with two serpent heads), lionesses, baboons, jackals, various birds, and other creatures. The Adept should formulate the heads of the Assessors as a Talismanic Yetziratic correspondence of the nature of each Assessor in accord with the Adept's own experience and understanding and contemplation, in consultation with her Higher and Divine Genius and with the Godform of the Ritual Officer in the Hall of the Neophytes Who corresponds to each Planet, always with the knowledge that she may modify the pattern and indeed totally transform the forms of the heads as her experience and understanding evolve. Typically heads should not be assigned to the individual Assessors until the clauses of the Negative Confession have been chosen and assigned to the 42 Subplanetary stations; the one exception may be if the Adept has chosen to assign Forms to the Assessors in Planetary groups (*e.g.*, lions and lionesses to the six Assessors of the Sun under Osiris, bulls and cows to the six Assessors of the Moon under Anubis of the East, hawks to the six Assessors of Mars under Horus, *etc.*).

The Names of the Godforms of the Assessors in the *Formulæ of Coming Forth by Day* are a diverse lot, mostly being otherwise unknown Names or Epithets. It is very worthwhile in this study to bear in mind that the dividing line between proper Names and Epithets is very permeable or even nonexistent in Egyptian theology, as many designations which we tend to treat as proper Names in fact have literal Epithetic meanings (*e.g.*, Duamutef, "Worshipper of His Mother"; Qabehsonef, "He Who Cooleth His Brother"; even the Name of the Child God Nofertum literally means "Beautiful Complete One"). The ancient catalogues include a few familiar Divine Names such as Nofertum, Ihi (the sistrum-playing Son of Hathor), and Tum. The unfamiliar names range from the noble (*e.g.*, Neb Maët, "Lord of Truth"; Neheb-Noferet, "Granter of Beauty") to the intentially terrifying (*e.g.*, Ambeseku, "Devourer of Entrails"; Sedqesu, "Breaker of Bones") to the puzzling (*e.g.*, Fendiu, "He of the Nose"). The Adept should devise and assign her chosen Names to the Assessors as Talismanic Yetziratic correspondences of the natures of the individual Assessors in accord with her own experience and understanding and contemplation, in consultation with her Higher and Divine Genius and with the Godforms of the Ritual Officers in the Hall of the Neophytes, always in the knowledge that she may modify the pattern and indeed wholly replace individual Names as her experience and understanding evolve. Typically Names should not be assigned to the individual Assessors until the clauses of the Negative Confession have been chosen and assigned to the 42 Subplanetary stations.

The following are a few examples of Divine Names—some anciently attested and some newly applied—which have been used for individual Assessors in these Actions, and some of which you may find applicable in your own Work, or which may inspire your own contemplations.

- Nofertum, Pakhet, Bes, Ihi, Kherti, Mafdet, Heret-Kau
- He of the Waters of Life and of Death
- Thresher of Grain
- She of the Binding Gaze
- Measurer
- Eyes of Fire
- Keeper of the Boundary Stones
- Nekhennu ("Infant")

The general form of address to the Assessors in the papyri is "Hail, NN [=Name or epithet], coming forth from PP [=Place name]." Since there are 42 Assessors and there were 42 nomes or territorial divisions of ancient Egypt, the idea has been suggested by some students that the Assessors come from the nomes. While there are certainly Assessors in the ancient lists Who are said to come forth from specific geographic locations in the nomes (Heliopolis, Hermopolis, Memphis, Saïs, etc.), others come forth from Underworld locations (Amentet, Rosetau) and from other regions unconnected with the nomes (the Abyss, the Sky, the Secret Place, the Cavern, etc.). Also, in the period when the Assessors and the Negative Confession first appeared in the texts, there were less than 42 nomes; so if there were any relationship between the Assessors and the nomes, it is likely to be that the number of nomes eventually was settled at 42 to reflect the significance of that Number of Power as it already had been reflected in the Assessors and clauses of the Confession.

The following is the form recommended for use by the Adept in Working with the Assessors, using the Assessor of Venus of Luna as an example: "Hail, NN, coming forth from the Gate of Venus in the Abode of the Moon," or, "Hail, NN, coming forth from the Gate of Venus in the Lunar Abode of Anubis of the East."

The Formulation of the Confession by the Adepta Major

The Negative Confession in the *Book of the Dead* was formulated by the priests and prophets for those who had served in powerful offices in the civil and religious hierarchies of ancient Egypt. So, while some of the clauses refer to *Isfet* or false action which no people should commit (*e.g.*, slaying or charging others to slay; causing pain or suffering; lying), others were crimes particular to Egyptians of high rank (*e.g.*, slaying a sacred bull, casting spells against the pharaoh), and others represented cultural taboos in that time and place (*e.g.*, homosexuality), while others in some versions of the Confession seem decidedly unworthy of a list of 42 principle evils a person may commit (*e.g.*, talking too much) or are simply mystifying to us as ethical crimes in their surviving form (*e.g.*, wading in water). In order to Work with the Assessors, the Adepta Major must formulate the Confession anew as a product of her own experience and understanding and contemplation, and in consultation with her Higher and Divine Genius, with the Godforms of the Ritual Officers

ON THE 42 ASSESSORS

in the Hall of the Neophytes, and perhaps with the occasional advice of an Adepta Exempta.

In formulating her own conception of the Negative Confession in support of the testing and purification of the Candidate, she should do so as much as possible from the perspective of an Adepta Minor (which she still remains, having added the grade of Adepta Major, not having deleted the grade of Adepta Minor, as a glance at her sash will remind her). She should also keep in mind that she may and should modify the Confession as her understanding and experience grow and evolve.

In formulating the Negative Confession in relation to her own life, Magical practice, and action in the Great Work, she should of course add the perspective of the Adepta Major (which always includes that of the preceding grade of Adepta Minor at the Heart of the Tree of Life). Again, she should also keep in mind that she may and should modify the Confession as her understanding and experience grow and evolve.

The following are a few examples of possible clauses for inclusion in the *Confessio Negativa* and possible Planetary or Subplanetary correspondences for them, to inspire your own contemplations. Of these possiblities, some are more obviously applicable to the Assessment of the Candidate, some to the Assessment of the senior Adept, and some to any person.

3, 9, 5, 6? → I have not been false or untrue; I have wrought no evil.
5? → I have neither slain nor caused to be slain.
8, 9, 6? → I have not committed fraud.
8, 5? → I have not stolen.
5, 8, 6? → I have not borne false witness.
4, 7? → I have not closed my heart or mind to the plight of poverty, but have given charitably to the poor.
3, 6? → I have not neglected my obligation to apply myself to the Great Work, which is to so purify

THE LIGHT EXTENDED

and exalt my Spiritual nature that with the Divine aid I may at length become more than human, and thus gradually raise and unite myself to my Higher and Divne Genius.

4, 7? → I have not acted from unbalanced Mercy, which is but weakness.

5, 3, 8? → I have not acted from unbalanced Severity, which is but cruelty and oppression.

5, 3? → I have not allowed evil to exist unopposed, thus making myself as it were a passive accomplice to that evil.

3, 4, 6? → I have not forgotten to give due honour and reverence to the Ruler of the Universe, Who Works in silence and Whom naught but silence can express.

8, 5, 6, 4? → I have not ridiculed the form of religion professed by another, for there is no true religion which does not contain a ray from the ineffable Light which I seek.

5, 6? → I have not been a source of strife or disharmony in the Order.

3, 5, 8? → I have not used my Magical knowledge or abilities for any evil purpose.

7, 9, 3, 6? → I have not neglected to be a steward of the natural world, preserving the ecological system on behalf of the creatures of nature and the generations yet unborn.

4, 5, 6? → I have not neglected my obligation to strive to the utmost to lead a pure and unselfish life.

9, 8, 6? → I have not neglected my obligation to support the admission and advancement of both sexes on a perfect equality.

4, 6? → I have not recommended a Candidate for Admission to the First Order without due judgement and assurance that she or he is worthy of so great a confidence and honour, nor have I unduly pressed any person to become a Candidate.

ON THE 42 ASSESSORS

4, 7? → I have not neglected my obligation to strive always to bestow fraternal love and forbearance upon my Fratres and Sorores in this Order.

5, 9, 6? → I have not clung to petty grievances and perceived slights.

3, 5? → I have not allowed anger or fear aroused by passing circumstances to degenerate into the corruption of long-term bitterness or hatred.

5, 6? → I have not allowed natural fear of dangerous circumstances to degenerate into cowardice, hatred, or fanaticism.

5, 9, 6? → I have not projected my own imperfections onto others.

4, 6? → I have not neglected to feel and express gratitude for the blessings which I have received in my life.

4, 6, 7? → I have not neglected to feel and express gratitude for the beauty of the world in which I live.

4, 7? → I have not neglected to feel and express gratitude for the love and friendship which I have received in my life.

5, 3, 8? → I have not judged others harshly and unfairly.

5, 3, 8, 6? → I have not judged myself harshly and unfairly.

9, 6, 5, 8? → I have not been an untrue or unfaithful Soror of this Order.

8, 5, 6, 4? → I have not ceased to study and practice, striving as an Adept to maintain and expand my knowledge and skills.

THE LIGHT EXTENDED

VII. Rituals for Working with the 42 Assessors

There are two primary areas of focus in which to undertake Work with the Assessors. The first is in relation to the Outer Order and the Temple. The second is in relation to the Magical Work of the Adepta Major herself.

Assessorial Actions in relation to the Outer Order will generally concern the Assessment of Candidates and, to a lesser extent, of Members, to protect the Order and its Egregore, to support the Members in their equilibrium, and in their adherence to their Obligations. Such Actions are best Worked in the Hall of the Outer Order, but may also be Worked in the personal Chamber of Praxis of the Adept which she will visualize as the Hall of the Outer Order, but *must not* be Worked in the Vault, as no banishing is ever done in that hallowed Sepulchre.

Assessorial Actions in relation to the personal Work of the Greater Adept will generally involve enhanced self-awareness, dedication to the Truth, integirt and positive transformation, and fulfillment of one's Obligations.

The most appropriate Implement for these Actions is of course the consecrated Phœnix Wand of the Greater Adept; if this is unavailable at the time of Working, the consecrated Sword of the Lesser Adept is an acceptable alternative Implement. If the Working is in relation to the Outer Order, and the Adept is the current Imperatrix of a Temple, the Imperatrix Ordinis, or the Adepta Secunda of the Inner Order, she may instead choose to use the Sword or Phœnix Wand of her Office.

The dominant factors to consider in timing your Workings are Planetary days and hours. Sunday, Tuesday, and Saturday are the best default days for Assessorial Operations. Nocturnal hours are slightly to be preferred to diurnal hours. The Planetary rulership of the hour chosen can follow the same preferences as the days, or may be chosen based on details of the particular Action. Our example ritual, to Work with the Venus Hexad of Assessors, is opened in the Venus hour of Sunday evening (the fourth nocturnal hour). Secondarily, if you wish to factor in the Lunar phases, the week around the half

ON THE 42 ASSESSORS

moons (first and third quarter days), when the face of the Moon is most equilibrated between light and darkness, are well-suited.

Should the Adepta Major wish to engage with each of the Assessors in a formulaically planned series of Actions, it is recommended that she Work with the six Assessors of one Planet at a time. This Work may certainly be done gradually over a long period of time; however, should her current Magical commitments and other obligations allow, she may operate with all 42 Assessors—one Planetary set of six each day—in the course of a single week, beginning with the six Lunar Subplanetary Assessors (♄ of ☽, ♃ of ☽, etc.) on a Monday and completing the cycle with the six Solar Assessors on the following Sunday. A more detailed—and daunting—schema is to Work with the six Assessors of one Planet in the course of one week, one individual Subplanetary Assessor per day, from Monday through Saturday, concluding with the Godform of the Officer on Sunday, unifying the six Subplanetary Assessors under the Presidency of the Godform of the Officer. This Work would occupy seven weeks.

The Adept will employ Hexagram Rituals for all Operations with Assessors, regardless of the part purpose, using a particular form of Lesser Hexagram Ritual to establish a proper Working Circle, and a particular form of Greater Hexagram Ritual to call upon the Assessors (or a particular Assessor or group of Assessors) within that Circle.

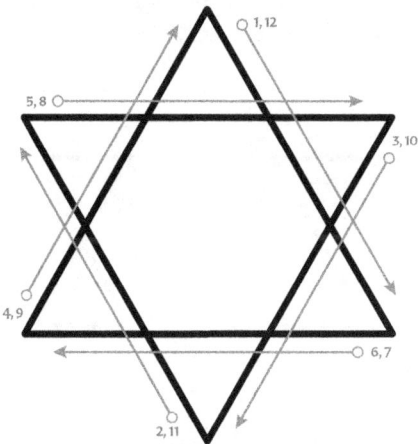

Fig. 44. The order of tracing the 12 triangles of the sixfold Invoking Lesser Officiary Hexagram

THE LIGHT EXTENDED

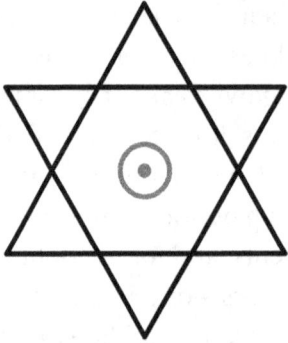

Fig. 45. *The sixfold Lesser Officiary Hexagram with the Hieroglyphic Sigil of the Sun*

Fig. 46. *The sixfold Lesser Officiary Hexagram with the Hieroglyphic Sigil of the Gods*

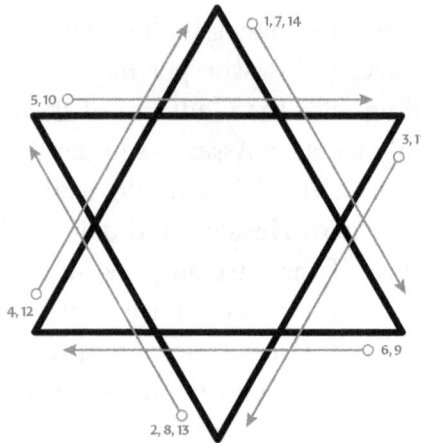

Fig. 47. *The order of tracing the 14 triangles of the sevenfold Invoking Lesser Assessorial Hexagram*

Fig. 48. *The Lesser Assessorial Hexagram with the Hieroglyphic Sigil of the Feather of Truth*

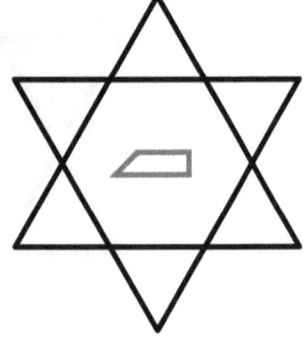

Fig. 49. *The Lesser Assessorial Hexagram with the Hieroglyphic Sigil of the Stone of Truth*

ON THE 42 ASSESSORS

Observations on the Lesser Hexagram Rituals of the Tetracontadyad[52]

Any time that the Adept operates with the Assessors or with an Assessor, she must cast a Magic Circle using the Lesser Invoking Hexagram Ritual of the 42 in the Four Quarters, and at the end of the Action she must close the Ritual with a Lesser Banishing Hexagram Ritual of the 42 in the Four Quarters. Scrupulous adherence to proper form is strongly indicated for Actions with the Assessors. Regardless of whether the particular Working is intended to be with a single Assessor, a Subplanetary Hexad of Assessors, or the 42 as a whole, the Circle is to be cast with the Hexagram Rituals of the Tetracontadyad, for the Assessors are in Their true nature a collective host or company of 42 Powers.

The Lesser Hexagram Rituals of the Tetracontadyad do not employ the four familiar Cardinal Transformations of the Hexagram (*viz.*, 🜂, 🜁, 🜄, and 🜃), as the foundational form of the Hexagram (✡) is so intimately connected with the Formulæ of the Assessors. Instead, two distinct compound Hexagrams using the foundational form are cast in each Quarter.

The first is the familiar compound sixfold Lesser Invoking Hexagram of the Sun (Fig. 44), which serves to invoke the Godforms of the Seven Ritual Officers of the Neophyte Hall as the rulers over the 42 Assessors, and can be distinguished as a Lesser Officiary (*i.e.*, pertaining to the Officers) Hexagram in this Working. One of two Sigils may be traced in the centre of the Hexagram, according to the *ingenium* of the Adept: either the Astrological Sigil of the Sun, which is also the Egyptian hieroglyph (Gardiner's Sign-list N5) of Rē the Sun (Fig. 45) or the hieroglyph (Gardiner's R8) signifying God or the Gods (Fig. 46), in this case referring to the Godforms of the seven Officers presiding over the 42 Assessors. The Divine Name to be vibrated in each Quarter after tracing this compound Officiary Hexagram is the Heptagrammaton *Ararita*.

---

52. *Tetracontadyad*: "A group of 42; also, the number 42 itself as a Platonic, Pythagorean, and Gematric entity." Tetracontadyad, from Greek Τετρακονταδυάς (*Tetrakontadyas*), is to Tetracontadigrammaton as Heptad is to Heptagrammaton. —APF

THE LIGHT EXTENDED

The second is a *seven*fold Lesser Invoking Hexagram of the 42 Assessors (Fig. 47), a compound Hexagram formed by tracing 14 Triangles which mark seven component Hexagrams. This Assessorial Lesser Hexagram is in form much like the sixfold, except that a *seventh* bicursal component Hexagram for the Sun[53] (beginning at the Saturn angle[54]) is traced after the Mars component Hexagram and before the Venus component Hexagram. Its triangular strokes are numbered 7 and 8 on Figure 47. The six triangular arms of each of the seven component Hexagrams represent and provide Triangles of Evocation for the six Assessors of one of the Planetary hexads. Either of two Sigils may be traced in the centre of the Hexagram, according to the *ingenium* of the Adept: either the Egyptian hieroglyph (Gardiner's Sign-list Aa11) of the Stone or Plinth of Maët (Fig. 48) or the hieroglyph (Gardiner's H6) signifying the Feather of Maët (Fig. 49). The Divine Name to be vibrated in each Quarter after tracing this compound Hexagram is the Tetracontadigrammaton *Avgithetz-qerashtan-nagdikash-betartzethag-cheqvetna-yegalpezaq-shequtzith*.

These two Lesser Hexagrams stand to some extent in the same relationship to one another as do a paired Spirit Pentagram and Elemental Pentagram, in that the casting of the Officiary Hexagram lays the Cosmic (Macro-, Micro-, or both, depending on the

---

53. The reason for the seventh component Hexagram is that the Asessors follow a Formula of 7×6 (*i.e.*, seven sets of six Subplanetary Assessors), and so the Assessorial compound Hexagram requires the arms of seven component Hexagrams to polygrammatically represent the 42 Assessors by valid sacred geometry. For by Names and Images (in this case the compound geometric Image of the Hexagram being a key factor) are all Powers awakened and re-awakened. —APF

54. The reasons that this component Hexagram for the Sun begins at the uppermost angle are threefold. First, the Saturn angle is the beginning point for a sixfold compound Solar Hexagram. Second, the Sun is the equilibrated centermost Planet of the Seven, corresponding to Tiphereth on the Tree, and its pair of triangles should be those whose defining angles are on the vertical axis corresponding to the Middle Pillar. Given this, if the two triangles of the Hexagram are considered Alchemically as the marriage of Fire and Water, Sulphur and Mercury, Sol and Moon, then the upright triangle is that of the Sun. Third, O Greater Adept, it is once more time to hear that familiar phrase which tests your aspiration to Stoic equanimity: It's outside of your Grade, as the third reason bears on a mystery of the *Tiqqun* which is specifically of the Grade of Adepta Exempta. —APF

ON THE 42 ASSESSORS

particular Working) Ground of Being which defines, generates, fulfills, and presides over the manifestation and operation of the 42-fold Power called forth by the Casting of the Assessorial Hexagram.

Working a Lesser Invoking Hexagram Ritual of the Assessors

The Adept may choose to assume the Godform of Osiris Onnophris (ⲟⲩⲱⲓⲡⲓ) to cast the Officiary Hexagrams and that of Maët (ϕⲙⲏ) to cast the Assessorial Hexagrams.

Let the Adepta Major come to the centre of the Hall, face East, and begin the Lesser Invoking Hexagram Ritual with a Qabbalistic Rose Cross, taking the opportunity to vivify her connection with her Higher and Divine Genius, as this is a prerequisite to Assessorial Work.

> *(Touching forehead:)* **Atah—**
> *(Bringing hand straight down to touch Tiphereth, visualizing Golden Light forming the vertical bar of the Cross from above to below:)*—**Malkhuth—**
> *(Bringing hand to touch Gevurah at right shoulder:)*—**ve-Gevurah—**
> *(Drawing hand straight across to touch Gedulah at left shoulder, visualizing Golden Light forming the horizontal bar of the Cross from right to left:)*—**ve-Gedulah—**
> *(Tracing clockwise Circle about Tiphereth from Gedulah to Gedulah, visualizing Ruby Light forming—in this case—a Rose of either seven or 49 petals:)*—**le-Olam.**
> *(Interlacing fingers before Tiphereth and inclining head:)* **Amen.**

Next, let her state her *Kavvanah* or Intention of the Action:

First, let her assume the Sign of Osiris Slain (which is also the Sign of the Cross of Obligation), and state the General Intention:

THE LIGHT EXTENDED

I, the <u>Very</u> Honoured <u>Soror</u> <u>Deo Duce Comite Ferro</u>, <u>Adepta Major</u>[55] and sworn Knight of this Order, <u>Past Hierophantis</u> of <u>Isis Urania</u> Temple, do cast this Circle of Art and commence this Operation as an endeavour in the Great Work, which is to so purify and exalt my Spiritual nature that with the Divine aid I may at length attain to be more than human, and thus gradually raise and unite myself to my Higher and Divine Genius. On this day and in this place, I die to the old life and am reborn to the new.

Then let her assume the Sign of Osiris Risen.

Next let her assume the Grade Sign of the Adepta Major and state the Particular Intention, formulated by her in relation to this particular Action, of which the following is one possible example:

Further, on this Day of <u>Sol</u> and in this <u>nocturnal</u> hour of <u>Venus</u>, I undertake this Action with <u>the six Assessors of Truth of Venus</u> that <u>I may gain a deeper understanding of Their Assessorial Work and Their relationship with Thaum-Ēsh-Nēith, the Office of Dadouchos, the Planet Venus, the Sephirah Netzach, and the Pillar of Mercy, that with the Divine aid I may be better able to empower and aid in the Formulation of the Godforms of the six Venereal Assessors and of all the Assessors of Truth about the bounds of the Hall of the Two Truths.</u>

Then let her advance to the East, salute the East, and trace the first Lesser Officiary Hexagram (Fig. 44), trace in its centre the Sigil she has chosen (either Fig. 45 or 46), and then vibrate **ARARITA**.

---

55. Should the Adept at first be surpised by some of the words (notably Very and Major) underlined as variables to be replaced according to the particular circumstances, she should understand that this Assessorial Work will also likely be undertaken at times by a Greatly Honoured Adepta Exempta, particularly by one serving as Imperatrix of a Temple, or as Adepta Secunda of the Inner Order. —APF

ON THE 42 ASSESSORS

Then let her trace the first Lesser Assessorial Hexagram (Fig. 47), trace in its centre the Sigil she has chosen (either Fig. 48 or 49), and then vibrate **AVGITHETZ · QERASHTAN · NAGDIKASH · BETARTZETHAG · CHEQVETNA · YEGALPETZAQ · SHEQUTZITH**.[56]

Then let her point her Implement at the centre of the Eastern Hexagrams and thence circumambulate to the South, tracing as she does so the first quarter of the Magic Circle.

Then let her trace in the South the second Lesser Officiary Hexagram, trace in its centre the Sigil she has chosen, and then vibrate **ARARITA**.

Then let her trace the second Lesser Assessorial Hexagram, trace in its centre the Sigil she has chosen, and then vibrate **AVGITHETZ · QERASHTAN · NAGDIKASH · BETARTZETHAG · CHEQVETNA · YEGALPETZAQ · SHEQUTZITH**.

Then let her point her Implement at the centre of the Southern Hexagrams and thence circumambulate to the West, tracing as she does so the second quarter of the Magic Circle.

Then let her trace in the West the third Lesser Officiary Hexagram, trace in its centre the Sigil she has chosen, and then vibrate **ARARITA**.

Then let her trace the third Lesser Assessorial Hexagram, trace in its centre the Sigil she has chosen, and then vibrate **AVGITHETZ · QERASHTAN · NAGDIKASH · BETARTZETHAG · CHEQVETNA · YEGALPETZAQ · SHEQUTZITH**.

Then let her point her Implement at the centre of the Western Hexagrams and thence circumambulate to the North, tracing as she does so the third quarter of the Magic Circle.

Then let her trace in the North the fourth Lesser Officiary Hexagram, trace in its centre the Sigil she has chosen, and then vibrate **ARARITA**.

---

56. Do not chastize yourself if you need to read this lengthy Divine Name in ritual. It is typically not a Name most Adepts will have often used. If you feel uncertain of your memory in this matter, it is far better to have the written Name before you to allow for a powerful and concentrated Vibration, rather than to stumble uncertainly (and unpowerfully) through its 23 syllables in your Invocation. —APF

THE LIGHT EXTENDED

Then let her trace the fourth Lesser Assessorial Hexagram, trace in its centre the Sigil she has chosen, and then vibrate **AVGITHETZ · QERASHTAN · NAGDIKASH · BETARTZETHAG · CHEQVETNA · YEGALPETZAQ · SHEQUTZITH**.

Then let her point her Implement at the centre of the Northern Hexagrams and thence circumambulate to the East, tracing as she does so the fourth and final quarter, completing the Circle of the Place as she reaches the East. Let her be clearly aware of the completion and integrity of the Circle and of the ongoing increasing attunement of the atmosphere within it to the Assessorial Work of Truth.

Then let her return directly to the centre of the Circle and perform either the LVX Signs in silence or the complete Analysis of the Keyword.

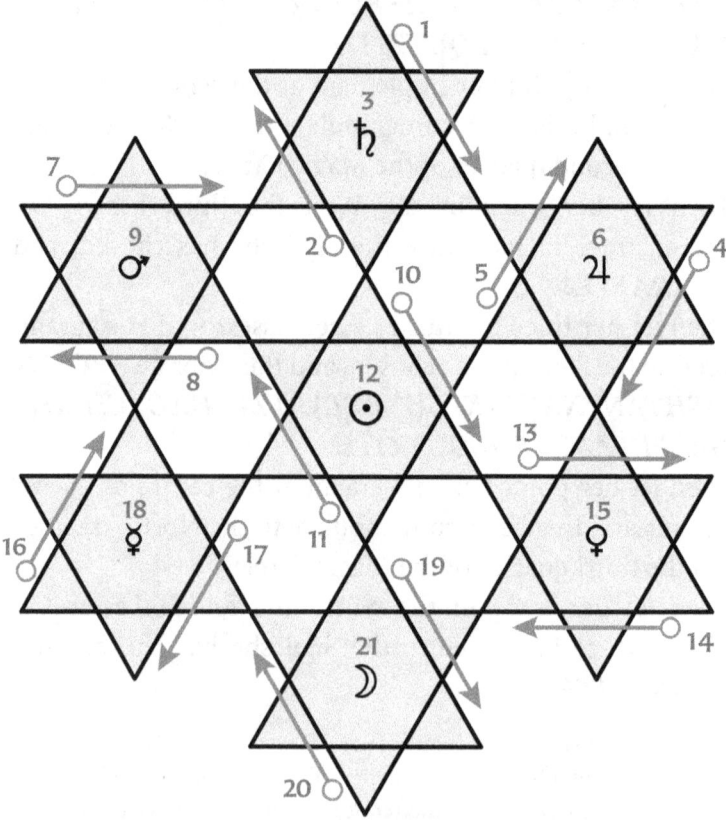

Fig. 51. *The order of tracing the 14 triangles and seven Astrological Planetary Sigils of the seven component Subhexagrams (seven bicursal Subhexagrams) of the less complex form of the Greater Invoking Assessorial Hexagram*

ON THE 42 ASSESSORS

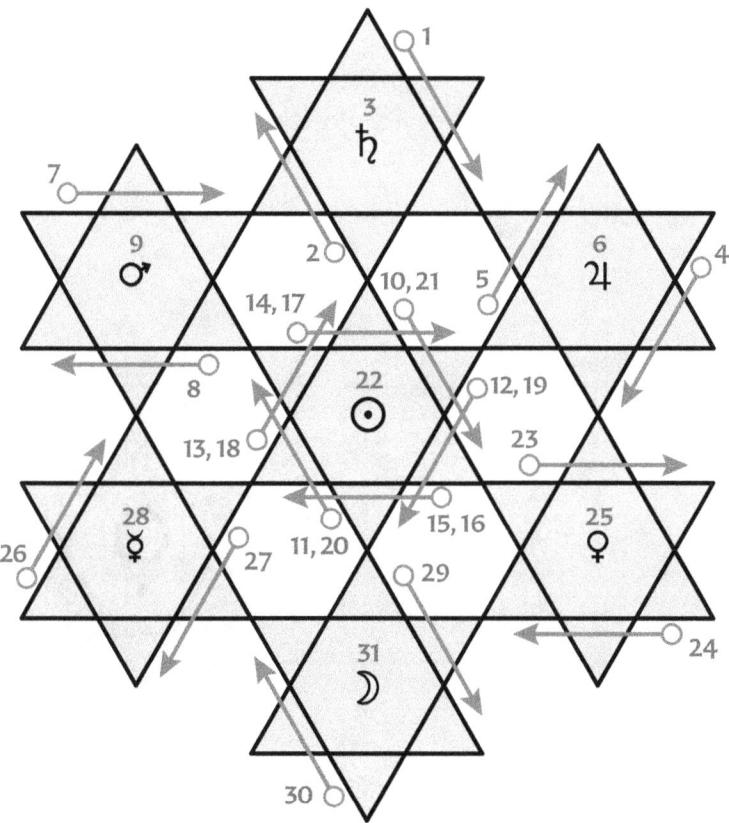

Fig. 52. The order of tracing the 24 triangles and seven Astrological Planetary Sigils of the seven component Subhexagrams (six simple Subhexagrams, and one sixfold Solar Subhexagram) of the more complex form of the Greater Invoking Assessorial Hexagram

Working a Lesser Banishing Hexagram Ritual of the Assessors

The process of Working a Lesser Banishing or Closing Hexagram Ritual of the Assessors will be easily discerned by the Greater Adept on the basis of the Invoking form, with one key proviso. In closing a Circle opened with the Lesser Invoking Hexagram Ritual of the Assessors, the Lesser Banishing Assessorial Hexagram will be cast before the Lesser Banishing Officiary Hexagram in each Quarter, as the 42 Assessorial Powers are closed before the seven higher Officiary Powers which unite and preside over them.

THE LIGHT EXTENDED

Fig. 53. The tracing of the Invoking Subhexagram of the Hexad of Assessors of Venus

Observations on the Greater Hexagram Rituals of the Tetracontadyad

Unlike most Greater Hexagrams, a Greater Hexagram of the Tetracontadyad is not cast in accordance with an electional horoscope in the direction of the Planet's current location about the Zodiacal Circle, but is cast facing the West, the place of the entrance to the Hall. The Greater Officiary Hexagram is normally from the Station of Hierophant in the East, and the Greater Assessorial Hexagram is normally cast from the Station of Hegemon between the Pillars.

In Invoking, the Adept must first trace the sixfold Greater Solar Officiary Hexagram which underlies and unites the 42 into 49 under the Presidency of Sol. She may, according to her own ingenium or

ON THE 42 ASSESSORS

the nature of the particular Action, trace either the six small Solar Sigils in the arms of the Hexagram and the single great Solar Sigil in the heart of the figure, or simply the single large Solar Sigil. She must then vibrate **ARARITA**.

Then the Adept must trace—superimposed over the Greater Solar Officiary Hexagram—the Sevenfold Greater Assessorial Hexagram (Fig. 51 or 52). While it may seem dauntingly complex at first appearance, on further study one sees that it is familiar complexity, consisiting of tracing the seven very familiar Planetary Hexagrams adjacent to one another in an array following the underlying framework of the Greater Solar Hexagram.[57] She may, according to her own ingenium or the nature of the particular Action, trace either a less complex (Fig. 51) or a more complex (Fig. 52) form of the Greater Assessorial Hexagram. The only difference between the two forms is that the less complex uses a simple bicursal Solar Subhexagram (as in the Lesser Ritual at the Quarters), and the more complex a sixfold compound Solar Subhexagram. Since Hexagrams are bicursal, each consisting of two triangles, the less complex form requires 14 strokes to cast the sevenfold Greater Assessorial Hexagram, while the more complex form requires 24 strokes (12 triangles for the central Solar Hexagram and two triangles each for the other six Planetary Hexagrams).The order and direction of tracing the 24 triangles is indicated in the figure.

After then tracing the seven Planetary Sigils in the centres of the Hexagrams, the Adept should vibrate the 42-Letter Name, aware as she does so of its structure as a Heptad of Hexads: **AVGITHETZ · QERASHTAN · NAGDIKASH · BETARTZETHAG · CHEQVETNA · YEGALPETZAQ · SHEQUTZITH**. The Name may be spoken at its full length at the conclusion of tracing the sevenfold compound Assessorial Hexagram, or, alternatively, it may be divided into its seven component Hexagrammata, with each spoken after tracing the component Hexagram (*e.g.*, after tracing the Saturn Hexagram,

---

57. Refer back to Figures 17-19 if necessary to more fully understand this relationship. In practice, one's visualization may be enhanced if rehearsed with a properly scaled large Greater Officiary Hexagram on paper or whiteboard in the Quarter to provide the framework before which to trace the components of the Greater Assessorial Hexagram. —APF

vibrate **AVGITHETZ**; after tracing the Jupiter Hexagram, vibrate **QERASHTAN**; etc.)

If it is her intention to Work with a particular Subplanetary Power or Hexad of Subplanetary Powers rather than the 42 Assessors as a whole, she may then choose to retrace the relevant Subhexagram and insert in its heart the Planetary Sigil of the Planetary Power and in its arms the Sigils of the Subplanetary Assessors (see Fig. 53). She should then vibrate **ARARITA** and the ruling Letter of the Planet from that Heptagrammaton (in the case of our Venus example, **YOD**), and then the appropriate component Hexagrammaton from the 42-Letter Name (in the case of our Venus example, **CHEQVETNA**).

Let the Adepta Major then affirm the Rosicrucian nature of the Hexagram Ritual and her authority to employ it by Analyzing the Key Word or at least giving the LVX Signs in silence. This will also serve as a Salutation to the Assessor or Assessors.

Working a Greater Banishing Hexagram Ritual of the Assessors

As with the Lesser Banishing Ritual, the process of Working a Greater Banishing or Closing Hexagram Ritual of the Assessors will be easily extrapolated by the Greater Adept on the basis of the Invoking form, with the same principal stipulation, *i.e.*, in closing a midpoint opened with the Greater Invoking Hexagram Ritual of the Assessors, the Greater Banishing Assessorial Hexagram will be cast *before* the Greater Banishing Officiary Hexagram, as the 42 Assessorial Powers are dismissed before the seven higher Officiary Powers which unite and preside over them.

Components of the Core Working Within the Temenos Provided by the Hexagram Rituals

The Hexagram Rituals are largely standard, but the contents of the Working executed within their framework is inherently individual and personal. It may at various times include prayer, simple contemplation, evocation, Talismanry, Skrying in the Spirit Vision, and Travelling in the Spirit Vision. Generally, when employing

ON THE 42 ASSESSORS

Visionary Work with the Assessors, it is recommended that the Adept first encounter an Assessor through Skrying, and only subsequently in Travelling.

Her Assessorial Work should always include Invoking the Highest Divine Names pertaining thereto, being the Tetracontadigrammaton and Ararita. She should always include her Higher and Divine Genius in such Work, along with Osiris, Maët, the Godform Who is set over any particular Assessorial Hexad, and of course the relevant Assessors Themselves.

She should develop and employ her rendering of the Negitive Confession in Assessorial Actions, in both those relating to the Order and the Temple, and those relating to her personal Magical Work.

In composing further verbal portions of her Assessorial Workings, the Adept may wish to study the Formulæ of the *Book of the Dead*, the *Coffin Texts*, and the *Pyramid Texts* and include elements having a more distinctly Egyptian voice; for example:

> I am pure! I am pure! My heart, which I have from my mother, my father, my ancestors, is pure. Osiris is pure; I am pure. I am pure with the purity of that sacred Bennu-Phœnix Who sacrificeth Himself unto Regeneration and is Reborn to the newer Life upon the Altar of the Sun. There is no part of me that is not Maët. Osiris is True of Voice; I am True of Voice.

Conclusion

May our study and practice of these Inner Rosicrucian Mysteries sustain and nurture us in the Great Work, which is to so purify and exalt our Spiritual Natures that, with the Divine aid, we may at length attain to be more than human, and thus gradually raise and unite ourselves to our Higher and Divine Genii.

And may we remain always

S V A T

ה ו ה י

THE LIGHT EXTENDED

APPENDIX

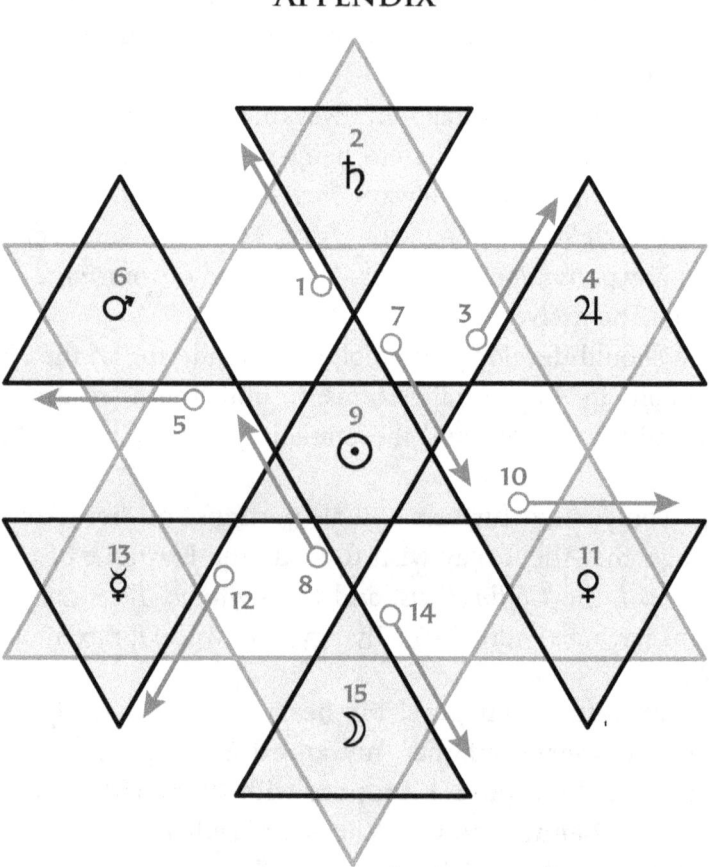

Fig. 54. EXPERIMENTAL *simplest form of tracing the eight Triangles which complete the seven component Subhexagrams: The order of tracing the eight triangles and seven Astrological Planetary Sigils of the simplest form of the Greater Invoking Assessorial Hexagram*

If the Greater Adept should choose to pursue this Work at some length, she may find that she has room for experimentation after mastering the basic forms. If so, she may wish to explore a simple, alternative form of the Greater Assessorial Hexagram with which I have recently (and briefly) experimented. As shown in Figure 54, after the Greater Solar Officiary Hexagram is cast, only those triangles required to complete the component Hexagrams are traced in casting the Greater Assessorial Hexagram. The positive characteristics of this approach which have so far presented themselves are: practically, the reduction

ON THE 42 ASSESSORS

in number of strokes required, and theoretically, the enhanced reflection of the sacred geometric relationship (Figs. 17–19) between the Officiary and Assessorial Hexagrams. Also, it is suggestive that the Solar component Hexagram requires two strokes rather than the one stroke of each of the others. Perhaps the most interesting characteristic is that the single triangle to be drawn to complete the component Hexagram is in each case (except for the Solar, which of course requires both triangles) is the second triangle, appropriately indicating that one is completing the component Hexagrams begun in the preceding Greater Officiary Hexagram.

About the Author

Adam P. Forrest serves, along with Chic and Tabatha Cicero, as a Chief Adept of the Hermetic Order of the Golden Dawn, an office he has filled for more than 30 years. He is a priest of the Hermetic Fellowship, and, along with M. Isidora Forrest, a founding steward of that organization.

He has been a ceremonial magician since he was a teenager and chalked his first Magic Circle and Triangle in the loft of an unused barn back in Tennessee. He is a Bakchos priest of Dionysos, and has also served as a priest of Hermēs-Thōth, Apollōn, Hekatē Persephassa, Jēsous-Osiris, and, like all Adepts, his Higher and Divine Genius.

At the request of Israel Regardie, he contributed a ritual of evocation to *The Complete Golden Dawn System of Magic* (Falcon Press, 1984). He was a regular contributor of articles, rituals, and illustrations to the *Golden Dawn Journals*. He also contributed his translations of two of the Orphic Hymns to *Written in Wine: A Devotional Anthology for Dionysos* (Bibliotheca Alexandrina, 2008). Most recently, he edited the anthology *Liber Spirituum: A Compendium of Writings on Angels & Other Spirits in Modern Magick* (Azoth Press, 2016).

He is by vocation a magus and priest, and by profession a graphic designer, illustrator, editor, and writer, and lives in the Pacific Northwest with his wife, Isidora, and a black cat named Pyewacket.

Ἑκάς ἑκάς ἐστε βέβηλοι
(HEKAS HEKAS ESTE BEBELOI)

by Soror DPF

Ἑκάς ἑκάς ἐστε βέβηλοί - (*Hekas Hekas Este Bebeloi*) is a ritual incantation, or 'Sacred Announcement' attributed to the ancient Eleusinian Mysteries in Hellas (Greece), much like the similar phrase "*Eskato Bebeloi*" which can be found in *Pythagoras and the Delphic Mysteries* by Edouard Shuré [1906], pg. 69.

In translation meaning "Far, far be removed the profane," it declares a form of exorcism, or purification (*katharmos* - Καθαρμός) prior to any Ceremonial gathering, Magickal invoking Ritual or honouring of Deity, as it is oft exclaimed at the intro to many Western Mystery Tradition Rites, including those of the Order of the Golden Dawn.

Its pronunciation being a mystery all of its own, firstly with the Classical Greek to Classical Latin translations by Erasmas in 1528, further by Sir John Cheke who was the first Regius Professor of Greek at Cambridge University, whom with his friend and fellow scholar Sir Thomas Smith, around 1540 through teaching, brought a broader study of the Greek language across Europe to Britain, changing with it as it traversed, the Classical Greek into the Byzantine form of spoken Greek which had already begun to birth, and is closer to the Modern Greek we hear today; Greek itself even in Athens changed over time into three separate forms; Classical, Hellenistic Koiné, and the Modern Greek.

So, how to pronounce it? There is a lot of research and a definitive thread to that final conclusion, of which is pertinent. Refraining from listing the various mispronunciations that have sadly become the norm, and misinformation splattered across the internet, in both academic and public sources, the focal point of the research gathered is thus:

The most common aspects to consider via the transliterations and therefore pronunciation, is the many versions of Greek through

Latin to the English, as well as accent's, vowels, and language itself. The main focus of contention was on the H in Hekas and the correct pronunciation of βέβηλοι (Bebeloi).

H in Greek; H in Greek is actually Eta, this gives a rather large clue as to the H of the English language versus the Eta of the Greek, however, this Eta comes from the Ionic Greek, whereas it originally took the letter H (as Hēta) from Phoenician Heth; yet when Greek dialects dropped the H in Eta, along with its 'sound' from their phonological systems, it changed the Hēta consonant into a new use as a vowel, and by 400 BC the majority of Greek speakers used the Ionic Eta.

Let us look at Ἑκάs (a version Walt Whitman used in his book The Liberator in 1860) vs. Hekas for a moment, you will see there is a 'daseia' before the - Ἐ - and above the second words - ἑ -. That left-hand single quote mark or 'spiritus asper' as it is known in Latin, actually stands for something, it is more than an accented Eh for Eh-kas, in place of a very harsh English H for Heh-kas; it is an aspiration, it is what the Latin translations left the English language with, essentially a Latin 'H'.

It is understandable how the English language has mispronounced this in part for so long, when a mixture of variant dialects of Greek, tinged with Latin through translation, ended with speaking it the somewhat erroneous harsh 'H' of the English language.

On a more spiritual note, H is Breath (aspiration!), perhaps leading to the added emphasis of the deliberate H in modern, especially English pronunciations; breath, however, is almost silent, alive yes, not completely inaudible, yet ... almost, silent. H in Classical Greek is a Voiceless glottal fricative, an Aspirated consonant, in the application of an Allophone (other sound/voice).

Taking the above into account, to use a form of 'breath' with the Latin H of ['] before the Ἐ/ἑ, makes perfect sense, and adds the power ascribed to the incantation. However, a strict omission of the H - (*Ehkas* for example) is as equally inaccurate as is using a very loud or harsh English H of Heh-kas! A somewhat level in-between exists, and will take time to master, perhaps like all mysteries with each element requiring each to master it.

Now on to βέβηλοι (Bebeloi). It appears it is not pronounced

Beh-Be-Loy, [though this has become the most common (mis) pronunciation], which is asserted as correct by Fra. P in the Additional Notes and Errata on pg. 245 of *Secrets of the Golden Dawn Cipher Manuscript* by Caroll Poke Runyon. Starting from the end 'oi', misconceptions in the English transliteration are that it is to be read as an 'o' followed by an 'i', whereas in Hellenic (Greek) this is a Vowel called δίφθογγο, belonging to a set of Vowels whereby the two letters together are as one. This 'oi' was further confused by the Erasmas period, with some scholars stating Attic Greek pronounced 'oi' as 'oy', whereas in Hellenistic Koiné onwards, along with the Vowel shifts across Greek/Latin and English has it pronounced as 'ee', as the 'oi' becomes a singular 'i', thus spoken like one would say Delphi - (Greek: Delfoi -> Delphi) - Del-fee.

Even today this is still an area of contention between Modern Greek linguists and those researching to acquire the most historic version of the pronunciation, debating the dipthong vs. vowel.

Moving onto 'βέβη(λοι) - there are three factors to consider:

1. β = Beta
2. Beta can be voiced as B or V
3. η = (one of those confusing letters), foremost the letter Eta lowercase 'h', yet used as a long open 'e' in words also.

Examples include βέβηλοι, and again in Ἑκάτη.

The same onomatopoetic [βη] from 'βέβηλοι' occurs in *The Frogs* by Aristophanes, pgs. 346-347, 361-362, leading to the question, should it be pronounced [bæ] or [vi]?

The jury is still out on absolute accuracy, depending on which dialect, Modern vs. Ancient Greek.

According to the *Glossary of Hellenic Mystery Religion - Part Two*:

> [Vǽvili - (Bebeloi; Gr. βέβηλοι, BEBHΛOI. Adjective pl. and verb.) Vǽvili is an adjective or verb referring to the profane or uninitiated. The rituals of the Mysteries open with the exhortation, θύρας δ' ἐπίθεσθε βέβηλοι,
> "Shut your doors, you who are profane!" Cf. Vǽvilos].

Therefore Veh-Ve-Lee seems to be most used by Greek native speakers, (this naturally could be due to the Modern Greek Language, and a reluctance to venture back to the earlier dialects,[1] for lack of use).

Internationally, albeit more the English, transcended from the Latin, tend to adopt Beh-Ba-Loy, which as discussed above, is somewhat inaccurate. A full pronunciation would seem to be most accurate as thus:

'Ekas, 'ekas - ['E - an aspiration of breath from the back of the throat as if finding it hard to breathe, therefore almost inaudible, followed by - Kahs – more emphasis on the Kah ending with a soft 's']

Este - [Ee-steh]
Bebeloi - [Veh-Ve-Lee]
In full: ['Ekahs, 'ekahs Ee-steh Veh-Ve-Lee]

---

[1] From audio files given by three separate Greek natives who also follow an ancient Hellenic spiritual path, it appears that the accurate pronunciation of this is indeed Veh-Ve-Lee.

About the Author

Soror DPF was born in the 'oldest recorded town in Britain', the Pre-Roman town of Camulodunum, now known as Colchester, in 1968. (The earliest record of the town's existence is a reference by the Roman writer, Pliny the Elder in AD77).

She has written a variety of media, for niche publisher's Anthologies, including Avalonia's *Hekate: Her Sacred Fires*; Magazines/eZines, including *Isis Seshat, Mirror of Isis,* and *Isian News, Isian Voices*, as well as articles published online for the Fellowship of Isis International Symposium.

Soror DPF is also a consecrated Adept and Priestess in training, in the Fellowship of Isis, and was also a founding Torchbearer of the Covenant of Hekate, though since has inaugurated a Hierón dedicated to Hekate/Εκάτη Própolos.

Her interests are eclectic, delving into pre-Hellenic, Thracian, Ancient Greek with their Eleusinian Mysteries, Babylonian, Ancient Egyptian Mysteries, Western Mystery Traditions, and in more recent years the Qabalah and the Golden Dawn systems.

Skrying in Theory & Practice

by Alex Sumner

This article derives from a talk I first delivered at a Golden Dawn Open Day held in London in August 2017. It came about because my magical associates and I had been discussing the subject of Skrying some months previously, and mentioning how important it is, when some of the more junior of my acquaintances indicated that they would appreciate a fuller explanation of what it actually consists.

Skrying is defined in the Oxford English Dictionary as:

> [t]o see images in pieces of crystal, water, etc. which reveal the future or secrets of the past or present; or to act as a crystal-gazer.

NB: Most modern dictionaries spell it as "Scry": "skry" is an old-fashioned spelling of the word. Interestingly, the first recorded use of the word "scrying," a shortening of to "descry," surfaces in the English language in early sixteenth century—a date to which I will have reference later on.

However the Golden Dawn uses the term "skrying" in a slightly different sense—we do not necessarily use apparatus such as a Crystal Ball—which has been termed the "lesser crystalline sphere"[1]—but we attempt to see visions before the Mind's Eye itself—which is the "greater crystalline sphere." Also, we do not necessarily attempt to see through Time, or Space, but into the Astral Plane. For a Golden Dawn Magician, skrying is an attempt to become visually conscious of at least part of the astral plane, without necessarily having the immersive experience of having a full astral projection.

Although the word "skrying" has only been recorded since the

---

1 I.e by Frater Achad (Charles Stansfeld-Jones) in "Crystal Vision through Crystal Gazing."

sixteenth century, the practice of obtaining magical visions in shiny or reflective materials is thousands of years old. Mind you: one has to be discerning when researching the origin of scrying. I have seen wild claims on the internet that it originated in China circa 3000 BC; that it took place in Ancient Greece, "in 2000 BC," and that it was practiced by the Ancient Celts. Note these supposed dates are all thousands of years before written records of anything existed in those places, so take any such claim with a pinch of salt!

It has also been claimed that Scrying occurred in Ancient Egypt. When I tried to find a concrete reference to this, however, the best I could find was that it was certainly an established magical practice by the late Ptolemaic or Roman period, roundabout the beginning of the Common Era. So although that is over two thousand years ago, technically that is *not* "ancient" Egypt!

Nevertheless: here is a good example of an Egyptian magical spell from two millennia ago, taken from the Greek Magical Papyri:

> *vii. Direct Vision Spell* "EEIM TO EIM ALALE'P BAR-BARIATH MENEBREIO ARBATHIAO'TH IOUE'L IAE'L OUE'NE'IIE MESOMMIAS, *let the God who prophesies to me come and let Him not go away until I dismiss Him,* OURNAOUR SOUL ZASOUL OUGOT NOOUMBIAOU THABRAT BERIAOU ACHTHIRI MARAI ELPHEO'N TABAO'TH KIRASINA LAMPSOURE' IABOE ABLAMATHANALBA AKRAMMACHAMAREI!"
>
> *In a Bronze Cup over Oil. Anoint your Right Eye with Water from a Shipwreck and the Left with Coptic Eyepaint, with the same Water. If you cannot find Water from a Shipwreck, then from a Sunken Skiff.*[2]

So right here we have evidence of a form of Divination in the true sense of the word—i.e. gaining knowledge by invoking a deity—in the form of staring into a shiny surface whilst reciting a spell at the same time.

Meanwhile, across the other side of the Atlantic Ocean, the first use of shiny dark mirrors in a ritual context occurred around about the same time in ancient Mesoamerica. Little is known about

---

2 [PGM V.54-69]

the actual practices of the time, but there appears to have been an established form of divination by dark-mirror scrying by the time the Spaniards arrived in the sixteenth century.

Despite clear evidence that skrying, in the sense of obtaining a vision by looking into some sort of reflective surface, was known about in ancient times, subsequent grimoires fail to mention the practice. The *Testament of Solomon* (ca. first to third century AD) seemed to believe that demons manifested to both visible and physical appearance. There is no mention of it in The Sword of Moses (tenth century), whilst the Sworn Book of Honorius (thirteenth century) suggests that visions may only be obtained either through dreams, or through "suffumigations"—the burning of incense composed of, inter alia, psychoactive compounds.

In The Key of Solomon (fifteenth century) there is a continuance of the notion that spirits appeared to actual physical appearance. The magician is told to perform the invocations from within the circle *"the which being said and done, thou shalt see them draw near and approach from all parts."* The implication is either there was no scrying necessary (as they actually manifested to visible appearance) or that scrying went without saying. Likewise in the Heptameron, which dates from 1496 though allegedly written by Peter de Abano two centuries previously.

However: Agrippa writes in his Three Books of Occult Philosophy (1509-1510) of the ancient arts of Hydromancy, Pyromancy and "Capnomancy" (divination by smoke). Edward Kelly famously skryed for John Dee using a Crystal ball (and an obsidian disk of Mesoamerican origin) in the 1580s, the same time that the *Lesser Key of Solomon* is estimated to have been compiled. This latter collection of grimoires contains blatant references to Crystal-gazing in the "Theurgia Goetia," "Ars Paulina," and "Ars Almadel."

There is a pattern emerging, to wit: Skrying is one of the many facets of knowledge which became lost during the dark ages and mediaeval times, and which magicians only rediscovered in Western Europe in the Renaissance. That Skrying was an art preserved in the East for some fifteen hundred years is attested by the re-birth of classicism which enabled Agrippa to write fluently about the ancient authorities, and that there is hardly any reference to it in any grimoire prior to the fall of Constantinople in 1485.

Remember I said earlier: "skrying" only appeared as a word in English at the beginning of the sixteenth century—that very time, the beginning of the Renaissance. My private theory is that not only was a lot of classical literature brought to western Europe at the start of the Renaissance, but so were a lot of secret Magical practices—such as Skrying—which had been forgotten in the west but preserved since ancient times in the East.

The Golden Dawn was founded in the late eighteen hundreds: its own practices of skrying have their roots from earlier in the 19th century. The middle of the 19th century—1848—saw the birth of Spiritualism in the modern sense, and whilst it proved sensationally popular, it also prompted a backlash amongst serious occultists. One of these was a gentleman named Fred Hockley. Hockley was a Mason and a Rosicrucian, but mostly he was a connoisseur of magical grimoires. He did not practice ceremonial magic *per se*, but he did practice skrying in conjunction with a number of people who acted as Seers for him. Hockley would perform the requisite magical invocations, whilst the Seer (usually a young lady) would stare into a skrying mirror on his behalf and describe what she saw.[3]

Figure 1 Frederick Hockley (1809—1885)

3   Hockley, Hamill *et al* (ed.) (1986)

Hockley also taught others how to go about skrying. From his letters it appears that he advocated a disciplined approach, modelled on that found in traditional grimoires.[4] It also appeared that Hockley was concerned that Spiritualists were going about it all wrong, in that in using an unstructured approach they were not exercising any kind of quality control over the visions they received.

The other main influence on the skrying practices of the Golden Dawn was the Theosophy of Madame Blavatsky. Theosophy made two positive contributions: firstly, it systematised the various different types of clairvoyance, giving them a rationale in terms of the etheric, astral and mental planes. This very much appealed to the then-mindset of the founders of the Golden Dawn and gave them a means of formulating a working theory of skrying based on interaction with the astral plane.

Figure 2 H P Blavatsky (1831—1891)

---

4 See, for example, Hockley, Gilbert (ed.) (2010)

SKRYING IN THEORY AND PRACTICE

The second contribution of Theosophy is that it brought with it knowledge of eastern, and in particular Indian, esoteric teachings, including the theory and symbolism of the Tattvas—of which I will more to say in a moment.

When the Golden Dawn developed its own methods of Skrying, it introduced two innovations. Firstly, it enabled the Initiate to do his or her own skrying. In the clairvoyant experiments of ceremonial magicians from the time of John Dee right up to Frederick Hockley, very often skrying would be done in pairs. One person—the evoker or magician—would perform the various conjurations, whilst the other—the Seer—would perform the actual skrying. They would in effect skry what the other person had conjured. The Golden Dawn however trains its initiates to be able to do their own skrying—to be both the evoker *and* the seer at the same time.

The second innovation is that it enabled students of the occult to explore the Theosophical theory of skrying in terms of the Qabalah and western ceremonial magick, as opposed to working in an eastern esoteric paradigm.

So what actually is Skrying in the Golden Dawn? I shall borrow some Theosophical imagery to describe it: imagine if you will an "Astral Current." This Current connects you to the Astral Plane like a telephone-line. Skrying thus consists of "seeing" along this Current or connection and receiving information from the Astral Plane. It is one of five types of Clairvoyance identified by the theosophist C. W. Leadbeater; of the other four, only one—that of projecting ones consciousness in the Astral Body (i.e. full astral projection) has been adopted as a Golden Dawn teaching, or at least *was adopted* at the time the founders of the order were still coming up with original teachings.[5]

So, we are concerned with establishing an Astral Current, and the Golden Dawn proposes that we can do this by visualising a powerful symbol: preferably one which is at the same time simple to use, but also invested with the appropriate magical significance. The first and foremost of such symbols are those of the Tattvas. These have the dual advantage of representing the five Elements—Fire, Water, Air, Earth, and Spirit—as well as constituting forms of distinctive shape and striking colours. An initiate of the Golden Dawn would learn

---
5 The five types of Clairvoyance are described in more detail in Leadbeater (1899).

THE LIGHT EXTENDED

to skry by starting with the Tattva symbols: however, once the basic technique is learnt, one can actually use almost *any* magical symbol to establish an Astral Current, for example: Geomantic symbols; Hebrew letters; Tarot cards; Planetary and Zodiacal signs; and more.

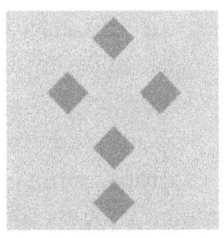 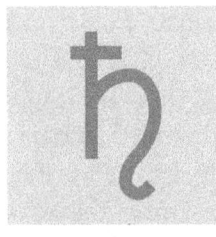 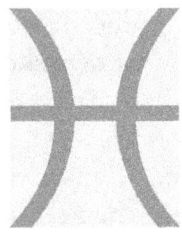

      Figure 3 "Puella"   **Figure 4 Saturn**   **Figure 5 Pisces**

Examples of potential symbols. For skrying purposes one would deliberately render them in colour: Puella, green on red to represent Libra; Saturn, Indigo on amber; and Pisces, ultra-violet crimson on yellow-green.

The Golden Dawn deliberately uses bright, vivid colours in its symbols, so that they "flash," that is to say that if you stare at them long enough, and suddenly stare at a blank white surface, you will see a particular negative image—because the intensity of the colours drains the corresponding pigment from the receptor cells in your eyes. So the initiate would stare at a given symbol intensely, and then quickly look at a blank surface: and then fix the negative thus formed in the mind's eye to visualise as an astral doorway—the one end of the Astral Current. Doing it in this way creates a more personal connection to the Symbol, because it transforms it from an image on a page or a card into an image burned into your optic nerves.[6]

So: why does the Golden Dawn encourage skrying in this

---

6 When originally delivering this talk in August 2017, I here interrupted my narrative to demonstrate this phenomenon using a Powerpoint slide (of the Fire Tattva, *see below,* as it happened), and a data projector. Quickly tapping the W key on the laptop provides a convenient modern method of suddenly looking at a blank white surface!

SKRYING IN THEORY AND PRACTICE

manner? Primarily, because it enables beginners to the Art to develop Clairvoyance from scratch. More importantly, however, by making a personal exploration of the astral reality of a symbolised force, one can discover esoteric teachings about that Element, Planet, Sign, or other force by *intuitive* means that one would not have discovered by book-reading alone.

Furthermore, when skrying into the astral plane, one can establish contact with Spirit Guides who will become valuable allies in ones magical career. For example, one might skry into the Water tattva, and meet a spirit guide who teaches you about the magical properties of the elemental Water, and later when you have the occasion to invoke Water you can make use of what that Spirit Guide taught you. You might also choose to invoke that Spirit Guide with which you first made contact whilst skrying its tattva. In this sense, Skrying thus becomes a hermetic / Qabalistic equivalent of shamanic vision-questing.

More generally, the Golden Dawn encourages skrying into not just the elements but also the other Qabalistic forces of the Tree of Life as a kind of Spiritual or psychological development. It is interesting to note that in this sense skrying is not dissimilar to Carl Jung's ideas about the use of "Active Imagination" in analytical psychology—except for the fact that the Golden Dawn thought of the idea first!

Skrying also helps prepare the initiate for more sophisticated forms of magick, e.g. Enochian. The Tattvas, and cognate symbols, are relatively simple. In the Enochian Magic of the Golden Dawn one combines multiple symbols into a complex, and uses quite specific invocations, but at its heart it still involves skrying, that is seeing on to the astral plane.

Quite separately, an Adept would be expected to regularly visit the Vault of the Adepti and investigate the symbolism found therein, again through Skrying.

Moreover: in an unpublished teaching of the Stella Matutina—which was a successor order to the original Golden Dawn—it was taught at the Adeptus Major 6=5 level that the basic tattvas which the Adept learnt in the previous grade could *themselves* be used for more advanced purposes than was commonly supposed, for example: gaining knowledge of past lives, making contact with disincarnate spiritual masters, discerning the astral history of this planet—and more.[7]

So now I would like to go into more detail about how the Skrying is actually done. Macgregor Mathers recommended that one should prepare for the skrying session by either painting the Symbol-in-Question on card or making it out of coloured paper. By way of a detail, he said that when making the Symbol for use, one should construct it magically. So for example, an Adept could do this by simply constructing the symbol in the appropriate, spiritual manner; or failing that, one could use an actual consecration ceremony.

The Skryer would then have the symbol before him, staring intently at it, before closing the physical eyes and holding the visualisation of the symbol before the mental vision. One then imagines passing through the Symbol as if it were a "magic door," or as if it one were drawing aside a curtain.

One would then vibrate the highest Divine Names associated with that Symbol, which serves to invoke the force associated therewith, and form and strengthen the astral current. One would follow that with the appropriate Archangelic and Angelic names, *"producing them mentally, visually, and by voice."*

This, incidentally, is why the Golden Dawn gets its initiates to memorise vast quantities of Qabalistic data—so they will be able to remember them easily when performing a Skrying experiment such as this, or when travelling on the astral plane.

The Order lays down some specific rules for practice—in this it follows the influence of Fred Hockley's advocacy of a structured approach, e.g. the Skryer should

> "... test everything in the vision, that is to say, everything at all doubtful to him."[8]

This the Skryer would do by calling mentally to them, using the appropriate symbols, grade signs, pentagrams or hexagrams, and

---

7 "The Aura of the Earth." This is an undated (but probably ca 1916) anonymous (but probably R W Felkin) typescript in a private collection whose owner is not likely to open it to the general public anytime soon, so there is little point in me providing a scholarly citation for it.
8 Flying Roll XXX—see King (1987)

SKRYING IN THEORY AND PRACTICE

again the Divine and Angelic names.

Mathers was also quite specific of not falling into a trance whilst doing this. Now technically skrying inevitably causes one to shift into an altered state of consciousness: however, Mathers was particularly concerned about the kind of mediumistic trances in which one loses control of ones thought-processes. One should always be "lucid" when performing Skrying, mainly so that one can remain discerning about the vision and test it in the appropriate manner. Becoming "unlucid" is regarded as a cop-out, and one of the main failings that occultists identified with the Spiritualist movement: i.e. they were unable to exercise any discernment during their trance, and they had no way of preventing any old astral entity, such as an undesirable one, taking control of them and telling them all kinds of nonsense!

Other general rules included that when first entering an astral landscape, first ask a Guide to appear, and then only explore in the company of that Guide. Also, one should start and end a Skrying session *properly*, i.e. one starts by going through a magic doorway, and one ends by mentally going back through the doorway, back along the Astral Current to normal consciousness.

All this is so that you can consciously verify that all is well throughout the experience.

Additional guidance given to initiates to make a scrying session more effective included that of noting the symbolism observed during a vision, as well as any names or words communicated. What is observed can be checked against known correspondences of that astral realm; whilst Gematria can be used to check the words. These can indicate whether one has actually made psychic contact with the forces in question. It can occasionally occur that random words and images pop up in the Spirit vision seemingly unbidden, and one is surprised to find that they correspond to the symbolism of that particular part of the astral plane in a way previously unknown: this can be indicative of a powerful spirit-contact.

Likewise, the order also recommends astrally formulating the double-letters of the Hebrew alphabet within the vision: these have the effect of guarding against influences from ones own psyche affecting the content. For example, in order to make sure what you beheld was not tainted by something from your own Memory,

THE LIGHT EXTENDED

you would use astrally formulate the letter Tav (Saturn); or if you suspected that your vanity might be affecting your skrying, you would use the letter Resh (Sun).

Initiates of the 5=6 grade of Adeptus Minor have to pass an exam in Tattvic Clairvoyance. MacGregor Mathers wrote that an adept

> "... should test everything in the vision, that is to say, everything at all doubtful to him. He should describe carefully and in detail the landscape etc. of the vision, and discover, if possible:
>
> The special attributes and varying natures of the Plane.
>
> Its Elemental Nature.
>
> The Inhabitants (Elemental, Spiritual, etc etc).
>
> The Plants, Animals, Minerals etc., which would be correspondent to the Nature of the Plane.
>
> The Operation of its Influence in the Universe of Macrocosm upon (a) this particular Planet (b) animals, plants and minerals.
>
> The Operation of its Influence upon the Microcosm, i.e. Man."[9]

Speaking personally, I would add that it is always good, before scrying into a tattva or other such Symbol, to spend some time meditating about it and the force it represents. To some extent this occurs naturally when consciously deciding to enter upon the skrying session with the right attitude. Brodie-Innes, for example, wrote:

> On taking any symbol whereof I know the meaning, such as a Tattva—or Tarot card, the abstract idea of the meaning of the symbol comes first—as fire, or water in the abstract—and a pose of mind cognate and sympathetic thereto, a desire for that particular element—not keen but perceptible—gradually the feeling of the physical effects of the element—as of warmth, moisture, etc—and especially the sound as of the oaring or crackling of fire, the rush—or

---

9 Ibid.

SKRYING IN THEORY AND PRACTICE

patter, or ripple of water.[10]

By preparing for the skrying in this way it helps one to attune oneself to the force in question, before you start to investigate it.

In addition to meditating on the physical qualities of the force, one should also consider the spiritual qualities. For example, Fire is not simply light and heat: it is also courage and initiative, creative force, and the Qabalistic world of Atziluth or Divinity. Likewise, Water is not just cold and moisture, but also sensuality, and the Archangelic realm of Briah.

Furthermore—if one is talking about the Tattvas specifically, one ought to remember that the beings one will encounter on the astral will be the Elementals, with which we communicate by contemplating love and sympathy towards them.

Quite separately, one ought to remember that although the Golden Dawn talks about making Adepts sit an exam, one should not look upon skrying as *exam-cramming*. Instead of expecting to accomplish everything in one visit, one should aim to make multiple visits that that one builds up a relationship with the corresponding spirits. The object of a Skrying-session should be not just to observe for curiosity or novelty, or go on an astral junket, but to make useful connections with spiritual forces. If one were making use of the "active imagination" as in Jungian Therapy one would not do it just the once, but one would replay the same imaginative scenario over several sessions: and then one would find that some aspects from earlier sessions lose their significance whilst others gain, as your understanding of the mindscape evolves. So it should be with skrying.

Finally: if a "mistake" occurs—such as a spirit that gives the wrong signs, or a something that is plainly inconsistent with the part of the astral plane being visited—it is always better to give it up as a bad job and try again later, than persist in a flawed vision. You may end up rejecting a lot of supposed visions this way, but it will save you from languishing in delusion, and help make the few genuine visions you have more valuable.

---

10 Flying Roll XXV — see King *op cit.*

Skrying Demonstration[11]

I should like to end by inviting you to participate in a skrying demonstration. On this occasion I will talk you through it: although you should remember that an initiate of the Golden Dawn would typically do such a session by him or herself.

There is a Golden Dawn rule of thumb: *invoke the highest first.* For this reason I propose investigating the Akasha or Spirit Tattva, which is normally depicted as a black egg or oval, thus:

Figure 6 Akasha tattva

I would therefore like to invite you to seat yourself, as for meditation, and to close your eyes, breathing deeply and regularly.

Breathe with the four-fold breath: in-2-3-4; hold-2-3-4; out-2-3-4; hold-2-3-4. Keep breathing in and out regularly.

Spend some moments relaxing each part of your body in turn.

Before we even begin to attempt to skry, let us first contemplate the nature of Akasha, so that we can get a feel for it, and attune ourselves to it.

Akasha is equivalent to "Spirit," which is the foundation of the other four elements. If you were to invoke any of the elements—Fire, Water, Air or Earth—it would be Spirit, the fifth element, which is the root which supports them.

Akasha has also been described by Dion Fortune as pure" mind-stuff,"[12] which transcends our own individual brains and minds, and permeates the whole Cosmos—existing outside linear time, as we understand it.

The yogi, Paramhansa Yogananda once said that a thought, once

---

11 This is a guided meditation on which I led those who attended my talk when I originally gave it in August 2017. Again, as I describe in note 6 above, Powerpoint and a data projector were used to help the attendees with the necessary visualisation.
12 Fortune (1935), p219.

thought, remains in existence, because it is imprinted in the Akasha: thus explaining the notion of the "Akashic Records."[13]

More importantly—in the Eastern tradition, especially in Hinduism, it is believed that the Universe was created from the vibrations set in motion when God spoke the first word: "AUM." It is further said that it is at the Akasha-level of our being that we become conscious of those Divine Vibrations.

So let us briefly consider our Earthy-nature, which is our physical bodies. In our Earthy-nature we experience the vibrations which affect us physically. Let us become aware that we observe what happens to us physically... but we are separate from and above it.

Realising we are more than our physical or Earthy-nature, let us withdraw our consciousness to our Watery-nature, which is not our physical body but the subtle-energy which animates our body. Know that our consciousness is separate to and above this also... and that we can with draw our consciousness to a higher level.

We therefore withdraw our consciousness to our Fire-nature. In the metaphysical element of Fire we experience what we believe to be light, and what we believe to be vision. But as we experience whatever images may appear before our mind's eye, let us consider we are not here interested in the things seen, but the truth which gives rise to those images. Therefore, let us try to discern the truth behind the images we experience, and in doing so, withdraw our consciousness from this plane to an even higher level.

The element of Air corresponds to the last remaining sensations we retain of our physical surroundings. The sounds we hear in this room. The sound of my voice. The sound of your own internal monologue. Become aware that your Akasha-nature is above even this—it is the Truth above the internal auditory sensations, just as it is the Truth above the images you may experience, and the truth above your physical sensations. Become aware, then, not of sounds playing in your head, but what the ultimate reality above and beyond those sounds must be.

That is the Akasha-level of your being. Remain still for a moment, calm, simply aspiring to the truth of what is above and beyond the thoughts which may occur in your mind.

---

13 "All thoughts vibrate eternally in the cosmos. By deep concentration, a master is able to detect the thoughts of any mind, living or dead." Yogananda (1950), p136.

THE LIGHT EXTENDED

Now, with your mind calm, slowly open your eyes… and stare at the symbol of the egg of Akasha. Try to stare at it unblinkingly, for as long as you can manage…

… And now stare at the wall next to the image. Without straining you should see a white oval—the negative of the image of the Tattva-symbol. Try doing this a couple of times, so you can get a clear idea of this negative-image.

Now, gently close your eyes again, concentrating on the Akasha-level of your being, the pure consciousness which is separate from and above all ordinary thoughts, and hold the negative image of the Akasha tattva before your mind's eye.

Know that this is one end of a connection—between you, and that part of the astral plane, which corresponds to Akasha.

The real nature of Akasha is above all ordinary thoughts. Therefore, the image before your mind's eye is not Akasha itself, but the gateway leading to the real meaning of Akasha.

In the Qabalah, there are two divine names associated with Akasha or Spirit: they are "Eheieh," which means "I Am," and "Agla," which means "Thou art mighty forever, O Lord." "Eheieh" is the active side of Spirit, whilst "Agla" is the passive. Whilst remaining in this Akasha state-of-mind, let us chant these divine names, once:

"EHEIEH."

"AGLA."

Silently, keep repeating these two divine names mentally, whilst remaining in this Akasha-state, whilst visualising the white oval before your mind's eye.

Now, imagine that in your vision, you are moving towards the white oval. You are moving *through* the white oval, as if you are passing through a veil. Imagine that you have passed right through, so that the white oval is now behind you.

Mentally repeat the names "Eheieh" and "Agla" to yourself and take note of the images which appear before your mind's eye.

Do not censor what may appear: just observe. Don't necessarily interact with what you may see, but just take note of what happens.

Always remember that you are safe whilst you are repeating the divine names "Eheieh" and "Agla."

Now I would like you to imagine that you are floating upwards—

rising straight up away from the ground. You look up, and see you are rising towards what first appears to be a barrier—but as you get closer you realise it is more like a veil, through which you can pass easily.

As you pass through this veil, the whole feel of the place seems different—as if this part of the astral plane has a more intimate, a more intense or more relevant connection to you—and you to it.

You rise even further. Looking up you see you are approaching another veil above you. As you rise you pass through this, at the same time feeling that the sense of connection between you and what you observe has become even more intense than before.

The rate at which you are rising slows, and you come to a stop. You are floating above a giant sphere, and you realise that it represents the entire influence of the Akasha upon the whole of our planet. The veils through which you have passed represent vibratory levels in the Akasha, surrounding the world of the elements like concentric spheres, or onion-like layers.

Looking up, you fancy you can see even higher layers, where you can experience the astral influence of the stars and planets upon this Earth.

Looking around, you realise that you can detect influences in the Akasha which are personal to *you*, including the Akashic records of your own past lives.

Looking down, you fancy you can make out more general influences, concerning your loved ones and family, your home country, and the world as a whole.

Realise that you can return at any time in the future to investigate further, by repeating this journey in the way you have made it today.

When you are ready, you begin to descend, floating gently back down through the veils through which you passed on the way up, down, all the way down ... until you the white oval, which is the gate through which you first passed to come to this place. You float gently down, and through the portal, and feel yourself coming back to your body, and gradually returning to normal consciousness.

THE LIGHT EXTENDED
BIBLIOGRAPHY

Betz, H. D. (editor), 1992, *The Greek Magical Papyri in translation, including the Demotic Spells—Volume one: texts,* second edition, The University of Chicago Press, London.

Fortune, D., 1935, *The Mystical Qabalah,* The Aquarian Press, London.

"Frater Achad" (Charles Stansfeld-Jones), 1923, *Crystal Vision through Crystal Gazing,* (reprinted 1976) Yoga Publication Society, Chicago.

Hockley, F., Gilbert, R. A. (editor), 2010, *Invocating by Magic Crystals and Mirrors,* Teitan Press, York Beach ME.

Hockley, F., Hamill J. (editor), Gilbert, R. A. (additional material), 1986, *The Rosicrucian Seer: Magical Writings of Frederick Hockley (Roots of the Golden Dawn series),* Aquarian Press, Loughborough, UK.

King, F. (editor), 1987, *Ritual Magic of the Golden Dawn—Works by S L MacGregor Mathers and Others,* Destiny Books, Rochester, Vermont.

Leadbeater, C. W., 1899, *Clairvoyance,* Theosophical Publishing House, Adyar, India.

(Paramhansa) Yogananda, 1950, *Autobiography of a Yogi,* Rider & Company, London.

About the Author

Alexander McAllister Sumner (born 1972), is a novelist and writer on the occult. After having written several non-fiction articles for the *Journal of the Western Mystery Tradition*, he came out with his first novel *The Magus* in 2008. He has written six novels in total, of which the most recent is *Eternal Witch* (2016).

He is also a ceremonial magician and amateur tarot reader and astrologer. His other interests include the Hermetic Order of the Golden Dawn, Rosicrucianism, and Freemasonry, and he is a member of several reasonably secret initiatory organisations. He lives in Essex, UK.

Thelema and the Golden Dawn
Spatting Siblings or Kissing Cousins?

by Frater D

I was recently asked about the relationship between Aleister Crowley and the Golden Dawn. I find myself uniquely positioned to answer, having received both Thelemic initiations and studied the work of TO MEGA THERION; and I am an initiate of the Golden Dawn. Some people would say these two things are in opposition or incompatible, while others would not.

In my experience there is a fundamental disconnect, a gulf between Thelemites and Golden Dawners, sometimes manifesting as animosity or mudslinging, while at other times uninformed write-offs of the other.

The Thelemite parrots Liber AL vel Legis, the Book of the Law, stating "Abrogate are all rituals, all ordeals, all words and signs", like a stroppy teenager looking at an outfit and exclaiming "that is soooo last year!". If you ask most thelemites to explain the meaning of this verse many are at a loss for words beyond the channelling of a stroppy teenager who throws the lines of an anarchical book as if a baby throwing toys from a pram, watching for a tired parent's reaction. The Thelemite also often assumes an equivalent knowledge base to the Golden Dawn initiate having read, and perhaps even learned and performed Crowleys adaptations of Golden Dawn rituals in his Liber O vel Manus et Sagittae, which includes the pentagram and hexagram rituals, both in significantly altered form. This is not the case and it is an offensive assumption.

Golden Dawners can be just as puerile, reading only the most yellow press accounts of Crowley and dismissing him as a morally devoid wretch who broke his oaths and 'destroyed the Golden

Dawn'. Golden Dawners also often work on the assumption that all of Aleister Crowleys works are derivative from the Golden Dawn and that Thelema is equally derivative and unoriginal in its scope and content. This is a gross over simplification of Crowleys magical legacy.

It is not hard to imagine animosity growing in the fertile ground of such oppositional positions, but in many cases these hard positions are built on shifting sand that a more nuanced view of each other would both be more fruitful, balanced position from which to consider the real relationship, legacy, differences and compatibilities of Thelema and the Golden Dawn.

OATHS AND INTEGRITY

Aleister Crowley is first and foremost charged with breaking his Golden Dawn neophyte oaths when in 1910 he published the rituals of the Golden Dawn… and he both did and he didn't. The contents of The Temple of Solomon the King in the Equinox was a definite "fuck you" to the Golden Dawn, giving outlines to the rituals, however they were not useable rituals by any stretch of the imagination. People wishing to enact or experience the rituals in any useable form, or who wanted the 'secrets' still had to join one of the branches of the Golden Dawn Family. If anything it probably raised the profile of the Golden Dawn and sent potential aspirants in their direction. Its redacted format was created by J.F.C. Fuller from the originals in such a way that they described processes rather than offering a workable system. Many who decry Crowley as an oathbreaker have never actually examined what it is that he published.

But for me this raises wider questions. As part of my oath I have promised to keep secret the papers and details of my initiation. I take that seriously. We live in an age where several people have published papers from the Golden Dawn including Aleister Crowley, Israel Regardie, R. G. Torrens, Pat Zalewski, Nick Farrell and others, others who have taken the same oath as I have, and of all of them, Aleister Crowley has made the least significant disclosure.

Much more significant was the disclosures of Regardie in 1938, the contents of which was a breach of copyright (being direct transcripts of the already edited Stella Matutina rituals being used in the Bristol Temple) and which gave rise to the self-start Golden Dawn movement. The excuse Regardie gave was "...it is essential that the whole system should be publicly exhibited so that it may not be lost to mankind. For it is the heritage of every man and woman – their spiritual birthright." It's amazing how Crowley was the devil because he published rough outlines that did not disclose the full ceremony, but Regardie is treated as the grand high poobah of Golden Dawn stuff when he did significantly worse. The fact that several prominent lines of the Golden Dawn today have either started from Regardies book, or trace downlines to him has led to a 'kind old grandfather' archetype never afforded to Crowley, though ironically perhaps some of Regardies own reminiscences on Crowley have something of this quality. A similar "get out of jail free card" has been afforded to various later 'exposers' of the Golden Dawn, all claiming initiation into the Golden Dawn.

We live in an age of instant information, google and a sense of entitlement to knowledge including knowledge which was previously hidden or private. I do not agree with this sense of entitlement. It is true that much is 'out of the box' about the Golden Dawn, and is widely available. This availability has fed into people's sense of entitlement to it. But what is out there is often fragmented, developed away from the source 'coherency' of its roots, outside its original context or even just plain wrong. Information is useless unless it can be correctly applied. You can have data or you can have lived experience. The latter is the Golden Dawn rituals in the context of a working temple and Order.

Crowley broke his oaths. This was wrong. But in the history of the Golden Dawn he is the person who revealed the least, but who is reviled the most for having done so. This hardly seems proportionate when even today Golden Dawn authors, bound by these same oaths, are releasing and profiting from 'previously secret documents' and are being patted on the back for doing so.

THE GOLDEN DAWN WAS SO MUCH MORE THAN CROWLEY REALISED

When Crowley joined the Golden Dawn he moved through the outer Order in a relatively short period, and was not advanced into the second Order in London. This was by-and-large due to his eccentric high-profile lifestyle including a rather open bisexuality and recreational drug use at a time when the former was illegal and the latter was not only legal, but in common practice among the middle classes. It is also undoubted that Crowleys flamboyance and rapid rise did not sit well with people – he was technically a good candidate, turning up, learning the lectures and testing out, but he was also fundamentally offensive to conventional Victorian ethics and decorum.

Mathers made clear his position on these matters – peoples private lives are just that, private, and had no bearing on membership of the Order. In reality this was not the case with Crowley. When not progressed in London, Crowley went to Mathers, then in Paris who was sympathetic to his predicament. It seems likely that the position of Mathers contributed significantly to the later work of Crowley with Rabelias' law of thelema, being "do what thou wilt shall be the whole of the law."

Crowley claims to have been initiated into 5=6, Adeptus Minor while in Paris, but we only have his word on this matter. I am not aware of any letters or records to confirm this fact, though a reactionary battlefield initiation does not seem impossible. If we look at the collections of Crowleys papers in the Warburg, we have the outer Order rituals in his own hand, however most of the material from the second Order, including the 5=6, came in the hand of, or with the name of Alan Bennett on them. The relationship between Crowley and Bennett was intense, collaborating in both magic and in the exploration of various drugs. It is clear the succession of the Golden Dawn work, and the oaths binding it were not strictly adhered to.

There are reams of material missing in Crowleys remnant papers from the RR et AC, and all evidence would suggest that much of the material he received and worked with from the Inner Order was patchy and illegitimately gained. His alleged 5=6 was proceeded by Crowleys attempt to seize the property and assets of the Golden Dawn in London, often referred to as the Blythe Road incident. This was proceeded by his abandonment of the Golden Dawn, travelling and so much more. He did not do the work of the Adeptus Minor and the subgrades and there is no evidence he had full access to the truly magical stuff of the Inner Order. He had access to aspects of it indirectly, but how piece meal this was is unclear.

ALEISTER CROWLEY'S THELEMA IS MORE THAN JUST THE GOLDEN DAWN RITUALS

There are certainly aspects of Thelema that are wholly derivative from the Golden Dawn, however there is much more than just this work in his writings. The work with yoga, begun during his mountain climbing days and deepened considerably during his time in Ceylon visiting Alan Bennett, then studying in a Buddhist monastery, is a core aspect to the magical system of Thelema. The work with the I ching, eastern thought and its marriage to those of the West was innovative. The integration of a syllabus including the study of Western thought and philosophy including naturalism was innovative. The work with 'recieved material' and the specific development of the idea of the HGA in the context of Thelema was innovative, if inspired by the Abramelin work. The work with sex magick was innovative.

There is much in Crowley that is not of or from the Golden Dawn, much of which has never been read by contemporary members of the Golden Dawn. It is not, and will not be to everyone's tastes, but at least we can seek an awareness that there is more to Thelema than the Golden Dawn, its rituals and ideas, as a firm foundation for exploration or critique.

ABROGATE ARE ALL RITUALS?

Abrogate are all rituals, all ordeals, all words and signs. Ra-Hoor-Khuit hath taken his seat in the East at the Equinox of the Gods; and let Asar be with Isa, who also are one. But they are not of me. Let Asar be the adorant, Isa the sufferer; Hoor in his secret name and splendour is the Lord initiating.

— Liber AL vel Legis I: 49

From a Golden Dawn perspective, the statement of all old rituals being abrogate, and many of its less measured interpretations, read very much like a stroppy teenager swearing at his parents. It is something which closes down conversation, and creates much of the gulf between the Golden Dawn and Thelema.

First off, Aleister Crowley carried a huge amount of baggage from a conservative Christian upbringing and as a queer man at a time when homosexuality was criminalised. His work is filled with contradictions that arise from a seeming contradiction in his own psyche. He had a decidedly reactionary anti-Christian attitude, much of which was only properly worked through in the 1920s, and much of what he projected on the Golden Dawn as problems, was part of his reconciling with his Christian past and with his social environment in Victorian England as a queer libertarian. Aspects of it, including the declaration of abrogation of the past is reactionary, but important in terms of the arising zeitgeist within a younger generation. He explains this abrogation as follows:

"49. The New Æon: All previous formulæ now obsolete. The New Initiation-Ritual indicated. All secret keys of the former Magick of the Æon of the Dying God are now useless, since the Lord of this New Æon of which I am the prophet is the Crowned and Conquering Child. Asar, the Man who suffers, is no longer the type of Godhead to which Man must aspire. He needs no more die and rise again: His great Work is now to come to know Himself as the Child ever-living, sinless, perfect, the all-shining Sun."[1]

The interpretation of Osiris as "the man who suffers" rings true from a certain perspective, the cross of suffering featuring in the 5=6. Consider now a man like Aleister Crowley, dubbed by his own mother as the Great Beast 666, who has revelled in a certain kind of martyrdom encountering the overtly Christian symbolism of Osiris/ Christ. It would not be difficult to imagine Crowley seeing this, in the context of his personal biography, as a deeply challenging encounter. The cross of suffering to such a person was more of the ordeal of Prometheus in Aeschylus' Prometheus Bound, being unjustly punished for daring to steal fire from heaven. His rejection of the Christian Rosicrucian context misses much of the death of the lower for the arising of the higher implied in this. The pathological conflict of sexuality and social repression, and his association of it with Christianity in all its forms has led to this 'new law'.

Thelema posits the stripping back of obscuring factors such as religious upbringing, social conditioning and more to arrive at "the Child ever-living, sinless, perfect, the all-shining Sun". This childlike state is achieved through simplifying and identifying with this glittering image, typified formulaically as Horus, and eventually as the Holy Guardian Angel.

In his monumental Book 4 he makes a minor concession for those not ready for this new paradigm:

> "The predominance of the Mother (Aeon of Isis) and of the Father (Aeon of Osiris) are of the past. Many people have not completely fulfilled these formulae, and they are still valid in their limited spheres; but the Masters have decided that the time has come for the administration of the Sacraments of the Aeon of Horus to those capable of comprehension."[2]

---

1 The Comment called D (Djeridensis Working. Tunis, 1923 e.v.) comment to Liber AL I:49
2 Book IV prt. III Chpt. V

THELEMA AND THE GOLDEN DAWN

Aleister Crowley and much of his work is a product of the juxtaposition of his lifestyle and life experience, and an Order (certainly in the London temple) and a society that would seek to impose strictures on these things fundamental to his identity and path in the world. Those drawn to Thelema are often initially re-enacting the revolt against the strictures of moral or social absolutism, whether in civic or religious life, but a more mellowed and mature attitude is less reactive, less adversarial and more focused inward toward the path of self-actualisation.

In spite of all of the above - the rejection of moral absolutism and external ideas of sin, evil and punishment, the figure of Osiris appears in the early stages of the A∴A∴. He appears as Ankh-af-na Khonsu, described as the self-slain God and echoes the sacrifice of Odin, "sacrificing myself to myself", and he appears as Asar-Un-Nefer, described as "myself made perfect."

> ASAR UN-NEFER: Whom no man hath seen at any time…" He acclaims his Angel as "Himself Made Perfect"; adding that this Individuality is inscrutable and inviolable. In the Neophyte Ritual of G∴D∴, the Hierophant is the perfected Osiris, who brings the Candidate, the natural Osiris, to identify with himself. But in the new Æon the Hierophant is Horus; therefore the Candidate will be Horus too. What then is the formula of the initiation of Horus? It will no longer be that of the Man, through death. It will be the natural growth of the Child. His experiences will no more be regarded as catastrophic. Their hieroglyph is "The Fool": the innocent and impotent Harpocrates Babe becomes the Horus Adult by obtaining the Wand. Der reine Thor seizes the Sacred Lance. Bacchus becomes Pan. The Holy Guardian Angel is the Unconscious Creature Self – the Spiritual Phallus. His Knowledge and Conversation contributes occult puberty. It is therefore advisable to replace the name Asar Un-nefer by that of Ra-Hoor-Khuit at the outset, and by that of one's own Holy

THE LIGHT EXTENDED

Guardian Angel when it has been communicated.[3]

The subtleties of the formula of Osiris are clearly struggled with, and are not rejected outright as a simplistic reading of the abrogate passage might suggest, but are an initial stage on the path. In the A∴A∴ Osiris is proceeded by Horus, who in turn is proceeded by the particular and intimate nature of the Holy Guardian Angel.

THE SS AND THE A∴A∴

One of the challenges is that Thelema is a broad designation, covering several distinct perspectives and 'beliefs'. There is the OTO or Ordo Templi Orientis, which is a body offering initiation for the masses, with no tests or criteria other than "don't be a dick" before their 4th degree. It is quasi masonic in structure and style. The OTO was not started by Aleister Crowley, though it was reformed under him to conform with the law of thelema. Appended to the OTO is the EGC, the Ecclesia Gnostica Catholica which performs the Gnostic Mass, a pseudo religious ritual built around the allegory of sexual union and creation. It also administers liferites including Baptism, Confirmation, marriage, and death rituals. The EGCs rituals are open to the public. There are few parallels between the OTO and EGC and the Golden Dawn, and while these are the most public and popular manifestations of Thelema, they are not the only ones. If we contrast and compare Thelema and the Golden Dawn we also must ask, which Thelema? Trying to compare pseudo masonic, or essentially 'churches' of Thelema is an exercise in futility. The face of Thelema comparable to the Golden Dawn is the A∴A∴, which is a reformulated version of the Golden Dawn.

The A∴A∴ was formed in 1907 with J.F.C. Fuller and G.C. Jones. It is clear from its history lection[4] that is considers itself a direct continuation of the Golden Dawn, and its own outer Order bears just this name. The name A∴A∴ stands for Astron Argron, Greek for Silver Star, the name of the third Order of the original Golden Dawn.

Unlike the Golden Dawn the relationship is with the work,

---

3 Excerpt from Liber Samekh Sub Figura DCCC, point II, Section A, August 30, 1921 e.v.
4 Liber LXI vel Causae

with guidance from one who has walked the path before. Those who progress through the Order also offer guidance to those who are walking the path after them. There is no social context to the A.'.A.'., no fraternising and though there are temple initiations, they are done using hooded officers. Unlike the Golden Dawn the A.'.A.'. only has rituals of initiation in the sephira of the middle pillar, with the Neophyte ritual (Troa) and the Zelator ritual (Cavederis) corresponding to the work of the Outer Order and Second Order (particularly 5=6) of the Golden Dawn respectively. The progress of a candidate from Dominus Liminis to Adeptus Minor in the outer is dependent on competence alone.

Golden Dawn	GD of the A.'.A.'.
	Student – is given a reading list and given an open book test based on that reading list. This forms a theoretical knowledge base.
0°=0▫ Neophyte – Temple Initiation, the candidate is welcomed into the Order. Given LRP, advised to keep a record. Given the first knowledge lecture. Must be tested before progression.	0°=0▫ Probationer – is given the task of keeping a record of a practice of their choosing from Liber E and Liber O. Inspected by supervisor. The probationers task is to gain an understanding of their own powers and nature.
1°=10▫ Zelator. Temple initiation, element of earth. Given knowledge lecture. Must be tested before progression	1°=10▫ Neophyte. Temple initiation – Liber Troa. Enters four elemental gates at once. Task perfecting the practices of Liber O (pentagram and hexagram rituals) and work of the astral plane. Makes Pentacle

2°=9☐ Theoricus. Temple initiation, element of air. Given knowledge lecture. Must be tested before progression.	2°=9☐ Zelator. Temple initiation – Liber Cavederis. Faced with the 'creature of the slime'/ Lesser Guardian. Die as Asar and arise as Horus. Formal acceptance of the Law of Thelema. Work to perfect asana and pranayama. Makes Sword
3°=8☐ Practicus. Temple initiation, element of water. Given knowledge lecture. Must be tested before progression.	3°=8☐ Practicus – No temple initiation. Intellectual training, especially the study of the qabalah. Divination. Destruction of stray thoughts. Makes Cup
4°=7☐ Philosophus – Temple initiation, element of fire. Given knowledge lecture. Must be tested before progression.	4°=7☐ Philosophus – No temple initiation. Tested in devotion to the Order. Talismanic work. Evocation. Makes Wand
Portal – initiate is considered a nominal 5°=6☐. Not a grade somuch as the portico of the RR et AC.	Dominus Liminis – Mastery of pratyahara and dharana.

Crowley in ceremonial garb

RR et AC	RR et AC in the A∴A∴
5°=6□ - Adeptus Minor – temple initiation into the vault of CRC. Work of the grade sub divided into sub grades recapitulating the work of the Golden Dawn in the Outer at a higher octave. Years of work follow discovering and developing the magical legacy of the Golden Dawn. Everything from this point on was absent from Crowleys Golden Dawn journey.	5°=6□ – Adeptus Minor in the outer. Adept builds own temple and administers a ritual for knowledge and conversation with the Holy Guardian Angel. This is specific to the A∴A∴ and is not, as many seem to think, the Abramelin working. Adeptus Minor in the Inner. Adept has achieved knowledge and conversation. Is admitted to the practice of the formula of the Rosy Cross on entering the College of the Holy Ghost (the marriage feast)
6°=5□ - Adeptus Major	6°=5□ - Adeptus Major – Achieves a mastery of practical magick under direct instruction of his or her Holy Guardian Angel.
7°=4□ - Adeptus Exemptus	7°=4□ Adeptus Exemptus – Completes in perfection all these matters. Writes magical thesis.

It is clear they are very different approaches, with a lot of the landmarks of the Golden Dawn dropped down the tree in the A∴A∴ and there is a noticeable focus on yoga and its disciplines in the A∴A∴.

The A∴A∴ then exceeds the Golden Dawn by putting the Third Order into action. The first Order is based on the meeting with the lesser Guardian or creature of the slime. The shadow side is exemplified in Horus' brother Set. The second Order is exemplified in Horus as a formula, and later the intimate knowing of the glittering image of the Greater Guardian of the Holy Guardian Angel. The Third Order of the A∴A∴ is focused on non-dualism and a radical embrace of all manifestations of ourselves as an ultimate unity. Crowley concedes that these attainments are states we visit, acquiring them as an insight filled revelation and that we are 'spit out' and find a functional resting place below the supernal triad. While the original Golden Dawn did not include the supernal triad, later branches developed these as grades. Crowleys acknowledgement that we do not constantly function from supernal consciousness strikes me as important, as the experiences and attainments he describes are akin to yogic and mystical states of transcendence, and not a functional baseline.

THE METHOD OF SCIENCE?

One of the major challenges in looking at Thelema is Aleister Crowleys claim to a method of science. The use of the record, and tests were a part of the Golden Dawn, and Crowley never really experienced the equivalent for practical experiment in the inner Order. In some senses methodical approach can be found in the A.'.A.'. through the record and its examination, and the testing of certain techniques, for example success in asana. On the other hand Aleister Crowleys religious upbringing had a heavy legacy in his life, and the thelemic mythos includes the reception of several channelled books which are not to be changed, the identification of Crowley as the 'prophet of the lovely star' and 'To Mega Therion' (all serving the function of a religious messianic cult), and the creation of social masonic and religious expressions of his Thelemic philosophy. His work and its debate has been dogged by dogmatic readings and decidedly unscientific features.

While fully committed to a methodical approach, and as one of the few magicians whose diaries have been printed, Aleister Crowley has also produced a cult of personality, with scores of people quoting him warmly, as if quotation is the proof of a theory and rushing to explain away some of the truly shitty things he did during his life time. Despite excellent intentions Aleister Crowley failed miserably to be the father of a more sensible, scientific Golden Dawn. He succeeded in bringing the body and yoga into magick. He succeeded in promoting a primary social law of "do what thou wilt!" but in the end a messianic cult has grown around his name and work that in the majority of cases is anything but scientific. This is sad, as Crowley himself would have hoped for better from those who followed after him.

THE WICKEDEST MAN: ATTACK OF THE PEARL CLUTCHERS

Many people will call me a Crowley apologist. I am not. The truth is, as a person I think he wasn't a role model by any measure, nor does genius excuse poor life decisions. He wrote some genius things, but also some repugnant things. Some of these repugnant ideas arise from the ideas of the time, and were generally accepted social norms.

Crowley was a prolific writer, and in later life shifted many of his more objectionable ideas as he freed himself from ingrained social conventions, however many of his writings need to be considered as brilliant, drug addled and morally objectionable in equal measure. Casting the morality of the 21st Century on someone born in the 19th and who died shortly after the Second World War is a problematic approach. In some senses his views were progressive, in some conservative, and in many there was an evolution. The tendency of both the followers of Thelema and Crowleys critics to cherry pick convenient quotes from a huge body of work to argue for and against various points, with often opposing positions being offered on the same subject is a tabloid approach devoid of the perspective history, biography and balance offer. The aspect of evolution, biography and humanity is absent from these superficial conversations.

People have written similar salacious accounts of Mathers going "look at how flawed he was". Adepts of ages gone by are mythologised and put in ivory towers of idealism because we know very little about their personal lives, and those whose lives we do know about are often held up with scorn as flawed geniuses, loved for their creations but loathed for their humanity.

By saying yes to a person's humanity, good and bad, and by putting them on no pedestal nor denying any aspect of their life, we put attainment within our grasp as we recognise that the adepts, like us were and are mortal, struggling and achieving through the vehicle of our humanity. I do not and will not pretend that I am only the glittering image, nor will I project angelicism or diabolism upon anyone else for being human.

One of the most important threads in the A∴A∴ are the two faces of the angel. There is the creature of the slime, the double and dweller on the threshold mirroring our frailties, inadequacies and those things that we both don't like about ourselves, and don't like to admit about ourselves. We know from a psychological perspective that blame and shame are destructive in exclusion, however self-acceptance and the wish to do better calls us to exceed. The acceptance of this 'fearsome face' of the Lesser Guardian as a part of our nature allows us to aspire onwards towards the glittering image of the Holy Guardian Angel, representing those elements which are idealised, strong, and representative of the ideal light. The thelemic initiate is told to achieve both weddings, being fully human by recognising that even in the aspiration to light there is a shadow, and one cannot exist without the other. The first Order of the A∴A∴ is the confrontation with the shadow, recognising it and persevering. The second Order is the fruit of that perseverance, the greater Guardian an image of potential brought to fruition.

Unlike the original Golden Dawn, Crowley goes a step beyond, saying the third order is within reach as a place where opposites stand not in opposition, but as equal truths and as a oneness. Crowley was all of the shadows cast upon him, a wicked man, and he owned this, and he was also the idealised image cast upon him by Crowley fanboys, but beyond the creature of the slime, beyond the glittering image is an adept who was not superhuman or deserving of a pedestal. He was a man who was fully human and did not deny any aspect of that humanity and that extreme embrace is offensive to those who would deny anything but the most virtuous parts of their nature.

NOT SUCH A NEW LAW

One of the major challenges for a Golden Dawn magician is the central ideas of Thelema, being "do what thou wilt shall be the whole of the law" and "love is the law, love under will" don't strike the Golden Dawner as actually anything new, much less the foundations of a 'new age'.

The idea of will is an explicit teaching of the second Order of the RR et AC. One example, from Flying Roll number I by G.H. Frater N.O.M. (Westcott):

> 'To obtain magical power, one must strengthen the will. Let there be no confusion between will and desire. You cannot will too strongly, so do not attempt to will two things at once, and while willing one thing do not desire others.
>
> Example: You may at times have passed a person in the street, and as soon as passed may have felt some attraction, and the will to see him again; turning round (you) may have found that he also turned to you. The will, though untrained, may have alone done this. But if you, untrained, walk out again, and decide to make an experiment of Willing that he who passes you shall turn round, and try it, you will fail. Because the desire of gratifying your curiosity has weakened the force of your will.'[5]

Sound familiar? – the will as the prime basis of magic, the singularity of will, and will free from desire, or in thelemic speak "for pure will, unassuaged of purpose, delivered from the lust of result is in every way perfect". In the light of these core concepts being integral to the Golden Dawn system, the declaration of a new law seems superfluous.

Flying Roll II addresses the first paradox of philosophy, part of some initiatic branches of Thelema in which one disciplines the will, adding restrictions to train the will. These examples are really only the tip of the iceberg and demonstrate that the "new aeon" and its rebellious law was in no way foreign to the Golden Dawn system of magic.

MODERN GOLDEN DAWN AND THELEMA

Israel Regardie, seen by many as the grandfather of the modern Golden Dawn was also an aspirant to the A.'.A.'.. He even had

[5] In *Commentaries on the Golden Dawn Flying Rolls*, page 23 (Kerubim Press, 2013)

students in this system. Chic Cicero, one of the prominent members of the modern Golden Dawn revival built a vault of the adepti in a Thelemic temple. He was allegedly told by Regardie that he needed to make a choice between the two by Regardie, however we know through Regardie's A∴A∴ students and from his continuing publishing of Aleister Crowleys work and ritual, often under his own name, that he did not make this clear cut.

On the other side of the fence there are several redacted forms of the Golden Dawn ritual being practiced that incorporate Horus as the initiator and the law of Thelema. The most publicly accessible of these is probably the Open Source Order of the Golden Dawn, however there are other temples working Thelemic Golden Dawn rituals.

I am of two minds about this. On one hand, do what thou wilt! If you want to construct a Golden Dawn tradition, work away. It does seem that self-identified thelemites are looking for temple based magical systems beyond the OTO. On the other hand I wonder how much of an understanding of the holism of the Golden Dawn system was held before it started being chopped and changed? It often seems that people want their own unique 'tradition' and set out to make radical changes, but are they really improvements or are they just the egotistical need to project a personal vision, regardless of original context? I am sure there are more and less intelligent syntheses and redactions, however it is very hard to judge the ritual of a group from without, and I am personally very wary of groups intent to throw out baby, bathwater and tradition in the name of progress.

ARE THEY INCOMPATIBLE?

I started out with an interest in the Golden Dawn at a time before there was an active Irish temple. I then joined a thelemic body and later the A∴A∴. As a probationer of the A∴A∴, I was working edited forms of the Golden Dawn rituals from Liber O, but I had no context for their meaning and original context. In many ways the study of Aleister Crowley's work supposes a knowledge of the Golden Dawn, so I made a decision to focus on that properly, and in doing so discovered compatibilities, differences, and old bones in new clothing.

I personally believe the systems can be worked side by side, in the same way that there are Christian Golden Dawners, Pagan Golden Dawners and Buddhist Golden Dawners, but it is important when working multiple systems to have a hygienic approach, keeping them separate and not projecting the context of one onto the other. There are those who would say the two cannot mix at all. This sounds awfully like dogma to me. By all means choose what's right for you, but please don't start telling me what my path should entail…

I know this essay will not address all questions, but it may stop so many pot-shots being taken at genuine aspiration, in whatever form it may take. In the end I believe we should trust in individuals and measure them, and not their religious/aspirational labels, on their own merits.

About the Author

Frater D has spent the last 15 years in service to various esoteric impulses including the A.'.A.'., the Golden Dawn and Rudolf Steiner's anthroposophy. His Work is withdrawn and focused in those organisations of which he is a member. In his muggle life he is a potter, visual artist and social sculpture.

"I HAVE PUT ON THE CLOAK OF THE GREAT LADY; I AM THE GREAT LADY"

THE ASSUMPTION OF GODFORMS AND THE KEY TO EGYPTIAN MAGIC

by M. Isidora Forrest

I am in the retinue of Hathor, the most august of the Gods, and She gives me power over my foes who are in the Island of Fire. I have put on the cloak of the Great Lady, and I am the Great Lady. I am not inert, I am not destroyed, and nothing evil will come to pass against me. I am the Great One Who Came Forth From Re, I was conceived and borne by Shesmetet, and I have come that I may weave the dress for my mistress. The dress is woven by Horus and Thoth and by Osiris and Atum; and indeed I am Horus and Thoth, I am Osiris and Atum.[1]

— *Formula 485, the Coffin Texts*

A series of Coffin Texts dealing with the weaving and wearing of the cloak of Hathor is among the clearest examples in Egyptian magic of what is most-often known today as the Assumption of Godforms.[2] As in the example above, the deceased puts on the cloak of Hathor and becomes Hathor. He is both the weaver and the wearer of the magical covering of the Goddess—Her "cloak," "dress,"

---

1 R.O. Faulkner, trans., *The Ancient Egyptian Coffin Texts* (Warminster, England: Aris & Phillips Ltd, 1973), Vol. 2, p. 130.
2 The term 'Assumption of Godforms' was coined by the magicians of the Golden Dawn. Modern witches sometimes refer to a similar technique as Drawing Down the Moon. Ancient Greek and Hellenistic philosophers and theurgists sometimes referred to this as Divine Possession, Divine Inspiration, or the Theurgic Union. An appropriate Egyptian term would be *Kheperu*, "Transformations" or "Forms." This article will employ the Golden Dawn term as it is most familiar.

or astral form.

The Assumption of God/dessforms may well be the most powerful magical technique human beings have available—in this or the afterlife. It was one of the vital keys to ancient Egyptian magic and it can still be a key to the working of powerful, sacred magic today.

We will look at how the ancient Egyptians may have developed this important technique, how they used it, and how it passed into the Western Esoteric Tradition. We will see how and why the technique was largely lost to us until being re-discovered and reconnected with its Egyptian roots by the magicians of the Golden Dawn at the end of the 19th century. Then, readers who would like to try this ancient technique for themselves are invited to use the brief ritual at the end of this article. It combines classical Egyptian and Hermetic theurgic formulae to assist you in Assuming the Godform of Amun, a Deity Who may be considered the God of God/dessforms.

The Key to Egyptian Magical Religion

The technique of the Assumption of God/dessforms is found throughout ancient Egyptian writing from the Pyramid and Coffin Texts, to the *Book of Coming Forth by Day*, to the Greco-Egyptian Magical Papyri, to Hermetic philosophical treatises and more. It is a genuinely Egyptian technique of magical religion. Most simply put, whenever we find the deceased, the priest, or the magician claiming TO BE a particular Goddess or God and speaking in the first person, we are likely to be witnessing the technique of the Assumption of God/dessform. It is the voluntary taking on of the astral or imaginal form of a Deity that enables the ritualist to share, albeit briefly, in the powers and Divine energy of that Deity, usually for the purpose of enhancing the effectiveness of a magical working or for deep communion with that Deity.

Unfortunately, no existing ancient texts discuss the technique, so we don't know precisely what the Egyptians intended or believed about it when they used it—or even by what name they called it. Scholars who have studied ancient Egyptian magic note the technique, but have apparently not recognized its central importance to the effectiveness of Egyptian magic. In point of fact, the Assumption of

THE ASSUMPTION OF GODFORMS

God/dessforms is a defining characteristic of Egyptian and Egyptian-derived magic. There are reasons to believe that it was more than mere convention to the Egyptians, that a real connection with the Deity invoked was both intended and achieved—at least by skillful magicians. The Assumption of God/dessforms was and *is* one of the most important ways we can empower our magic.

The Pharaoh & the Form

In the beginning, it was probably only the pharaoh who assumed Divine powers through sacred forms or images, the earliest being those of animal powers. A number of early Egyptian palettes show animals—perhaps intended to represent the ruler in Animalform—destroying enemies.[3] Indeed, Egypt's earliest-recorded kings took the names of dangerous, powerful, and sacred animals such as Scorpion, Kite, and Cobra.

The idea that a human being could be god-like is found throughout Egyptian literature. In the *Instruction for Merikare*, wisdom literature from the First Intermediate Period, it is said that the deceased is "like a god" in the beyond and refers to humanity as the "likeness of God." Humankind is called the "herd of God" and is "his likeness which came forth from his flesh." A human being with great knowledge is also said to be a likeness of God. It may be said that the Egyptians recognized a fundamental kinship between the human and the Divine.[4]

Naturally, it was easiest to recognize this Divine kinship in Egypt's Divine king. When the pharaoh is "manifest" to his people, the actions he takes are "not the work of men" and his words are "the utterances of God himself."[5] The pharaoh is often described as acting like a particular Deity or "being in the likeness" of that Deity.[6] Ramesses was said to be "like Montu." He appeared to his enemy

---

[3] Erik Hornung, *Conceptions of God in Ancient Egypt, the One and the Many*, translated by John Baines (Ithaca NY: Cornell University Press, English version, 1982), p. 105.
[4] *Ibid.* p. 138.
[5] *Ibid.*, p. 139.
[6] John Baines, Leonard H. Lesko, David P. Silverman, edited by Byron E. Shafer, *Religion in Ancient Egypt, Gods, Myths, and Personal Practice* (Ithaca & London: Cornell University Press, 1991), p. 66.

as "Seth Great of Strength" or "Baal in person."[7] The human-Divine pharaoh operated in two worlds.

From his dual perspective, the pharaoh mediated between Heaven and Earth. His mediation was vital because without the king playing his proper role, *Ma'et* or Right Order could not be maintained. Yet, as important as the pharaoh's share in Divinity was, if he was to be a true mediator, his humanity was equally vital. Interestingly, as a human being, the pharaoh was not considered infallible; the king's foibles are portrayed in numerous Egyptian stories. Furthermore, the king is not always Divine. He receives his Divinity through ritual. A Coffin Text provides a ritual conversation between the dead-but-now-renewed king and his inheriting son. It reveals that the son must journey to the underworld to inherit his father's power. Realizing this, the son asks:

> Do you say that I should be brought to this sacred land in which you are, your seat which is in the realm of the dead, that I may inherit your dignity? Transfer to me your power in order that I may take over for myself your office and say: My power is equal to yours![8]

The son states that his father has "god-like power" while he is in the West (the underworld) and asks him to "be kindly, be god-like, be god-like in this sacred land in which you are." Unlike a Deity Whose Divine power is intrinsic and eternal, a human being—even a pharaoh—must receive his power through right ritual and through actions that are in accord with Ma'et. The idea that ritual and right action could make one god-like has important implications for our discussion of the Assumption of God/dessforms, for while one does not literally *become* a Deity while in God/dessform, like the pharaoh, one can become god-*like*—and specifically through ritual and other preparations.

---

[7] Jeremy Naydler, *Temple of the Cosmos, the Ancient Egyptian Experience of the Sacred*, (Rochester, VT: Inner Traditions, 1996), p. 156.
[8] Faulkner, *Coffin Texts*, Formula 38, Vol.1, pp. 30-31.

THE ASSUMPTION OF GODFORMS

Beyond Pharaoh: Magic for All

As time went by, mortuary beliefs began to undergo "democratization." Beliefs about what happened to the pharaoh after death began to be applied more broadly. Ritual texts that had been carved on the pyramids (the Pyramid Texts) to assist the pharaoh during his journey to the land of the dead began to be written on the coffins (the Coffin Texts) of nobles, clergy, and other wealthy people to assist them. Like the Pyramid Texts, the Coffin Texts recognized the deceased as a god-like being. Eventually, even those who could not afford expensive mummification and ritually inscribed coffins could gain the magical protection of the sacred texts with a portable *Book of Coming Forth by Day* written on papyrus and placed with the body. By the time of the New Kingdom, an ordinary person could claim a "god-like omniscience."[9]

Furthermore, even ordinary people were used to employing magic or *heka* on a regular basis. The Egyptian wisdom literature had long said that heka was given to human beings so that they could use it "to ward off the blow of events."[10] Essential to the Egyptian universe, magic was inseparable from a relationship with the Deities. Heka is part of religion, part of life, and part of Nature. It is understood to be infused in things both Divine and natural, although Divine things have a greater share.

This magical world is a participatory world. In Jeremy Naydler's book *The Temple of the Cosmos*, he comments that the Egyptians believed human beings depended on the Deities, but that the Deities also depended on human beings even to the extent of relying on human action to help mobilize heka in the universe through the temple rites. Both Deities and humanity must uphold Ma'et or the universe will be thrown into chaos. Thus human beings have an innate power and influence, although they cannot hope to match that of the Goddesses and Gods.[11] In this worldview, it was theoretically possible for a human being—especially one who had acquired a lot of heka—to cause chaos in the universe. If humans are part of the cosmic order, they can affect the cosmic order. This is why we

---

9 Shafer, *op. cit.*, p. 73.
10 Robert Ritner, *The Mechanics of Ancient Egyptian Magical Practice* (Chicago: Oriental Institute of the University of Chicago, 1993), p. 20.
11 Naydler, *op. cit.*, p. 164.

sometimes find threats made against the Deities in Egyptian magical formula. The idea that human beings have the power to do this stems from the interrelatedness and interdependence of the human and the Divine worlds. "The expertise of the magician lay in bringing together the spiritual and material levels in a deliberately engendered and powerful coalescence. Magic did not function exclusively on the physical or the psychic or the spiritual planes but on all three together."[12] And a most effective way of joining Heaven and Earth was through the Assumption of God/dessforms.

A Living Relationship with Magic

In addition to being a natural energy, magic is also a living Being, a God. Therefore to truly know *Heka*, one has to enter into a relationship with Him.[13] The ancient Egyptian magician was not a mere technician, but a technically proficient priestess or priest. Heka is a primordial power—the first-created thing. He is the power by which the spiritual becomes manifest.[14] And He is the power by which the magician assumes a God/dessform, drawing spiritual forces into manifestation within and around her- or himself. As one could become other Deities, one could become Magic. Speaking to the assembled Deities in the Pyramid Texts, the deceased Pepi states that "it is not I who says this to you, you gods; it is Heka who says this to you, you gods."[15]

The energy of magic was considered to have a semi-physical aspect and may have been conceived of as a field of energy that surrounded the Deities, providing the power with which They maintained the natural order. As a semi-physical quantity, magic could be moved or directed. Texts also refer to heka being eaten or swallowed. This taking in of magic is volitional; and this is another important key to Egyptian God/dessform work. The Deity is specifically invited—even claimed—by the magician. This is why modern magic workers say they assume, take on, or draw down a God/dessform; they choose and activate this particular relationship with Deity.

---

12 *Ibid.*, p. 173.
13 *Ibid.*, p. 124.
14 *Ibid.*, p. 125.
15 R. O. Faulkner, *The Ancient Egyptian Pyramid Texts* (Warminster, Wiltshire: Aris & Phillips, Bolchazy-Carducci Publishers, 1969), Formula 1324, p. 208.

THE ASSUMPTION OF GODFORMS

The Assumption of God/dessforms in Egyptian Texts

In his study, *Conceptions of God in Ancient Egypt, the One and the Many*, Egyptologist Erik Hornung defines Egyptian Deities by three criteria: *Onoma* (the name of the Deity), *Logos* (words or knowledge about the Deity), and *Eidolon* (the image of the Deity). All three, combined with ritual, are also used in the Assumption of God/dessforms as we see it expressed in Egyptian texts. A longish passage from the Coffin Texts illustrates these principles and highlights some of the characteristics of God/dessform assumption.

> The Pelican prophesies, the Shining One goes forth, the dress of Hathor is woven, a path is prepared for me that I may pass by. I know this path (even of) him who is skilled in his movements, one whose face is hidden from those who see him. The Sistrum-Player is in my body, the pure flesh of my mother, and the dress will enclose me. I don the dress of Hathor, my hands are under it to the width of the sky, my fingers are under it as living uraei, my nails are under it as the Two Ladies of Dep, and I kiss the earth, I worship my mistress, for I have seen her beauty. She creates the fair movements which I make when the Protector of the Land comes; the gods come to me bowing and praise is given to me by the gods, they see me at my duty, and I am initiated into what I did not know, I cross the retinue of this Great Lady to the western horizon of the sky, I speak in the Tribunal.
>
> "This path of yours; whence is this path of yours?" say the horizon dwellers to me.
>
> "I have come here from the river-bank of Hu on my ascents of the Mountain of the sehseh bird, so that I may don the cloak of this Great Lady who is in the bow of the bark of Re and in the middle of the bark of Khopri. I found her when she repeated her manifestation and trebled her faces, the Serpent of Terror being on her brow, and her shape is distinguished above [those of] the gods."
>
> "The god who protects the land comes," say they of

THE LIGHT EXTENDED

the southland concerning me when they see me having taken my seat and occupied my throne, and having acquired what I found there. I am one wide awake and not weary, I am in the retinue of the king of the sky.

"The god who protects the land comes," say the horizon dwellers concerning me. "The god comes, having gone aboard the bark," say they who are about the shrine, who sit in the sides of the bark, who eat their food. They see me as the Sole One with the secret seal. I don the dress, I wear the robe, I receive the wand, I adorn the Great Lady in her dignity. Her Sistrum-Player is on her lap, and he has built mansions among your great ones, he has presented offering cakes, so that he may live thereon and that he may celebrate the monthly festival in his hour in company of those who are in linen, for he has looked at his face. So says the occupant of the throne of the Great Lady concerning me.[16]

We can be sure that the deceased is intended to be in God/dessform because when he "dons the dress of Hathor," "the Sistrum-Player is in my body," it is She Who "creates the fair movements which I make," and the horizon dwellers "see me as the Sole One with the secret seal." He employs the *Onoma*, the names and epithets, of Hathor in his formula. He has knowledge of Her *Logos* for he describes Her place in the sacred barques of the Gods and undoubtedly refers to myth when he says She "repeated her manifestation and trebled her faces." He also uses Her *Eidolon*, symbolized as the dress of Hathor, building up the Goddess' image through the description in the text and donning Her dress or image. As in this example, the Assumption of God/dessform is often characterized by a multiple consciousness. Here, the deceased perceives as himself, as Hathor, and as the Sistrum-Player—Who may be either Hathor Herself, or Hathor's son, also called the Sistrum-Player. He is the Great Lady and he is Her worshipper. He is both human being and Divine Being. Like the pharaoh, he mediates between Heaven and Earth, partaking of and blending both.

There are many more casual—if I can use that term for something this profound—assumptions of God/dessform. In the Coffin Texts,

---

16 Faulkner, *Coffin Texts*, Formula 484, Vol. 2, p. 128.

THE ASSUMPTION OF GODFORMS

the funerary priest says to the deceased, "I am Isis, I am Nephthys, Horus has addressed you!"[17] He cautions, "Do not say it is I who say this. It is Geb and Osiris who say this to you."[18] In another text, the deceased himself says "I will travel as Isis."[19] In the *Book of Coming Forth by Day*, the dead person is identified with Re, then states "I have arisen as Horus, I have sat down as Ptah, I am strong as Thoth, I am mighty as Atum..."[20] The sick often identified with Horus while healers identified with Isis. And even though many of these formulae show up in funerary texts, they were not only for the dead. "As for him who knows this spell on earth [...] he will proceed to a very happy old age," says one text. Another states that anyone who knows the spell will "complete 110 years in life,"[21] while many others explain that the formula is beneficial for anyone who does it.

While these simple identifications may have been more *pro forma* than full-fledged Assumptions of Godforms, there were many others that were clearly formal assumptions—such as the Hathor spells above. Another excellent example is a formula "for the Soul of Shu and for Becoming Shu":

> I am the soul of Shu the self-created god, I have come into being from the flesh of the self-created god. I am the soul of Shu, the god invisible of shape, I have come into being from the flesh of the self-created god, I am merged in the god, I have become he.[22]

In this spell, the magician spends considerable time making statements that identify him with Shu. He tells the full myth of Shu, and beautifully ends the formula with "I am invisible of shape, I am merged in the Sunshine-God." I have no doubt that if you worked this spell today—as written and while in the proper frame of mind—you could indeed Assume the Godform of Shu.

The proper frame of mind is, however, crucial. The magician's ordinary consciousness must be expanded in order to contact the

---

17 Ibid., Formula 74, Vol. 1, p. 69.
18 Ibid., Formula 72, p. 67.
19 Ibid., Formula 182, p.153.
20 R.O. Faulkner, *The Ancient Egyptian Book of the Dead* (New York: Macmillan Publishing Company, 1972, revised 1985), Formula 11, p. 37.
21 Faulkner, *Coffin Texts*, Formula 228, Vol. 1, p. 181.
22 Ibid., Formula 75, p. 72.

energy of the Deity invoked. She must cultivate a state of mind that is larger than her subjective self. Says Naydler, "in various magical situations a person might identify with a transpersonal energy, or god, to such an extent that their psyche became wholly absorbed into this transpersonal power. They were no longer themselves but experienced themselves as a 'god' and were—or could be—so experienced by others."[23]

Ritual is the means of cultivating this expanded state; *Onoma* and *Logos* provide its framework. Many readers will already know the importance the Egyptians placed on the magic of names and words. This is because these were thought to contain the essence and energy of their subject. Even as late as the 2nd or 3rd centuries CE, Egyptians knew their own language to be the true sacred language. A Hermetic treatise from that period, says that

> The very quality of the speech and the [sound] of Egyptian words have in themselves the energy of the objects they speak of [. . .] We [. . .] use not speeches but sounds full of action.[24]

If words and names contain the energy and essence of the thing they represent, then one participates in that essence or energy by speaking. Isis, the Lady of Words of Power and a mighty magician, spoke Her spells never halting or stumbling over a word and human magicians tried to emulate Her. In addition to words and names, magicians participated in the Divine energy by making themselves into magical images by putting on masks or using ritual gestures. Depictions of priests wearing Anubis masks are known and examples of the masks themselves have been found. The mask obscures the human identity, outwardly enabling the magician to become an image of the Deity, and inwardly to identify more fully with the Deity. Other types of costuming may have been a part of God/dessform assumption as well. Just as the magician astrally donned the "dress of Hathor," put on "the fringed cloak as Re in the sky," or "donned the white-and-bright fringed cloak of Nun which [. . .] gives light in darkness,"

---

23 Naydler, *op. cit.*, p. 176.
24 Brian P. Copenhaver, *Hermetica, the Greek Corpus Hermeticum and the Latin Asclepius in a new English translation with notes and introduction* (Cambridge: Cambridge University Press, 1992), Corpus Hermeticum XVI, 1-2, p. 58.

THE ASSUMPTION OF GODFORMS

perhaps he literally was "clad as Horus" or "robed as Osiris."[25] Ritual gestures could turn the magician into "a hieroglyph; an icon bearing symbolic meaning."[26] Through sacred gesture, the magician's actions are no longer personal, but become archetypal, contributing to the expanded state. She may also have prepared herself on a psychic and energetic level: "I have come into you, having opened up my head and aroused my body..."[27]

In addition to words of power, ritual costuming, and gesture, visualization is another highly effective mechanism for the Assumption of God/dessform. No ancient text specifically says one should "see this in the mind's eye," yet there is no reason not to assume such an instruction was given orally. Furthermore, the reading of the spell itself may be used to build up the visualization—as in this example from the *Book of Coming Forth by Day*:

> I am the Radiant One, brother of the Radiant Goddess, Osiris the brother of Isis; my son and his mother Isis have saved me from my enemies who would harm me. Bonds are on their arms, their hands, and their feet, because of what they have done evilly against me. I am Osiris, the first-born of the company of the gods, eldest of the gods, heir of my father Geb; I am Osiris, Lord of persons, alive of breast, strong of hinder-parts, stiff of phallus, who is within the boundary of the common folk. I am Orion who treads his land, who precedes the stars of the sky which are in the body of my mother Nut, who conceived me at her desire and bore me at her will...[28]

By reading the description, no doubt the reader began to picture himself as Osiris—or the priest began to see the deceased as Osiris. By visualizing the form of the God, recalling the myth, using the sacred words and names, and standing in the archetypal postures, the magician attuned himself to the energy of Osiris, thus becoming Osiris. So much so that he could eventually say "I am indeed Osiris, I indeed am the Lord of All, I am the Radiant One, the brother of the

---

25 Faulkner, *Coffin Texts*, Formula 910, Vol. 3, p. 60.
26 Naydler, *op. cit.*, p. 144.
27 Faulkner, *Coffin Texts*, Formula 467, Vol. 2, p. 95.
28 Faulkner, *Book of the Dead*, Formula 69, pg. 70.

THE LIGHT EXTENDED

Radiant Lady; I am Osiris, the brother of Isis."[29]

Another *Book of Coming Forth by Day* formula identifies the deceased with Re, quality by quality, again allowing for visualization:

> His sun disk is your sun disk;
> His rays are your rays;
> His crown is your crown;
> His greatness is your greatness;
> His appearings are your appearings;
> His beauty is your beauty;
> His majesty is your majesty;
> His savor is your savor;
> His extent is your extent;
> His seat is your seat;
> His throne is your throne;
> His heritage is your heritage;
> His panoply is your panoply;
> His destiny is your destiny;
> His West is your West;
> His goods are your goods;
> His wisdom is your wisdom;
> His distinction is your distinction;
> He who would protect himself does
> indeed protect himself—and vice versa.[30]

Once the God/dessform is assumed, the Deity is perceived within: "Hail to you, Khopri within my body..."[31]

Some texts offer hints about what the Egyptians thought was going on during the Assumption of God/dessforms. Formula 250 of the Pyramid Texts seems to understand the *process* of the assumption. Early in the text, the king states "I become Sia who bears the god's book." Later, he says "I, even I, am Sia who is at the right hand of Re." First, he *becomes* Sia, then he *is* Sia. The Coffin Texts say that the deceased "appears as Horus" or walks "on my feet like Osiris." Coffin Texts Formula 513 has the deceased state that he "will go up and take possession *in the shape of Anubis*. . ." In Formula 78 of the *Book of*

---

29 Faulkner, *Coffin Texts,* Formula 227, Vol. 1, p. 179.
30 Faulkner, *Book of the Dead,* Formula 181, p. 180.
31 Faulkner, *Coffin Texts,* Formula 460, Vol. 2, p. 88.

THE ASSUMPTION OF GODFORMS

Coming Forth by Day,

> Horus has invested me with his shape [...] I am the falcon who dwells in the sunshine, who has power through his light and his flashing. [...] My arms are those of a divine falcon, I am one who has acquired (the position of) his lord, and Horus has invested me with his shape.[32]

Texts like these show that in many cases, the Egyptians were making a clear differentiation between the God and the God*form* in which the deceased or the magician appears to be like the Deity.

Uses for the Assumption of God/dessform

The reasons one might want to Assume a God/dessform included increased heka for a good outcome after death, for protection, as well as for accomplishment of a variety of tasks, such as healing and the usual human reasons of gaining love and money.

Ritual theater is another possibility for the use of God/dessform. We know that theater was used in Egyptian religion—we even have the script from a sacred play about the conflict of Horus and Set. Since these were religious rites, not mere entertainment, it is possible that the actors Assumed a God/dessform for the performance.

Oracular use is another possibility. Many of the most famous oracles had a built-in God/dessform: the sacred statue of the Deity that had been magically enlivened by the Ceremony of the Opening of the Mouth. Archeological evidence suggests that some of these oracular shines had a bronze pipe that may have served as a speaking tube for giving oracles through the sacred image. We have no specific details about how the priests may have prepared for such an oracular audience. Assuming they were not complete frauds, I suggest that those giving the oracular utterances were in God/dessform.

But in addition to these uses, it is also possible that the ancients used the Assumption of God/dessforms as many sacred magicians do today—for communion with the Divine:

> I will go into the Moon-god, so that he may speak to me, that the followers of the gods may speak to me, that

---
32 Faulkner, *Book of the Dead*, Formula 78, p. 76.

the sun may speak to me, that the sun-folk may speak to me.³³

Greco-Egyptian God/dessforms

Egypt's dramatic, magical religion strongly influenced the many cultures surrounding it. Its defining influence on the way magic was worked is evident in Greek texts and extends deeply into Greek culture. Indeed, most Greek magic cannot be explained except by Egyptian antecedents.³⁴ So the next place we'll look for the Assumption of God/dessform is the Greek Magical Papyri. While these texts were written in Greek, they were written in Egypt and employ largely Egyptian magical techniques.

Greek magicians seem to have held the Assumption of God/dessform in high regard but used it more sparingly than their Egyptian counterparts. They often reserved it for the key part of the spell, the compulsion or culmination of the spell, or at another point when especially powerful magic was required. The Greek texts often clearly demarcate between the time before and after the magician has assumed the God/dessform. Often, an invocation is spoken to the Deity or Deities involved—until it comes time for the culmination. Then the magician Assumes the God/dessform and speaks as the Deity; this is still the most common way the Assumption of God/dessform is used today.

The Greek Magical Papyri provide numerous examples of the Assumption of God/dessform for increased magical effectiveness. One of these is a working for a sacred vision in which the magician declares himself to be a prophet *about to call* upon a powerful name, then he declares himself *to be* the Deity he has just called upon. Only then, in Godform, does he command Anubis to appear to him.³⁵ In a less-clear example, the magician first calls herself a slave of the most high God then declares herself to be the most high God—and can command Eros:

---

33 Faulkner, *Book of the Dead*, Formula 124, p. 115.
34 Garth Fowden, *The Egyptian Hermes, A Historical Approach to the Late Pagan Mind* (Princeton, NJ: Princeton University Press, 1986), p. 66.
35 Hans Dieter Betz, *The Greek Magical Papyri in Translation including the Demotic Spells* (Chicago and London: University of Chicago Press, 1986), PGM VII 319-34, p. 126.

THE ASSUMPTION OF GODFORMS

...inasmuch as I am a slave of the most high God, who controls the universe MARMARIOTH LASIMIOLETH ARAAS . . . SEBARBAOTH NOO AIO OIER AAAAA EEEEEE OOOOOOO. I give orders to Eros, who is charged with carrying out my commandments, inasmuch as I am God of all Gods, IAON SABAOTH ADONAI ABRASAX IARABBAI THOURIO THANAKERMEPH PANCHONAPS.[36]

The spell seems to be constructed for the magician to assume the form of God of all Gods during the speaking of the first set of magical words (MARMARIOTH, etc.). Then, in Godform, she continues with the second set to complete the working.

A text often called the Mithras Liturgy, which is a working for Divine communion and a holy vision of Mithras-Helios-Aion, offers a striking example of how Godform assumption was used. In the text, the ritualist acknowledges that it is impossible for a mere mortal to do the things he wishes to do. Therefore, he Assumes a Godform, and no longer a mere mortal, he confidently asks to be received among the Deities:

> . . . for today I am about to behold, with immortal eyes—I, born mortal from mortal womb, but transformed by tremendous power and an incorruptible right hand and with immortal spirit, the immortal Aion and master of the fiery diadems—I, sanctified through holy consecrations—while there subsists within me, holy, for a short time, my human soul-might, which I will again receive after the present bitter and relentless necessity which is pressing down upon me . . . Since it is impossible for me, born mortal, to rise with the golden brightnesses of the immortal brilliance, OEY AEO EYA EOE YAE OIAE, stand, O perishable nature of mortals, and at once receive me safe and sound after the inexorable and pressing need. For I am the son PSYCHON DEMOU PROCHO PROA, I am MACHARPH [. . .] N MOU PROPSYCHON PROE.[37]

---

36 *Ibid.*, PGM XII 14-95, p. 154.
37 *Ibid.*, PGM IV 475-829, p. 48.

THE LIGHT EXTENDED

As the working continues, the magician draws in "breath from the rays" and he feels himself being lifted into the air. Eventually, he finds himself among the Gods and declares "I am a star wandering about with you, and shining forth out the deep..." Like the Egyptian who after death is joined to his star, the magician in this text is also a star, a God in the company of Gods. As the vision continues, he sees many Deities and spirits. Finally, there is the great revelation of Mithras-Helios-Aion. Before the God, the magician declares that "I am dying, while being born from a life-generating birth; I am passing on, released to death—as you have founded, as you have decreed, and have established the mystery. I am PHEROURA MIOURI."[38]

Modern magicians will note that the first Godform the magician appears to assume is that of his Higher Soul. He asks to be received because he is "the son PSYCHON;" *psyche* is soul in Greek. Many modern magicians would readily agree that the Higher Soul or Higher Self is an excellent God/dessform to assume in order to achieve a sacred vision of this very personal, initiatory type.

As grandiose as the Mithras Liturgy is, there are many examples of less complex Godform Assumptions, such as this one in which the intimacy between the magician and the God he invokes is simple and beautiful:

> For you are I and I am you, your name is mine and mine is yours. For I am your image [...] I know you, Hermes, and you know me. I am you and you are I.[39]

Divine Possession & the Assumption of God/dessforms

In addition to the papyri, another area in which we find the use of God/dessform in the Greek and Hellenistic worlds is in relation to oracles and the oracular shrines, especially the most famous shrine of them all, the Oracle of Delphi.

Yet Delphi was not the oldest oracle in Greece. According to legend, Greece's first oracle was the Oracle of Zeus at Dodona. And according to what Herodotus relates of the story told by the priestesses at Dodona (called *Peleiads* or Doves), the oracle's origin was Egyptian. The Doves told him that two black pigeons flew from

---

38 *Ibid.*, p. 52.
39 *Ibid.*, PGM VIII 1-63, p. 146.

THE ASSUMPTION OF GODFORMS

Thebes in Egypt, one to Dodona and one to the Siwa Oasis in Libya. Each bird alighted in a tree and, speaking in a human voice, told the people to set up an oracle of Zeus in each place—which was done. Herodotus learned another version of the tale from Egyptian priests. They said that the Phoenicians kidnapped two Theban priestesses of Amun and sold them, one in Dodona and one in Libya. In those two places, the priestesses founded oracles. The Egyptians had searched for the priestesses without success and only later learned what had become of them. Herodotus felt the Egyptians had the more plausible story.

It is likely that both divinatory lots and inspired prophecy were employed for oracles at Dodona. Plato tells us that the Dodona priestesses become "mad." But by madness, he does not mean what we usually mean today. Indeed, in the *Phaedrus*, Plato's character Socrates says, "the greatest of blessings come to us through madness."[40] Plato refers to a Divine madness that, "when it comes by gift of the gods, is a noble thing."[41] So inspired by the Divine is the mad one that she is no longer herself; she is perceiving in an extraordinary, god-touched way. In other words, madness is an altered state of consciousness.

An ancient Greek term to describe this state is *enthusiasmos*; yes, it is the origin of English "enthusiasm." A prophet in this state is *enthusiastikos* and a prophetess in this state is *enthusiastike*. The word ultimately derives from the Greek term *entheos*, literally, en-godded—having a God inside.

This brings us to a question. What is the difference between Assuming a God/dessform and Divine Possession? In some cases, none. It may be correct to say that the Assumption of God/dessform is a subset of the larger category of Divine Possession; it is one way of being possessed. Earlier, I characterized the Assumption of God/dessform as voluntary (usually, but not always, true with Divine Possession). It may further be characterized by first-person expression; the prophetess or prophet speaks as the Deity, acts as the Deity. It is also a ritual technique, requiring ritual preparation of some type. Finally, it involves the form or image of the Deity in some

---
40 Plato, *Phaedrus*, 244a, Harold N. Fowler, trans., *Plato in Twelve Volumes*, Vol. 9 (Cambridge, MA: Harvard University Press; London: William Heinemann Ltd. 1925), p. 465.
41 Ibid., 244c, p. 467.

manner. Today, this is usually done by visualization. In the Egyptian texts and the papyri the opportunity for visualization is in the written descriptions of the Deities and through priestly costuming or the temple's sacred statue. In the case of the Greek oracles, we simply do not know whether visualization or other images were employed, although the other conditions for the Assumption of God/dessform appear to have been met. During the hundreds of years that the Greek oracles operated, it is more than likely that different prophetesses and prophets employed different methods according to their personal propensity and/or training.

This seems very probable when we read the varying accounts of the trance of the Pythia at Delphi. Some describe the Pythia as wild and incomprehensible while others have her speaking in controlled verse. The Neoplatonic philosopher Iamblichus notes a wide variety of possession experiences available to the ritualist:

> For either the god possesses us, or we become wholly the god's property, or else we exercise our activity in common with him. And sometimes we share in the god's lowest power, sometimes in his intermediate, and sometimes in his primary power. And sometimes there is a mere participation, sometimes a communion, and sometimes even a union; from these inspirations, either the soul alone benefits, or it shares also with the body, or even, again, it is the composite living being that benefits.[42]

As a result, he says, there are many and contradictory signs of Divine Possession: movement or stillness, calm speech or halting, an increase in (physical) size or a diminishment—a variety that we also see today in those who Assume a God/dessform. Of the Pythia's possession, Iamblichus says she "gives herself absolutely to the divine spirit, and is illuminated by the ray of divine fire. [. . .] whenever she is found on the seat of the god, she is in harmony with the divine, unwavering oracular power."[43]

Plato identified four types of Divine madness. The prophetic

---

[42] Iamblichus, *On the Mysteries*, 3.5, Emma Clarke, John Dillon, and Jackson Hershbell, trans., *Iamblichus, On the Mysteries* (Atlanta: The Society of Biblical Literature, 2003), p. 131.
[43] *Ibid.*, 3.11, pp. 148-9.

THE ASSUMPTION OF GODFORMS

madness of the Pythia he called Mantic. There are also Erotic, Poetic, and Telestic madnesses. Both Mantic and Telestic madness are of interest to our discussion of the Assumption of God/dessform. Telestic madness has been variously translated as "ritual," "initiatory," and "mystic" madness. In the Greco-Roman world, perhaps the best examples of Telestic madness are the Bacchants, the worshippers of Dionysos (also called Bakchos). Their Divine madness was evidenced by ecstatic dancing, wild cries, running, and generally "raving," usually in an outdoor setting, traditionally the mountains.

The most well-known group of Bacchants are the Maenads, certain groups of Dionysos' female devotees. In myth, the Maenads are Divine Nymphs, the Nurses of the young God and They share His attributes. Like Him, They are graceful and fierce, life and death-bringing. Like the God Who is called the Prophet of the Thracians, They also prophesy in their madness. Human Maenads too imitated their God in these ways. In Euripides' famous play, *The Bakchai*, the blind prophet Teiresias says, "The Bacchic ecstasy and frenzy hold a strong prophetic element. When he [Dionysos] fills irresistibly a human body, he gives those so possessed power to foretell the future."[44] The Greek verb *baccheuein*, which is used of both the female and male devotees of Dionysos, means "acting like Bakchos." (Quite appropriate for this God of Theater.) The Bacchants ritually danced until entranced, undergoing the mystic communion and the initiation of Dionysian madness, identifying with the God through the movements of their dance, their ritual cries, and their prophecies.

If they acted like Bakchos through their ecstatic dance and wild behavior, they also attempted to wear the form of Bakchos. Like the God, they wrapped fawn skins about their shoulders, let their hair fly loose, and carried the *thyrsos*, the ritual wand and weapon of Dionysos. Like them, the God sometimes wore long, feminine robes. Thus the God and His followers shared a Divine image—a Godform. By invoking the manifestation of Dionysos within themselves through their ritual dance and outwardly wearing His form through costuming and the transformations of ecstasy, we can surmise that at least some of the Bacchants did indeed Assume the Godform of Dionysos. They acted as Bakchos just as the Egyptian magician

---

44 Phillip Vellacotte, trans., *Euripides: The Bacchae and Other Plays* (Harmondsworth, New York, Victoria, Ontario, Auckland: Penguin Books, 1954 & 1972), p. 201.

walked as Horus.

Hermes and the Assumption of God/dessforms

If the Bacchants were acting like Bakchos, there were others who were acting like Hermes. In fact, we have already met some of them, the magicians of the papyri who Assumed the Godform of the most famous magician of all, Thrice-Greatest Thoth or in His Hellenized form, Hermes Trismegistos. Trismegistos was believed to be the Divine author of thousands of sacred writings—all of them, if you asked the Egyptians. Egyptian paintings sometimes show Thoth's sacred baboon perching on the shoulder of a writing scribe. I have wondered whether that image was intended to indicate that the scribe was in the Godform of Thoth as he wrote, thus the words were not his, but the God's.

As Hermes Trismegistos entered the Hellenistic and Roman worlds, He continued to be associated with literature, including works on cosmology, healing, magic, astrology, and alchemy. He was also considered the author of a number of philosophical dialogs, some of which have come down to us today as the *Corpus Hermeticum*. Some scholars divide the Hermetic texts (dating from 300 BCE to 300 CE) into the technical or magical texts and the theoretical or philosophical texts. In some cases, this is a fairly arbitrary distinction. The "theoretical Hermetica present a theory of salvation through knowledge or *gnosis*, yet this theory was the product of a culture that made no clear, rigid distinction between religion as the province of such lofty concerns as the fate of the soul and magic as a merely instrumental device of humbler intent."[45] Indeed a common Hermetic attitude is expressed in the philosophical treatise *Kore Kosmou* that says "no prophet about to raise his hands to the gods has ever ignored any of the things that are, so that philosophy and magic may nourish the soul and medicine heal the body."[46] Thus all knowledge is part of the Hermetic spiritual quest for gnosis.[47] It may be that the Hermetic texts that have come down to us in the philosophical *Corpus* were all that remained after the more magical texts were purged from the Hermetic collection, perhaps during its

---

45 Copenhaver, *op. cit.*, p. xxxvii.
46 *Ibid.*, p. xxxviii.
47 *Ibid.*, p. xxxviii.

stay in Christian Byzantium.[48]

But before we go further, it must be said that there was and is no unified Hermetic doctrine. The surviving texts are contradictory. Some express a positive attitude toward the manifest world; some find it a trap for the soul. Some are positive about ritual; some contend prayer as the only appropriate way to approach the Divine. Nor was there a single Hermetic school. More than likely, the earliest Hermetics were small groups of seekers, perhaps under the guidance of a teacher, loosely organized in much the same manner that many spiritual groups are today. Furthermore, the *Hermetica*, technical and theoretical, bear the marks of the diverse cultures that blended under the Light of the Pharos lighthouse of Alexandria, Hermeticism's most fertile home.

Yet the *Hermetica* have an Egyptian core and there are some unifying themes in the texts. One of these is that human beings are of a dual nature, both human and Divine. They share in Divinity through the "rational part of the soul" that "stands unmastered by the demons, suitable as a receptacle for god."[49] The treatise called *Asclepius* notes that "mankind is the only living thing that is twofold: one part of him is simple, what the Greeks call *ousiodes*, [and] what we call a form of divine likeness..." while the other part is the body that houses the spark of Divine mind. Later in the text, Trismegistos states that God "shapes mankind from the nature of soul and body, from the eternal and the mortal..."[50]

Human beings share in the Divine nature, they are god-like—and can become more so through Hermetic knowledge. The first treatise of the *Corpus Hermeticum* has the Divine instructor of Hermes Trismegistos, Poimandres, tell him that human beings are created in the Creator's image, and God, being in love with His/Her (Trismegistos clearly states in the *Asclepius* that God is of both sexes) own image gave human beings the god-like ability to create as well. When human beings die and shed the material body, "they rise up to the father in order and surrender themselves to the powers, and having become powers, they enter into god. This is the final good for those who have received knowledge: to be made god."[51] This is

---
48 *Ibid.*, p. xli.
49 *Corpus Hermeticum XVI* (trans. Copenhaver, *op. cit.*, p. 60).
50 *Asclepius*, 7-8 (*ibid.*, p. 70).
51 *Corpus Hermeticum I* (*ibid.*, p. 6).

a human birthright, for "the human is a godlike living thing, not comparable to the other living things of the earth, but to those in heaven above, who are called gods."[52] Probably because of our kinship with the Divine, human beings wish to know the Divine—just as the Divine wishes to be known. To assist human beings in their search for knowledge, the Divine bestows some of Its own power on Hermetic initiates.[53]

Sprung from the Egyptian soil, Hermetic philosophy is clearly descended from ancient Egyptian concepts. Both see human beings as sharing in Divinity. Both understand the possibility that human beings, with the proper knowledge, can become god-like. Both consider "divinization" a process of evolution, of "becoming." The ancient Egyptian passed through the underworld by her knowledge of the proper names and words, undergoing various transformations until she became a god. The knowledgeable Hermetist surrendered to the Powers, became a Power, then entered into God. In both philosophies, the seeking human being can unite with the Divine.

If the themes were Egyptian, it is reasonable to assume that the methods of gaining the knowledge required to claim one's Divine birthright might also ultimately derive from traditional Egyptian methods—such as the Assumption of God/dessform. We have already seen how the Assumption of God/dessform was used in the magical papyri, which as works of Thoth are by definition *Hermetica*. Scholars of the *Hermetica* have specifically noted Hermetic use of the Assumption of Godform—even using that specific term and without knowledge of it as a living magical technique. Garth Fowden, Research Director of Athens' Historical Research Foundation, writes in *The Egyptian Hermes*, that the Hermetic initiation does not bring external knowledge of one being about another but "an actual assumption by the initiate of the attributes of God: in short, divinization. The way of Hermes is the way of immortality and its end is reached when the purified soul is absorbed into God, so that the reborn man, although still a composite of body and soul, can himself fairly be called a god."[54]

Hermes Trismegistos puts it this way:

---

52 *Corpus Hermeticum X* (*ibid.*, p. 36).
53 Fowden, *op. cit.*, p 104.
54 *Ibid.*, pp.110-111.

THE ASSUMPTION OF GODFORMS

> Thus, unless you can make yourself equal to god, you cannot understand god; like is understood by like. Make yourself grow to immeasurable immensity, outleap all body, outstrip all time, become eternity and you will understand god. Having conceived that nothing is impossible to you, consider yourself immortal and able to understand everything, all art, all learning, the temper of every living thing. Go higher than every height and lower than every depth. Collect in yourself all the sensations of what has been made, of fire and water, dry and wet; be everywhere at once, on land, in the sea, in heaven; be not yet born, be in the womb, be young, old, dead, beyond death. And when you have understood all these at once—times, places, things, qualities, quantities—then you can understand god.[55]

In another treatise, Trismegistos tells His students that God's image is in all things and God may be experienced in all things. In the text quoted above, He says one must actually become all things in order to know God. The only way this can be accomplished is through the imagination for Trismegistos advises, "coming to be is nothing but imagination."[56] Through the creative imagination (that is, visualization) one can experience the Divine in all Its forms. This lengthy task must be done by assuming Godforms—the many and varied forms of the Divine that are all around us. Human beings can do this by virtue of their own many-formed nature:

> The form of humankind is multiform and various: coming down from association with the [higher form] just described, it makes many conjunctions with all other forms and, of necessity, makes them with almost everything. Hence who has joined himself to the gods in divine reverence, using the mind that joins him to the gods, almost attains divinity.[57]

Human beings are encouraged to use their own multiform nature in

---
55 *Corpus Hermeticum XI* (trans. Copenhaver, *op. cit.*, p. 41).
56 *Corpus Hermeticum V* (*ibid.*, p. 18).
57 *Asclepius 5* (*ibid.*, p. 69).

order to experience and understand the multiform nature of God. By being all things, we come full circle, finally participating in our Divine heritage.

The Theurgic Union

Disapprovingly, Archbishop Cyril of Alexandria (5th century CE) calls Hermes Trismegistos a theurgist.[58] Theurgy is a term that came into use during the 2nd century CE for what is now sometimes called High Magic, ritual magic for spiritual development rather than for material ends. Theurgy is religious magic and literally means God-Working or Divine Working. By their name, theurgists differentiated themselves from *theologoi* in that theologians *talk* about the Divine while theurgists *work* with the Divine. Theurgists act—they do ritual—and one of their primary methods is the Assumption of God/dessform.

The development of theurgy was influenced not only by Hermetism, but by the spiritual system expressed in the *Chaldean Oracles* and by Neoplatonism. Key members of the Neoplatonic school—some of whom considered themselves theurgists—interpreted both the *Hermetica* and the *Oracles* along Platonic lines.

A father-and-son team of mages, the father, Julianus the Chaldean, and the son, Julianus the Theurgist, who lived in the latter part of the 2nd century CE, probably coined the term "theurgy." The two Juliani are most well known as authors of the *Chaldean Oracles*. The *Oracles* are extensive revelations of the Deities received through the theurgic workings of the two magi. The *Oracles* offer a cosmology and a course of purification, spiritual development, and salvation of the soul. All we have left today of the numerous books of the *Oracles* are bits and pieces quoted within the writings of the Neoplatonists. Another important book by Julianus the younger, entitled *Theurgy*, has (sorrowfully) not survived.

Three main operations are key to theurgy: *autopsia*, or evocation; *telestika*, the ritual consecration and animation of sacred images of the Deities; and *systasis*, or conjunction—the Assumption of God/dessform in which the human being becomes a *docheus* or vessel for a Deity. All operations are performed for the purpose of receiving information from the Divine, increasing *gnosis*, and elevating the

---

58 Copenhaver, *op. cit.*, xlii.

THE ASSUMPTION OF GODFORMS

soul of the theurgist to the Divine in a mystical union that will so purify it during life that after death it may be released from Fate and return directly to its home in the Divine.

This theurgical elevation is ultimately in the hands of the Deities but requires human spiritual, intellectual, and moral preparation—in addition to the sacred ritual.[59] According to Iamblichus, true theurgists were "without vice or unmindful passion." Instead, they were filled "with divine fire and truth." They were immune to evil spirits and were modest, non-violent, and non-thrillseeking. Theurgists were sacred magicians, true priests and priestesses.

Each of the theurgic operations mentioned above can be loosely considered God/dessform work in that each deals in some way with the image of the Deity and the invocation or evocation of the energy of the Deity to or through that image. Proclus (412-485 CE), head of the Athenian Neoplatonic school, echoes this breadth of theurgic concern when he describes theurgy as "a power higher than all human wisdom, embracing the blessings of divination, the purifying powers of initiation, and in a word all the operations of divine possession."[60] In this discussion, however, we are most concerned with *systasis* or the Theurgic Union. I will use the terms Theurgic Union and Assumption of God/dessform interchangeably.

The most extensive commentary left to us on this type of theurgy is in a text known today as *On the Mysteries of the Egyptians, Chaldeans, and Assyrians*. It was attributed by Proclus to Iamblichus, a highly influential Syrian Neoplatonist living in Egypt around 300 CE. Iamblichus is said to have studied under Porphyry, himself a student of Plotinus, the founder of the first Neoplatonic school. Iamblichus eventually founded the Syrian Neoplatonic school and gathered a large number of students during his lifetime. Soon after his death, he gained his most famous devotee, the Roman Emperor Flavius Claudius Julianus, whom the Christians called Julian the Apostate because he rejected his Christian upbringing to return to Pagan religion and philosophy. Julianus declared himself "greedy for Iamblichus in philosophy."[61]

---

59 Sarah Iles Johnston, *The Development of Hekate's Archaic and Classical Roles in the Chaldean Oracles and Related Mystic Literature*, thesis presented to Cornell University faculty (Ann Arbor: Dissertation Information Service, 1987), p. 139.
60 Proclus, *Theologia Platonica*, quoted in E. R. Dodds, *The Greeks and the Irrational* (Berkley, Los Angeles, London: University of California Press, 1951), p. 291.
61 Julian, Epistle 12, cited in Dodds, *ibid.*, p. 288.

THE LIGHT EXTENDED

There is a question as to whether or not Iamblichus was indeed the author of *On the Mysteries* for the text was written under the pseudonym of the Egyptian priest Abammon (Heart of Amun) in answer to a letter full of theosophical questions from Porphyry and addressed to another Egyptian priest, Anebo. Supposedly Abammon, Anebo's superior, decides that the questions are important enough to be addressed by himself. We don't know what the actual story is on the writing of this text, but if it was a communication between Porphyry and Iamblichus, it would seem to be a construct so that Iamblichus could answer questions, perhaps those of some of his own students.

On the Mysteries is a theurgy-positive work and addresses the Assumption of God/dessforms:

> In all of theurgy, the magician maintains a dual aspect: one as a human, which keeps our natural place in the Universe; the other is supported by divine signs because it is connected with the Higher Powers; under their direction it moves harmoniously, and is indeed able to assume the Form of the Gods. In accordance with this distinction, the magician naturally invokes as Higher Beings the Powers of the Universe, since he who invokes them is human; yet he also commands these Powers, since by his arcane formula he has assumed the sacred Form of the Gods.[62]

As we have seen, a key reason why human beings can even attempt anything like the Assumption of God/dessform is that there is an underlying harmony between human and Divine beings. Abammon/Iamblichus reiterates this essential Egyptian concept when he says that the human soul is joined to the Deities by knowledge of an "eternal identity." This, he says, cannot be known by the mere intellectual effort of conjecture or opinion or syllogism but only through a noetic perception that the soul has been continually receiving from the Gods and Goddesses throughout eternity and which unites us with Them. Knowing the Deities is unlike any normal way of knowing; it is an experience of *gnosis*—deep, inner Knowing.

Iamblichus explains that we can distinguish the higher "essences"

---

[62] Iamblichus, *On the Mysteries*, 4.2, translated by Adam P. Forrest.

THE ASSUMPTION OF GODFORMS

from the lower, the Divine from the human, by their varying energies. So that while the lower orders of beings could be said to vibrate at a lower frequency than the Divine essences, they are nevertheless connected with the higher Divine energies and that this Divine energy is implanted within all human souls. This offers a construct for how human beings can be elevated to Divine levels. By raising our own energies through spiritual, mental, and moral preparation, through correct theurgic ritual, and by receiving the Divine grace of benevolent Deities, we can follow the Ariadne's thread implanted in us since birth and find our way home into the presence of the Goddesses and Gods.

Yet our achievement of the Theurgic Union, Iamblichus insists, is due to the foundation of Divine Love and Goodness that supports the process. The Deities do not respond to theurgic invocation because They are in any way forced to, but because of Their great benevolence. They

> unstintingly shed their light upon theurgists, summoning up their souls to themselves and orchestrating their union with them, and accustoming them, even while still in the body, to detach themselves from their bodies, and to turn themselves towards their eternal and intelligible first principle.[63]

The Form of the Gods: Divine Images

The essential harmony that exists between the human and the Divine also extends throughout the Universe because it is as if the universe is "a single living being"[64] and though the parts of it are in separate places, it is all of one nature and the various parts are irresistibly drawn to each other. In this, Iamblichus is expressing the well-known Theory of Correspondences or Universal Sympathies with which modern magic users are familiar. Colors, plants, minerals, astrological phenomena, certain words, names, and more are said to correspond to each other by virtue of a similar nature. Iamblichus explains that the base cause of the attraction is Good and the principle of Love. By their Magical Art, theurgists could increase this

---

63 *On the Mysteries*, 1.12, *op.cit.*, trans. Clarke, Dillon, Hershel, pp. 51-52.
64 *Ibid.*, 3.16, p. 159.

spontaneous attraction by employing these divine signs and symbola of the Deities they invoked.

Proper use of correspondences can turn objects into fit receptacles for the energy of the Goddesses and Gods. For example, a copper statue is appropriate for Aphrodite because of the essential harmony between the Goddess, the Goddess' planet Venus, and the metal copper. Iamblichus states that the Egyptians believe that the Deities rejoice in images that resemble Them and wish to fill them with Good. Correspondences could also be employed by a theurgist who wished to Assume a God/dessform. In addition to spiritual preparation, the theurgist might employ the appropriate Divine signs within the working chamber and wear the appropriate symbola, making herself into a fit *docheus* (receptacle or vessel) for the Deity.

Yet the physical symbols and images of the Deities are not Their only images. They also have astral manifestations are "in accordance with their true natures, their potentialities and activities. For as they are, so do they appear to those invoking them; they display their activities and manifest forms in agreement with themselves and their own characteristic signs."[65] The theurgist must be able to recognize Divine beings by the quality of Their energy and appearances, as well as by Their symbola. Iamblichus states flatly that unless the theurgist can see these sorts of visions, he cannot truly know what he is doing on a theurgic level. Thus it is vital for the theurgist to develop his astral vision or psychic abilities.

Iamblichus offers a detailed description of the luminous appearances of Divine Beings for guidance. The energy of the Deities, he says, is uniform. Daimonic energy is changing; angels are simpler than daimons. Archangels are similar to Gods; archon energy varies depending on what they preside over. The Light of the Gods is brighter than light; that of the archangels is a supernatural light. Daimon light is like smoldering fire, angelic light is just described as bright. The light of the Gods appears enormous; archangels are accompanied by a light that precedes them and the world shakes; angelic light is less dramatic than archangelic. Overall, the higher the level of the Being, the clearer the image. Yet the quality of the light is more substantial with lower-level Beings, so that daimon light is more like physical fire than the supernatural astral light of higher Beings.

---

65 *Ibid.*, 2.3, p. 87.

THE ASSUMPTION OF GODFORMS

With knowledge of the symbola, the paradigmatic physical images, and astral appearance of the Deities, the theurgist is ready to attempt the Theurgic Union.

Divine Fire

Prayer is highly recommended to the theurgist. Iamblichus says that extended prayer nourishes the intellect and makes the soul more able to receive the communications of the Deities. It is the Divine key that opens the world of the Deities to us and accustoms us to the "brightness of divine light" and "brings to perfection the capacity of our faculties for contact with the gods, until it leads us up to the highest level of consciousness."[66] Prayer raises us up and stimulates communion, friendship, and Divine Love. It purifies us and inflames the Divine part of the soul. Through prayer we excite that which in us is Divine and encourage it to seek that which is similar to itself. Through prayer we increase our yearning for the Divine and develop our relationship with the Goddesses and Gods.

Once enflamed and purified by prayer, the theurgist can turn her attention to that part of herself that can assume the sacred Form of the Gods. In discussing the means of working employed by oracles, Iamblichus mentions the "aether-like and luminous vehicle (*augoeides ochêma*)," a body of light that surrounds the soul and, once purified, may receive the Deity. The luminous vehicle is also concerned with the reception of Divine visions "set in motion by the gods' will, [which] take possession of the imaginative power in us." It is controlled by the Deities as They please.[67] Iamblichus also speaks of the fire of the Gods filling, having dominion over, and encircling the theurgist who is possessed by the Divine. This astral fire is the sure sign of true inspiration from the Divine.

It is the luminous vehicle or astral body of the theurgist that, being shaped and moved by the Deity invoked, Assumes the God/dessform, producing or receiving a *phantasm*, an imaginative or mental image of the Deity. It is interesting to note that while the image and energy of the Deity appear to be drawn down into the aura of the theurgist, it is the soul of the theurgist that is being drawn upward to the Deities. Proclus comments, "In invocations of the

---

66 *Ibid.*, 5.26, p. 277.
67 *Ibid.*, 3.14, p. 155.

Gods, and when they are clearly seen, divinity, in a certain respect, appears to approach to us, though it is we that are extended to him [Them]."[68] Once the Theurgic Union has been made, the energy of Divine Fire shines forth from the theurgist and witnesses may even be able to see this Divine Fire, which has the luminous appearance appropriate to the particular Divine Being invoked. The theurgist

> through the power of arcane symbols, commands cosmic entities no longer as a human being or employing a human soul but, existing above them in the order of the gods, uses threats greater than are consistent with his own proper essence [. . .] [which] power he holds through his unification with the gods...[69]

Through the Theurgic Union, the soul is purified, gains a new life, and becomes more than human. Theurgists are advised to work the Theurgic Union many times, for each working further uplifts the soul and frees it for its great journey beyond to the Divine.

"It Is I Who Speak, the Lord Jesus"

Use of the Assumption of God/dessforms crossed religious lines as well as national boundaries. The technique is also found in early Christian texts, the majority of which are Coptic[70] Christian and from Egypt. It is no surprise that Egyptians were not about to give up this powerful, traditional method of connecting with the Divine just because the Deities now had different names. They merely made some adjustments.

In addition to employing new Divine names, the Copts also increased their use of a technique already familiar from ancient Pagan texts—the use of *historiola*, myth as a way to connect with the energy of the Deity. Many mortuary texts and magical formulae asked the Deities to do such-and-such on their behalf as was done

---

68 Proclus, *Alcibiades*, cited in Thomas Taylor, trans. *Iamblichus, On the Mysteries of the Egyptians, Chaldeans, and Assyrians* (San Diego: Wizards Bookshelf, Secret Doctrine Reference Series, 1984), note, p. 168.
69 Iamblichus, *On the Mysteries*, 6.6, trans. Clarke, Dillon, Hershel, p. 287.
70 Coptic is a late form of Egyptian written with Greek letters with additional letters to represent Egyptian sounds not found in Greek. It offers researchers some hints about ancient Egyptian pronunciation.

THE ASSUMPTION OF GODFORMS

for so-and-so in myth. As Isis healed Horus, so too, the magician hopes to heal the sick. This is a less-direct form of assumption and allows the magician to avoid the egotism of calling herself a Deity. At least in the Coptic communities, a negative attitude toward the Assumption of God/dessforms may have been slowly growing. Among a list of harmful things in a curse text is a Being "which went up to heaven, calling out, 'Eloi Ei Elemas. I myself am god.'" After naming this as a negative, the magician assumes a reverent posture: "As for me, then, I beg and invoke you today..."[71]

The following example of this oblique form of God/dessform assumption is for relief of childbirth pains. It tells the story of Jesus' meeting with a pregnant doe:

> [O holy] of holies, unshakable, indestructible rock! Child of the maiden, firstborn [of your father] and mother! Jesus our Lord came walking [upon] the Mount of Olives in the [midst] of his twelve apostles, and he found a doe [. . .] in pain [. . .] in labor pains. It spoke [to him in these words]: "Greetings, child of the maiden! Greetings, [firstborn of your father] and mother! You must come and help me in this time of need." He rolled his eyes and said, "You are not able to tolerate my glory, not to tolerate that of my twelve apostles. But though I flee, Michael the archangel will come to you with his [wand] in his hand and receive an offering of wine. [And he will invoke] his name down upon [it] with the name of the apostles, for 'whatever is crooked, let it be straight.' Let the baby come to light!"
>
> The will of my heart happens quickly. It is I who speak, the Lord Jesus.[72]

This formula enables the magician to partake of some of the power of the Assumption of God/dessform while only *quoting* Jesus—Who naturally speaks in the first person. A similar example is a prayer labeled as the prayer Jesus Christ uttered upon the cross and which the magician, too, now utters:

---

71 Marvin Meyer and Richard Smith, ed., *Ancient Christian Magic: Coptic Texts of Ritual Power* (HarperSanFrancisco, 1994), p. 221.
72 *Ibid.*, p. 96.

THE LIGHT EXTENDED

I am Jesus Christ. I took to myself a chalice of water in my hand and gave an invocation over it in the name of MARMAROI, the force standing before the father, the great power of BARBARAOTH, the right forearm of BARABA, the cloud of light standing before YAO SABAOTH. So I poured my chalice of water down into the sea, and it divided in the middle. I looked down and saw a unicorn lying on a golden field, that is named SAPPATHAI.

He spoke to me saying, "Who are you if thus you stand in this body or this flesh, you who have not been given into my hand?"

I spoke to him saying, "I am Israel El, the force of Yao Sabaoth, the great power of Barbaraoth."

So he hid himself from before me.[73]

Godform could also be avoided by simply asking for the powers of the Deities rather than claiming to *be* Them. "Give me the power of Yao, the strength of Abrasax, the favor of Sabaoth..."[74] This too has antecedents in the ancient Egyptian magical texts as do spells that make statements such as "It is not really I who ask you, nor other humans, but Sabaoth..."[75]

Still, there were Christians who knew powerful magic when they saw it and dared to retain the ancient forms. When Christian magicians did assume Godform, among the most popular was the Godform of Jesus. We also have examples of people assuming the form of "Seth, the Son of Adam, the first revelation of the unformed hands,"[76] and of the archangel Michael: "I am Michael; my name is god and humankind..."[77]

Here are two examples in which the God/dessform is that of the Virgin Mary:

Reach out and listen to us today, Sabaoth. For I am Mary,

---

73 *Ibid.*, p. 290.
74 *Ibid.*, p. 87.
75 *Ibid.*, p. 126.
76 *Ibid.*, p. 304.
77 *Ibid.*, p. 327.

THE ASSUMPTION OF GODFORMS

who is hidden in the appearance of Mariam. I am the mother who has given birth to the true light.[78]

I am Mary, I am Miriam, I am the mother of the life of the entire world, I am Mary. Let the stone break, let the darkness break before me. Let the earth break. Let the iron dissolve. Let the demons retreat before me. Let the [. . .] appear to me. Let the archangels and angels come and speak with me until the holy spirit clears my path. Let the doors that are shut and fastened open for me.[79]

Problems with the Assumption of Godforms

Nevertheless, after the institutionalization of Christianity throughout the Mediterranean and into the rest of Europe, the use of the Assumption of God/dessform in magic declines further. This is because, under the Christian Empire, there were at least three major problems with using the technique: the "God" problem, the "form" problem, and the magic problem.

The God problem is obvious. Since there was now supposed to be only one God (or perhaps a Trinity), all the other Gods—the Deities Whose names filled the traditional magical books—must be demons and devils. It was bad enough to speak Their names during an invocation, but it was worse still to claim to BE one of Them.

Magicians found it relatively easy to avoid these problems by using the theologically and politically acceptable Divine names. (Some papyri-type spells were secretly retained, of course, and the Deities turned into demons. We can find their rather pitiful remains in some of the Medieval grimoires.) Yet as time passed, more and more Western magicians were Christian themselves and naturally applied their own religion to their magic. To avoid claiming to be God, they could use the less-direct types of Divine contact already discussed to empower their workings.

The form problem is a little more interesting. It concerns sacred images and the question of idolatry. Two of the great radical monotheisms, Judaism and Islam, specifically forbade the making of Divine images. The God of the Jews condemned the making of graven

---
78 *Ibid.*, p. 130.
79 *Ibid.*, p. 283.

images and was not to be represented Himself. Islam, too, allowed no representation of its God. Catholic Christians found themselves in an interesting position, for while their churches and cathedrals were full of exquisitely beautiful Divine images, they still had to deal with the prohibition against idolatry—idol worship. Originally, this was directed against the use of Pagan sacred images. Because Pagans liberally employed sacred images in their worship, early Christian propagandists were able to redefine *any* Pagan worship as idol worship. By calling Pagan sacred images false gods, and claiming that Pagans worshipped the image rather than the reality behind the image, they denigrated Pagan worship. (Certainly some uneducated Pagans confused the image with the reality, just as some uneducated Christians today seem to worship their sacred book before the God Who is supposed to be its author.)

Then there was the considerable problem with magic itself. Like "idolatrous" Pagan worship, magic employs images—lots of them. Symbolic images of the Deities reveal Their attributes. Talismanic images correspond to Divine energies and retain the energy invoked into them. Astrological images fill the literature. And, as we have seen, visualized images are used in the Assumption of God/dessform. Paganism, idolatry, and magic shared the same heretical bed and were duly persecuted. However, we must remember that although the Christian Empire may have been more severe and far-reaching in dealing with magic users, they were neither the first nor only ones to prosecute it. If magic is acknowledged to exist, there is always someone sure to be accusing someone else of evil magic—and often the authorities get involved. To the powerful Christian Church, which reserved all miracles (and thus all magic) for itself, freelance magic could only be considered dealings with devils.

Given all this, it is not hard to understand why the magical technique of the Assumption of Godform fell out of use and began to be lost.

The Assumption of Godform Obscured

So magic went underground. Magicians modified their spells to become prayerful pleas *to* God rather than requiring the operator to *become* God. In a Medieval grimoire known as the *Sworn Book*

THE ASSUMPTION OF GODFORMS

of Honorius, the magician prays, "O God of all mercy, I, although unworthy—or, full of iniquity, deceit, and wickedness—[...] so too deign to hear me..."[80]

We continue to find examples of more oblique ways to contact Divine energy than the Assumption of Godform throughout the magical literature. In this one, myth is used as precedent, and identification is implied—but not stated—between the magician and God, as well as between the magician and Moses and Aaron:

> Just as God commanded the Jordan and it stood still that the children of Israel might walk across without hindrance, so do I command you to obey my precepts day and night, at all hours and moments [and be subject] to my precepts. Just as the Red Sea obeyed Moses and Aaron when it divided and presented a dry path for the children of Israel, so by invocation of Our Lord Jesus Christ I command you to obey me without delay, without harm or deception to me or any living thing...[81]

A 9th Century West Frankish exorcism employs another familiar one-step-removed spell booster; and this will sound quite familiar from ancient Egyptian precedent:

> It is not I who command you, nor my sins, O most unclean spirit, but the immaculate lamb, Jesus Christ Our Lord, the Son of God, commands you.[82]

A 15th-century exorcism retains the same type of formula:

> He commands you, accursed devil, who walked on the sea with dry feet...He commands you, accursed devil, who commanded the winds and the sea and the storms. He commands you, accursed devil, who ordered that

---

[80] Honorius of Thebes, *Sworn Book* CXXXVII in Joseph Peterson, ed. and trans., *The Sworn Book of Honorius, Liber Iuratus Honorii, by Honorius of Thebes* (Lake Worth, FL: Ibis Press, 2016), p. 287.

[81] Richard Kieckhefer, *Magic in History: Forbidden Rites, A Necromancer's Manual of the Fifteenth Century* (University Park: University of Pennsylvania Press, 1998), p. 140.

[82] *Ibid.*, p. 145.

you be cast from the heights of heaven to the depths of Earth...[83]

These exorcism formulae are likely to have been adapted from Catholic exorcisms of their time. Even today, the traditional Catholic exorcism commands the possessing devil similarly.

> Do not think of despising my command because you know me to be a great sinner. It is God Himself who commands you; the majestic Christ who commands you. God the Father commands you; God the Son commands you; God the Holy Spirit commands you...[84]

Interestingly, a 1999 Catholic newsletter of the Committee on the Liturgy informs us that the Church undertakes exorcism "united with the Holy Spirit," and that "In exorcising evil spirits, the Church acts not in her own name but in the name of Christ the Lord, to whom even the devil and the demons must be obedient in all things."[85] The Church rather than the individual priest takes on the Godform of the Holy Spirit to enable its minister to exorcise in the name of Christ. This maintains the humble attitude of the priest while the power of the connection with the Divine is reserved for the institution of the Church.

In addition to the individual magicians working during the centuries following the fall of Paganism, we can also look to the monasteries to find magicians aplenty. Monks were people involved in a spiritual search, they were educated and literate, and best of all, monasteries were often the repositories of ancient books—including books on magic that had survived the burnings. One such a person is a monk called John who was apparently enamored of ritual magic, but consumed with guilt (and perhaps well-founded fear) about his attraction. As a result, he began to have dreams of the Blessed Virgin Who offered him an alternative to the magical arts in the form of a new, more acceptable, form of magic: a course of prayers

---

83 Ibid., p. 147.
84 The Rite of Exorcism from the *Roman Ritual*, 1952. The Rite was updated October 1, 1998 to remove some of the 'medieval' sounding references to devils, replacing them with more psychologically based concepts.
85 Catholic newsletter of the Committee on the Liturgy, Vol. XXXV, Jan-Feb., 1999.

THE ASSUMPTION OF GODFORMS

and visualizations. The story of John's reception of Her teachings, between 1304 and 1307, is found in his book called *John the Monk's Book of Visions of the Blessed and Undefiled Virgin Mary Mother of God*.

The Virgin teaches John through images, not only through dream images, but also through the specific God/dessform in which She appears, for John states that the Virgin taught him "certain truths" by Her posture. Passing Her teachings on to others through his book, he notes that one should not say the particular prayer in which the posture teachings occur unless the Virgin's statue has been transformed: "this is that most holy and wonderful part of the prayer that nobody should say unless the most blessed, the Virgin Mary, has transformed her wooden or stone or other image before the one who prays."[86] It is likely that John is referring to a seeming animation of Mary's sacred image, just like the God-filled, living statues in the Hermetic *Asclepius*.

Natural Magic, New Magic

In fact, the subject of animated statues would make a comeback as Europe undertook its cultural rebirth, the Renaissance. This is because many ancient Pagan texts, including the *Hermetica* with the *Asclepius* in which such living images were discussed, were rediscovered at that time—and went on to inspire Renaissance art, science, and spirituality. Writings of the Platonists, Neoplatonists, and Hermetics, as well as Arabic magical, alchemical, and astrological texts were particularly influential. Sacred magic too was rediscovered and reborn in a lighter, brighter form. It emerged from the Medieval broom closet under the guiding hands of two Italians, Marsilio Ficino and Pico Della Mirandola.

Ficino was a physician and a priest who wished to help students adversely affected by the "melancholy Saturnine influences of their studies" by applying Solar correspondences, from sunlight and flowers to music and the hymns of Orpheus. He eventually developed a whole system of Natural Magic based on rediscovered and newly translated Pagan works. Ficino's Natural Magic makes

---

86 Claire Fanger, *Magic in History: Conjuring Spirits, Texts and Traditions of Medieval Ritual Magic* (University Park, Pennsylvania: University of Pennsylvania Press, 1998), p. 172.

great use of sacred images to draw celestial energies into talismans, but that's about as close as he gets to any kind of Assumption of God/dessform. Magical texts, such as the 12th-century Arabic text, the *Picatrix*, which records information from earlier Hermetic works, offered Ficino information on the "true forms" of the Gods that should be employed in such talismanic work. Jupiter, for example, is described as a man sitting on an eagle with eagles beneath his feet, and is to be inscribed on a talisman to draw beneficent Jovial influences. Ficino uses images such as these extensively, but gingerly, noting in the introduction of one book that if the reader does not approve of such astronomical images, they may be omitted.[87] He also cautiously opines that it is the natural materials from which the talismans are made, not the images, which make them effective. Ficino is struggling with the form problem, trying hard to balance it with the image-filled Hermeticism he finds so appealing.

Ficino's younger contemporary, Pico Della Mirandola, eagerly accepted Ficino's Natural Magic, but added Qabbalah to the mix, bringing the invocation of higher powers—the powers of God Himself—to magic. His was a blend of Hermeticism and Christian Qabbalah, which called on the names of God, archangels, and angels as well as the "natural gods," that is, the Pagan Deities that were attached to astrological principles. He too used images and sacred names, and agreed with Hermes Trismegistos that the dual nature of human beings enables them to "sculpt thyself into whatever shape thou dost prefer" and to "grow upward from thy soul's reason into the higher natures that are divine."[88] From the Qabalistic side, he says that "the more secret Hebrew theology at one time reshapes holy Enoch into an angel of divinity [...] and at other times reshapes other men into other divinities."[89] Della Mirandola never precisely says whether he does magic that involves the Assumption of Godforms. Yet in his *Oration on the Dignity of Man*, in which he reiterates the Hermetic/Egyptian concept of the Divine nature of humankind, we can perhaps find hints:

---

[87] Francis A. Yates, *Giordano Bruno and the Hermetic Tradition* (Chicago: Routledge and Kegan Paul, The University of Chicago Press, 1964), p. 62.
[88] Pico Della Mirandola, *On the Dignity of Man*, in Charles Glenn Wallis, trans., *Pico Della Mirandola, On the Dignity of Man and Other Works* (New York: Macmillan Publishing Company; London: Collier Macmillan Publishers, 1985), p. 5.
[89] *Ibid.*, p. 6.

THE ASSUMPTION OF GODFORMS

> And if it is right to make public, even enigmatically, something of more hidden mysteries . . . let us call Raphael, the heavenly physician that he may free us by morals and dialectic, as by saving medicines. When we are restored to good health, Gabriel, the strength of God will now dwell in us. Leading us through the wonders of nature and pointing out the power of God everywhere, he will finally hand us over to the high priest Michael, who will distinguish the veterans in the service to philosophy with the priesthood of theology as with a crown of precious stones.[90]

Francis Yates, author of a fascinating study on the Hermetic Tradition in the Renaissance asks, "did Raphael, Gabriel, and Michael come to dwell with Pico Della Mirandola?"[91] And we may wonder, if They did, did They dwell with Pico through his Assumption of Godform? Unfortunately, we simply cannot know.

Qabbalah & the Godform

Though Pico is credited with introducing Qabbalah to the magical mix, in truth, Hebrew mysticism and magic had been mixing with gentile mysticism and magic for a very long time. The Greco-Egyptian magical papyri contain numerous formulae with Hebrew Godnames; one of the most-often-invoked Deities in the papyri is IAO, the Greek rendering of the Hebrew Yahweh.

Qabbalah *per se* began as a Jewish religious movement of the Middle Ages and reached its popular height in the 16th and 17th centuries. Legend has it that *Qabbalah*, or The Reception, was knowledge Adam received from God Himself. Torah, Talmud, Midrash, Merkabah mysticism, Hellenistic philosophy, Neoplatonism, and more are all part of the Qabalistic current. Since a study of sacred images in Qabbalah would take a whole book unto itself, several interesting examples will have to suffice for now.

A 1509 publication of earlier 13th or 14th century texts called *Shushan Sodoth* ("The Flower of Secrets") discusses prophecy as an encounter of the human being with an astral image of himself that

---
90 *Ibid.*, p. 17.
91 Yates, *op. cit.*, p. 103.

"resembles its Former," that is, God.

> The deeply learned Rabbi Nathan, of blessed memory, said to me: Know that the complete secret of prophecy to a prophet consists in that he suddenly sees the form of his self standing before him, and he forgets his own self and ignores it. . .and that form speaks to him and tells him the future. And concerning this our sages said, "Great is the power of the prophets, who make the form [appearing to them] to resemble its Former."[92]

This astral form of the prophet can also be conceived of as a personal angel in whose form the Qabbalist wraps himself. Rabbi Isaac ha-Cohen of Soria, writing in the 13th century, says:

> In the prophet and the seer, all kinds of [physical and spiritual] potencies become weakened and change from form to form, until he enwraps himself in the potency of the form that appears to him, and then his potency is changed into the form of an angel. And this form, which is changed within him, gives him the power to absorb the prophetic potency [which is an influx from above], and [this angelic form] is engraved in his heart in a spiritual, visual way. And when the angel has completed his mission, the prophet becomes stripped of the form of the form that has appeared to him and takes on the power of his original form; he removes one form and puts on another form.[93]

The prophet clearly assumes a Divine Angelform. He enwraps himself in it and he takes it off again, returning to his human form once the angelic mission is complete. Also note that the form is "engraved in his heart in a spiritual, visual way." The characteristics of God/dessform assumption are here, even to the use of visualized images. Eventually not only prophets but all human beings were

---

92 *Shushan Sodoth*, in Gershom Scholem, *On the Mystical Shape of the Godhead, Basic Concepts of the Kabbalah* (New York: Schocken Books, 1991 ed., originally pub. 1976), p. 253.
93 *Ibid.*, pp. 259-260.

considered to have such a personal angel by virtue of their creation in the image of God. Some Qabbalists believed that this angel could be purposefully evoked while others denied it.

Christian Mystics & the Godform

While some Qabalists were assuming an image of God as a personal angel, Christian mystics were experiencing their own unity with the Divine. Although they would attribute their perceptions to Divine grace rather than a theurgic assumption and none spoke for God in the first person, many were intentionally trying to emulate the Christ. Some employed the image of the Christos in their meditations and most experienced a vision of some kind with which they interacted or into which they were absorbed. Their experiences usually followed intense prayer and either isolation or abstention, so their work was ritualized and volitional. Especially when these mystics saw or otherwise perceived themselves as joined to God or Christ, we can say that they were indeed experiencing the Assumption of Godform. Here are just a few examples of the mystics who experienced such a connection with their God.

St. Francis of Assisi received the stigmata—actual bleeding wounds, spontaneously formed, which corresponded to the wounds of the crucified Christ—through identification with the image of a crucified angel, a seraph. Toward the end of his life, Francis went on retreat to a hermitage at Mt. Alvernia. He fasted there for weeks and contemplated Christ's sufferings. Following a night of prayer, just as the sun was rising, he had a vision of the crucified, six-winged seraph. As he watched the vision, he felt sharp stings, mingled with ecstasy, as he received the wounds in five places on his body.

The 24th of 25 children, St. Catherine of Siena, another Italian, had from an early age vowed herself to a life of asceticism and holiness. She had intense personal mystical experiences, particularly around the concept of the Precious Blood, the blood shed by the Christ during His crucifixion. Like Francis, this intensity of devotion eventually took the outward form of the stigmata. She describes receiving the stigmata like this:

> I saw the crucified Lord coming down to me in a great

THE LIGHT EXTENDED

> light [. . .] Then from the marks of His most sacred wounds I saw five blood-red rays coming down upon me, which were directed towards the hands and feet and heart of my body. Wherefore, perceiving the mystery, I straight-away exclaimed, 'Ah! Lord, my God, I beseech Thee, let not the marks appear outwardly on the body.' So great is the pain that I endure sensibly in all those five places, but especially within my heart...[94]

Catherine's intense devotion to the suffering Christ caused her to take on the form of His suffering, the Godform of the crucified Christ.

A German metaphysician who believed in the essential unity of God and the soul, Meister Eckhart distinguished between God and the Godhead. God is the "person" we can know and become unified with by virtue of the divine spark in our souls. The Godhead is the ground of Divinity behind God. To become unified with God, Eckhart believed, we must withdraw from the world, practice asceticism, detachment, silence, forget ideas and concepts, and not love anything created. Like the ancient Egyptians and Egyptian Hermetics, Eckhart believed that human beings shared in the Divine, and must seek the Divine in order to come to that place of unity. Unlike (at least some of) them, he believed that we must turn away from all earthly things, including ideas and concepts, in order that the soul may know God as Godself.

St. Teresa of Avila in Spain specifically employed the contemplation of a Godform in her mystical work. She wrote that she often contemplated the picture of Christ within her and that sometimes there would come to her "such a feeling of the presence of God as made it impossible for me to doubt that He was within me, or that I was totally engulfed in Him."[95]

To conclude this too-brief glimpse of Christian mystics, I would like to mention a visionary who actually used a term precisely equivalent to Godform, which came to her in a vision of Christ. In a book called *Enochian Walks with God*, Jane Leade (mid 1600s) writes of the visionary experiences of "the Spirit of my mind" and the Christ. In one such vision, the Christ tells her that one who has

---

94 Ursula King, *Christian Mystics, the Spiritual Heart of the Christian Tradition* (New York: Simon & Schuster Editions, 1998), p. 89.
95 *Ibid.*, p. 140.

THE ASSUMPTION OF GODFORMS

put on the "deiformation" of the Christ is heir to His energy:

> And it was replied to me, 'Yea, surely, it will so follow to be, to the soul that has put on the deiformation of Christ the Lord, such hath a good and right claim to his Person and possessions.'[96]

Christ promises that such a soul should receive from God grace, wisdom, love, and power. He instructs Jane that to accomplish this deiformation, she should turn away from the exterior world and create an empty, still space within herself into which the Holy Spirit may flow. He further tells her that this deiformation "will be the manner of my coming in this latter day, to stand upon the earth." As Christians gradually put on the form of Christ, they will share His attributes and the gifts of God His Father and "the dark corners of the earth shall become light."[97]

The Assumption of God/dessform Reborn

The Assumption of God/dessform is a true technique of Divine contact. It was communicated to the ancient Egyptians and used for both sacred and profane purposes throughout the Hellenistic and Roman worlds. Under pressure from Christianity, it was largely lost because of its connection with magic and the demands of monotheism. No longer in common use, the technique was transformed and employed in some esoteric Qabalistic circles in relation to the personal angel; and it was re-discovered by some Christian visionaries—even being specifically restated to Jane Leade as putting on the deiformation.

Yet it was not until much later, with the decipherment of the hieroglyphs and a subsequent resurgence of interest in ancient Egypt, that the Assumption of God/dessforms was fully reconnected with its ancient Egyptian roots. The magicians of the Hermetic Order of the Golden Dawn reintroduced the technique to the Adepts of the Order.

In the published higher-grade materials of the Golden Dawn,

---

96 Jane Leade, *Enochian Walks with God*, in Arthur Versluis, *TheoSophia, Hidden Dimensions of Christianity* (Hudson, NY: Lindisfarne Press, 1994), pp. 209-217.
97 *Ibid.*, p. 210.

there are frequent references to Godforms and the Assumption of Godforms. A great deal of information is given on the specific forms of the Deities that the Adepts are to use, but little instruction is given on the assumption of those forms. These teachings were, and are, largely oral. The Z Documents, which explain in detail the symbolism and formulae of the Neophyte Ritual, offer this guidance to the Hierophant in his Assumption of the Godform of Osiris:

> Thus should he act. Let him remember what particular God he represents. Exalting his mind unto the contemplation thereof, let him think of himself as a vast figure, standing or moving in the likeness of that God, colossal, his head lost in the clouds, with the light flashing round it from the head-dress of the God—his feet resting upon Earth in darkness, thunder and rolling clouds, and his form wrapped in flashes of lightning—the while vibrating the Name of the God. Thus standing, let him endeavor to hear the voice of the God whom he represents and of the God-Forms of the other officers as previously explained.
>
> Let him speak, then, not as if unto an assembly of mortals but as to an assembly of Gods. Let his voice be so directed as to roll through the Universe to the utmost confines of space. Let the Candidate represent unto him, as it were, a world whom he is beginning to lead unto the knowledge of its governing Angel.[98]

The Hierophant builds up the image of Osiris and animates it in his imagination. He lives in it, acts from it. Repeatedly, he vibrates the name of the God to energize the form, "for by Names and Images are all powers awakened and reawakened," as the Golden Dawn Neophyte Ritual opening states. Yet most important of all, he must first exalt his mind unto the contemplation of the Deity. Before endeavoring to awaken the Power by Names and Images, he must invoke the Highest. He must make a true connection with the Divine energy of that particular Deity or all else is mere imagination rather than magical, creative Imagination.

---

98 Z3 in Israel Regardie, *The Golden Dawn* (St. Paul: Llewellyn Publishers, 1937), pp. 132-3.

THE ASSUMPTION OF GODFORMS

Other magicians working at the same time as the Golden Dawn, as well as afterwards, employed the Golden Dawn's concept and use of God/dessform as the basis for their own explorations. A number of them connected God/dessforms with C. G. Jung's archetypes. Israel Regardie, who wrote much on the psychology of magic, considers the Deities to be expressions of the omnipresent Divine Life. Corresponding to Them, within the human psyche are the Jungian archetypes. Activating these archetypes within ourselves is the first step on the ladder that enables us to ascend to the Divine. The Assumption of God/dessform is a key method for doing so:

> As far as western Theurgy is concerned, centuries of effort have shown that one of the most potent adjuncts to spiritual experience, as aiding the assimilation of the lower self into the all-inclusive psyche, is the astral assumption of the magical form of a divine force or a god. By means of an exaltation of the mind and soul to its presence, whilst giving utterance to an invocation, it is conceded that there may be a descent of the Light into the heart of the devotee, accompanied *pari passu* by an ascent of the mind towards the ineffable splendor of the spirit.[99]

He also comments, like the ancient theurgists, that when the magician performs this exaltation and assumption, it is not actually the Deity that is assumed, but the magician who is assumed into the Divine. This is precisely why the Assumption of God/dessform is a valuable adjunct to spiritual growth.

In another work, Regardie comments on the famous Bornless Ritual, which Aleister Crowley adopted as his personal rite, but which derives from the Greco-Egyptian Magical Papyri and was adapted from a published translation of the text by MacGregor Mathers. Regardie writes that the purpose of the rite "is to so open the mind of the aspirant by continuous and concentrated application, that he becomes conscious of—or, if you like, possessed by—another

---

[99] Israel Regardie, *Foundations of Practical Magic, An Introduction to Qabalistic, Magical and Meditative Techniques* (Wellingborough, Northamptonshire: The Aquarian Press, 1979), p. 10.

spirit, the Holy Guardian Angel."[100] Like the magician of the Mithras Liturgy who Assumed the Godform of his Higher Self as Psychon, the ancient theurgists who invoked their personal daimon or angel, and the Qabbalists who enwrapped themselves in the form of their personal angel, so the Bornless Ritual, as it was worked by Crowley, was to enable the Assumption of the Form of the Holy Guardian Angel or Higher Self.

Dion Fortune, who trained in psychotherapy as well as magic, speaks of evoking to visible appearance "racial images" in the subconscious; that is, the archetypes—particularly those that belong to one's own culture. She explains that Deities and Archangels are cosmic powers with an astral form that has been built up by worshippers throughout the ages. The astral forms are a key component of what we know as Goddesses, Gods, and Archangels.[101] The magician builds up the form of the Deity or Angel in her imagination, but it is the part of her own psyche that corresponds to the Deity that ensouls the image while the magician's own astral body provides the basis for the manifestation.

Fortune gives an excellent description of the Assumption of the God/dessform of Isis in her novel, *Moon Magic*. Her character Vivian Le Fay Morgan uses visualization to take the magical novice Rupert Malcolm and herself into Isis' realm. Gazing into a mirror, she sees her own face in the mirror and it no longer seems to be her own:

> Then behind me, there began to be a warmth and a power. Isis was formulating. Above my head, I saw Hers. I was not longer conscious of the agony in my hands or the strain on my body. All I felt was the power flowing through me in electric heat [. . .] Over the man and myself there formed a cloud, a silvery cloud of palest moon-mist, slowly glowing to gold and growing warm as it glowed. It was the aura of Isis emanating from us, formed from our united magnetism…[102]

---

[100] Israel Regardie, *Ceremonial Magic, A Guide to the Mechanisms of Ritual* (Wellingborough, Northamptonshire: The Aquarian Press, 1980). p. 67.
[101] Dion Fortune, *Aspects of Occultism* (New York: Samuel Weiser, Inc., 1962), p. 5.
[102] Dion Fortune, *Moon Magic, Being a Memoir of a Mistress of that Art* (London: The Aquarian Press, 1956), p. 133.

THE ASSUMPTION OF GODFORMS

> There was nothing of the human left about me. I was vast as the universe; my head among the stars; my feet on the curve of the earth as it swung under me in its orbit. Around me, in translucent space, stood the stars, rank upon rank, and I was of their company. Beneath me, all Nature lay spread like a green-patterned carpet...[103]

W.E. Butler, a student of Dion Fortune's, also connects the God/dessforms with Jung's archetypes. In his explanation of the technique, he writes that the Divine manifests energy in different qualities or aspects, symbolized in Qabbalah by the different Sephiroth, and that it is living, conscious energy (like the Egyptian Heka). A God/dessform built up in the human imagination may be linked with its corresponding archetype in the greater Divine realm. It is most efficient to activate this link through images that other human beings have been building up in the astral for thousands of years. That is why contact with ancient Deities is effective. The form, already enlivened by the archetypal energy, is there waiting for us to tap into. The images not only connect with Divine energy and transmit archetypal energy, but they stimulate the corresponding archetype within the human psyche. This activation in turn stimulates a great chain of similar energies, but on different levels.[104] Of the actual Assumption of God/dessform, Butler says:

> Now the method of assuming the God-form is a certain technical method of auto-hypnosis. When by this operation a lesser change of consciousness has been effected, it is as though a self-starting mechanism has been switched on. The personality of the magician is overshadowed and flooded by the power of his deeper Self, and this is illuminated and charged through the entity who has been commemorated, and through the channel of the linked personalities the cosmic energy rushes down into the psychic and magnetic conditions of the magician. The effect of this downrush of power is to cause the buried archaic images to rise into his

---

103 *Ibid.*, p. 155.
104 W.E. Butler, *Magic, Its Ritual, Power, and Purpose* (Wellingborough, Northamptonshire: The Aquarian Press, 1975; first pub. 1952), p. 49.

temporarily exalted consciousness, and these images allow the invoked power to effect definite and far-reaching changes in the character of the initiate.[105]

Assuming the God/dessform Today

Modern practitioners who assume God/dessforms often draw on the Golden Dawn materials, Crowley, Regardie, Fortune and other such sources for their basic information, though with more widespread access to information, more people are now also turning directly to the theurgy of Iamblichus, his followers, the *Chaldean Oracles,* and the Greco-Egyptian Magical Papyri.

The Assumption of God/dessform is most commonly used so that the ritual actions one takes are informed by the energy of the Deity invoked. The Assumption of God/dessform enables the magician to tap into an energy source greater than her own psychic powers to aid in accomplishing the purpose of the working. It is a step beyond reaching out in prayer because it offers the opportunity to take an active part in creating a path—through oneself—into which the immanent Divine energy may be drawn. When properly done, the Assumption of God/dessforms puts the magician in touch with a deeper wisdom that should serve as guide in any act of magic, mundane or spiritual. It means no more, and no less, than placing the Divine part of the self in contact with a greater Divine power. The potential that this offers for spiritual development as well as for mundane magical workings is immense.

Hermetic and other ceremonial magicians commonly use the Assumption of God/dessforms for rituals of all kinds. Modern theurgists, including Hermetists, focus mainly on magic that aids the spiritual journey. In some Wiccan and Witchcraft circles, the priestess regularly embodies the Goddess by "Drawing Down the Moon," an ancient, beautiful, and romantic term for the Assumption of God/dessform. Typically, Wiccans, Witches, and Neo-Pagans will employ such Divine energy to empower rites of celebration and initiation.

Magic users differ in their definitions of God/dessforms. Some consider the God/dessform to be a purely human psychological construct. Some consider the imaginal form to reflect an archetype,

---
105 *Ibid.,* p. 55.

which in turn reflects a Divine Being or Reality. Most will consider the God/dessform to be a little of both—a sacred and enlivened image to which both humanity and Divinity contribute.

To be a God/dessform, I believe that a sacred image must have a true connection with Divine Reality. It is not *only* a human construct, although humanity adds greatly to it. A God/dessform is an image that interprets the Divine energy of that particular Being or aspect of the Divine to the human being. Normally, it would be an image that has some history behind it, an image that has been invested with human magico-spiritual, mental, and emotional energy for hundreds, even thousands, of years. To continue using Jungian terms, it is an image recorded in the Collective Unconscious. By assuming the form, we make it conscious rather than unconscious. Like the sacred statues of the *Asclepius*, these images are alive by virtue of the energy, Divine and human, invested in them. The invocation of a Deity by the Assumption of God/dessform becomes a great, sacred cycle of inflowing and outflowing energy, from human to Divine, Divine to human.

As far as practical techniques for actually assuming the God/dessform, Golden Dawn and Golden Dawn-heritage sources generally serve to supply the most information for modern magicians. These texts speak of "exalting the mind" by aspiration unto the Divine, building up the image of the Deity in the imagination, enlivening the form of the Deity by invocation, including vibrating or chanting the name of the Deity, expanding your human consciousness to fill the image of the Deity, and then using the highest part of your human perception to identify with the consciousness of the Deity, as translated to you through the God/dessform. If the assumption has been successful, a psychically sensitive person should be able to see or sense the God/dessform around the ritualist on the astral and to perceive the quality of the energy.

Putting on the Cloak of the Great Lady

Like the ancient Egyptian who put on the cloak of the Great Lady and became the Great Lady Hathor, a modern Adept can put on the God/dessform of Hathor and become Goddess-like. If she succeeds in doing this, she will certainly know it—for the feeling is very unlike any normal state of consciousness. She may feel as if her body, soul, mind, and spirit are tapped into a stream of energy coming from outside herself, a stream that extends beyond the physical and touches invisible realms. She may perceive herself as enormous, towering over the earth or suspended in space. She may have a feeling of expansion in the heart or little rushes or spasms of energy throughout her body similar to the *kriyas* that occur in some forms of yoga. She will, without doubt, feel the golden, shimmering presence of Hathor the Beautiful and may participate in the ecstatic passions that are a part of that Goddess' nature. Through the image of Hathor—perhaps seen as the image of the Adept's Higher Self wearing the turquoise dress and horned headdress of the Goddess— she will be able to use some of the power of the Goddess Herself to initiate, empower a rite, charge a talisman, or commune with the Divine.

She will also discover that true Divine contact, though very powerful, is humbling and does not idly flatter the ego. She may come to believe, as did the theurgists and Hermetists of old, that the Divine Ones participate in our assumption of Their Forms not merely because of Their harmony with the images, symbols, and names employed by the magician, but because of Their goodness and Divine love for us. She will see that when we expend our effort to reach out the Them, They will in turn stretch out Their hands to us, guiding us, assisting us in our magic, and most importantly, helping us grow spiritually.

An Assumption of the Godform of Amun

If you would like to see for yourself what the Assumption of Godform might be like, you are invited to try this theurgic assumption of the Egyptian Godform of Amun. Although experienced ritualists will certainly have no trouble with this Working, beginners may find that they need a little more practice. Nonetheless, contact with Amun— whether you achieve the full assumption or not—is always beneficial.

THE ASSUMPTION OF GODFORMS

BECOMING AMUN
A THEURGIC ASSUMPTION OF THE GODFORM OF AMUN, LORD OF GODFORMS

Introduction to the Rite: Amun is one of the Primordial Deities of Egypt. As Amun-Re, He came to be considered the King of the Gods and was compared by the Greeks to Zeus. His oracular shrine in the Siwa Oasis of Libya was as famous in the ancient world as the Greek oracular shrine of Delphi. Amun is a very mysterious God, for His name means the Concealed or Hidden One. He is a Creator, a Wise King, a Mighty Magician, a God of Fertility, and a Protector of the Weak. Among His epithets are He Who Abides in All Things, The Soul of All Things, Maker of Ma'et (Ma'at), Lord of Life, Eternal One, The Beautiful Power, The Beloved Child, Eldest Born of the Dew, Untiring Watcher, Lord of Intelligence, Lord of Repeating Life, He Who Listens, and Lord of Joy of Heart. Amun is said to protect the eyes, and so He may also be considered the God of Vision and Visions.

Perhaps most important to us for this rite is the fact that Amun is known as the Lord of Transformations, the Form of Many Forms, and the God Who Created the Divine Transformations. *Kheperu*, the Egyptian word for transformations or forms (*kheper*, singular), is also an appropriate word for God/dessforms. Thus Amun can be considered the God of God/dessforms and, since He is also an oracular Deity, can teach us about the art of assuming God/dessforms. Many-named and many-formed, Amun's truest nature is concealed beyond all these names and forms.

His sacred animals are the ram, the goose, and the lion. He is called the Lord of the Two Horns and the Fierce, Red-Eyed Lion. He is sometimes associated with the wind or breeze because He, like the wind, is unseen, but not unfelt. When Amun is represented, He is usually shown in human form enthroned like a pharaoh, although He may sometimes be shown with a ram's head and human body. He often has blue, lapis-lazuli skin and wears a high, double-ostrich-plumed crown with sun disk. Each plume has seven countercharged divisions and thus Amun's sacred number is seven, a number associated by the Egyptians with plurality, wholeness, and universality. The countercharged divisions also refer to Amun's balanced nature. In His hands, He holds the Ankh and the Phoenix Wand, the powers of Life and Transformation.

Many-formed and Mysterious of Form, Amun is an especially interesting subject for Godform assumption because He offers us such a great depth of possible perceptions. He is at once an unseen and unknown High God and an earthy God of Fertility; He is a Divine King and a Divine Child; He is the Soul that Abides in All Things. For readers who may be Qabbalists, Sephirotic correspondences for Amun (as we will invoke Him) are Yesod and Kether. As Lord of Kheperu, Amun is a God of the multi-formed Yesodic astral, yet He is also the Primordial One, the Maker of Everlastingness, and is hailed as "Thou Form Who Art One," the unified Deity of Kether.

So that we may assume the Godform of a Deity Who actually has a form, we will be working primarily with the Yesodic Amun of the astral realms and employing His anthropomorphic, lapis-skinned, golden-crowned image. However, we should remain conscious of the fact that He offers an ever-open conduit to the Supernal unity.

This open connection with the Supernal is another reason Amun is an appropriate choice for this working of sacred theurgic magic. For if we would lift up our souls in Theurgic Union, it would be well to invoke a God capable of uplifting us, such as the Supernal Amun. As a theurgic working, this rite involves purifications, prayers and invocations, magical correspondences—the signs and symbola—and visionary work. Beyond being an exercise in the Assumption of Godform, this rite seeks to unite our souls with the Divine, if only briefly. By this contact, we hope to gain information about the meaning and use of the technique of the Assumption of God/dessform as well as about our own souls.

Signs and Symbola of the Rite: The following are among the many correspondences that may be used in this rite. Obtain as many of them as seems good to you and wear them or place them within your temple or working area in an aesthetically pleasing manner: an image of Amun (this may be a digital image, printed out); frankincense, censer and lighter (these are required); image of a ram, goose, and/or lion, or something to represent the animal, such as ram's wool, a goose feather, or (imitation, please) lion's claw; an Egyptian eye

THE ASSUMPTION OF GODFORMS

amulet (such as the Eye of Horus) or other representation of an eye; the color purple; the color white; purple and/or white flowers; purple and/or white candles; the Moon; a mirror; the Circle; the Point; lapis lazuli—the stone itself or the stone mounted as jewelry; ostrich plumes; purple and/or white ritual robes.

Temple Arrangement: An altar should be placed in the center of the working area and a chair in the East, facing West. Place the signs and symbola about the chamber and upon the altar as you see fit.

Pre-Ritual Preparations: There is a set of elemental purifications to perform sometime before the working. You may either perform them on several days leading up to the rite or all on the day of the rite itself. As you perform each purification, ask the Supernal Amun to purify you of anything that would keep you from communion with Him as *Neb Kheperu* (Lord of Transformations). If knowledge of your own shortcomings arises in your mind during these purifications, thank Amun for this knowledge and ask to be purified of these things. (Of course, you will also need to continue work on personal improvement following the rite.) Aspire to the Supernal before each purification and perform each one slowly and deliberately. Use as much time as you desire and need.

Fire Purification: Bathe in the sunlight of Amun-Re for at least 20 minutes. Ideally, you will have your chest (and heart center) bared to the sun at this time (use sunscreen if you tend to burn).

Air Purification: Fumigate yourself with frankincense, the teardrops of Amun.

Water Purification: Charge a bowl of cold water as the "Primordial Waters of Nu" and wash with them.

Earth Purification: Abstain from meat, alcohol, and sexual relations for at least one day before the rite.

THE LIGHT EXTENDED

OPENING THE TEMPLE

Enter the temple and stand West of altar, facing East. Cross your hands on your chest and bow before Amun.

Theurgist: Great, Concealed, Hidden, and Mysterious Amun, Thou Form Who Art One, I call upon Thee and I call upon Thy Forms to aid me in this Work of Transformation.

Light the charcoal and offer frankincense upon it. Elevate the censer.

Theurgist: Neb Kheperu, I offer unto Thee this sweet frankincense, the teardrops of Thine own vision-revealing eyes.

Carry the incense to the East of the temple, then circle the temple clockwise, visualizing the smoke creating an enclosing circle about the temple.

Theurgist: (*While walking and addressing the incense*) Teardrops of Amun, you have become as the wind that He is—an invisible Power. Therefore, go forth and invisibly encircle this Temple of Amun, the Invisible God, the Hidden One. (*Addressing the God*) O Amun, Maker of Ma'et, make this temple fit for Thy indwelling. (*Chanting thrice*) Amun, Maker of Ma'et, make this temple Right.

Complete the circuit, then return the censer to its place and stand West of altar, facing East.

INVOCATION OF AMUN

If you have candles upon the altar, light them now. Stand for a few moments looking upward with closed eyes, aspiring to Amun. Kindle within your breast the desire to see and know the Hidden God. Only when this desire is truly felt should you continue.

THE ASSUMPTION OF GODFORMS

Theurgist: O Soul of All Things, Who Abides in All Things, Amun Neb Kheperu, I invoke Thee, Thou Hidden One, Holy Form—Beloved, Terrible, and Mighty in His Arising. Thou art the Sacred Soul Who Came into Being in the Beginning, the Eternal One—Hidden of Aspect, Mysterious of Form. I invoke Thee as the Form Who is One. I invoke Thee as the Supernal God, Mysterious, Wise, and Benevolent. Arise now in this Thy temple and come at the prayers of this Thy theurgist. (*Vibrating thrice*) AMUN!

As Thou art the One Who Listens, hear now my voice. As Thou art the One Who Protects the Deities with His Shadow, protect me in my Transformation. As Thou art the One Who Comes at the Voice of the People, come now to this human being. O Amun, Lord of Life, send down a ray of Thy Self into the World of Formation, into the astral realms, the place of the astral images. Let me see Thy Form. O Thou Who didst create the Earth and Sky by the thoughts of Thy Mind, create now a Form that I may see—that I may *Become*.

Begin to visualize the Form of Amun upon the throne in the East. See Amun as an enormous and beautiful God, seated majestically upon His throne. He wears the double-plumed crown and has blue, lapis-lazuli skin. His eyes are dark; one cannot make out their color, but they flash reddish gold. The roaring of deep-chested lions sounds about Him and a huge, dark-maned lion sits beside His throne. Between its paws, a magnificent goose is settled, unharmed. On the other side of Amun's throne, a ram with spiraling horns stands guard. Let yourself be aware of the scent of the beasts, clean and strong. Hear their cries and the sound of wind rushing, and feel the invisible air move with power.

Theurgist: Millions of years have passed over the World, O Amun, and I cannot know the years that Thou hast seen. Beautiful God, Beautiful Power, Beautiful Face Who Comest from the Divine Land, I honor Thee. Thy beauties take possession of me and carry away my heart and the hearts of all humankind.

THE LIGHT EXTENDED

Let yourself become aware of the center of energy above your head (Kether). Whisper the name of "Amun" into that center. Let yourself become aware of the energy center beneath your feet (Malkuth). Speak forcefully the name of "Amun" into that center. Then let yourself become aware of the center of energy at your heart.

Theurgist: O Amun, Lord of Joy of the Heart, I open my heart unto Thee! (*Vibrating seven times*) AMUN! (*and visualizing a "door" in your heart opening wide*).

Approach the East and the image of Amun enthroned. Once more bow to Amun and see the image arise from the throne as you do so.

Theurgist: Hail, Amun! Let me make supplication unto Thee for I know Thy name and Thy Transformations are in my mouth and Thy Form is before my eyes. Come, I ask Thee to place Thine heir and Thine image—which I am—into the Everlasting with Thee. O Amun, O Amun, O God, O Amun, I adore Thy name, grant this to me that I may better understand Thee.

Assuming the Godform

Note: If you can memorize the following brief invocation and the speeches of Amun, so much the better.

Turn to face the West with Amun behind you. Be aware again of the energy centers above, below, and in the heart—and of the corresponding centers in the Godform of Amun.

Theurgist: Amun, Thou Who Openeth the Way in Heaven and on Earth, I ask Thee: lift up my soul now in Theurgic Union with Thee; likewise, descend unto me, let me take Thy Form and, O Lord of Knowledge, give answer to what shall be asked. O Form of Many Forms, O God Who Created the Divine Transformations, I assume Thy Godform...

THE ASSUMPTION OF GODFORMS

Take one step backward into the larger Godform of Amun. Become aware of the transparent, shining image of the God on all sides of you, much larger than yourself. Reaffirm the visualization of the energy centers and see them glowing like white suns. With the next vibration, imagine yourself growing in size until you are the size of the Godform and can match your energy centers with those of the God.

Theurgist: (*Vibrating strongly*) AMUN!

Visualize the face of Amun before your face; the arms of Amun upon your arms; the chest of Amun breathing as you breathe; the loins of Amun energizing yours; the legs of Amun upholding you.

Theurgist: (*Vibrating into the center above*) AMUN! (*Vibrating into the center below*) AMUN! (*Vibrating into the space before you*) AMUN! (*Vibrating into the space behind you*) AMUN! (*Vibrating into the space to the right of you*) AMUN! (*Vibrating into the space to the left of you*) AMUN! (*Vibrating into your heart*) AMUN!

Having Assumed the Godform of Amun, be seated upon the throne of Amun and explore the image as your own body: the blue skin, the Ankh and Phoenix wand in the hands, the weight of the golden crown upon the head, the animals beside the throne. Seek to understand their meanings.

Amun/Theurgist: I am Amun, Form of Many Forms, in Whose Form the Earth began to exist. I am Amun, the God of Godforms, and I shall teach you of the Holy Form.

Allow time now for meditation to learn what Amun will reveal about the Godform. To do this, the still-human part of you should silently ask the God to "teach what Thou wilt of the Holy Form." The answer comes as images arise in your God-touched mind and imagination. You may also ask if the God has a personal message for you about the needs of your own soul. When this is complete, say:

THE LIGHT EXTENDED

Amun/Theurgist: I am Amun, Form of Many Forms, in Whose Form the Earth began to exist. I am Amun, the God of Godforms. Meditate on what I have communicated to you of the Holy Form.

In vision, reverse the procedure your undertook when Assuming the Godform. Imagine your own body becoming smaller and human sized. Be aware of the now-separate energy centers. Then, slowly, rise and step forward out of the Godform of Amun. Turn to face the God as He is reseated.

Theurgist: (*Touching your heart, then extending your hand toward the God*) O Amun, Great in Majesty, Living in Ma'et, I thank Thee for this gift of Theurgic Union. Though Thy True Name and Thy True Form are unknown, hidden from the Gods and humankind, I have been touched by one of Thy Holy Forms and for this I thank Thee.

Theurgist returns to West of altar facing East.

Theurgist: Hail, Amun! From the heights of the Sky to the breadth of the Earth to the depths of the Sea, Thou art praised. Thy Light is our guide, O Amun Whose name is sweet and beloved.

    Lord of Transformations, I thank Thee in Thine astral aspect as the Form of Forms and the Soul Who Abides in All Things. I thank Thee in Thy Supernal aspect as the Holy One Who is Unknown, Hidden of Aspect, Mysterious of Form.

    Hail, Amun, and farewell. Be in peace, Amun, be in peace.

Move to the East and circle the temple counterclockwise one time.

Theurgist: (*Chanting*) Be in peace, Amun, be in peace.

Exit the temple.

About the Author

M. Isidora Forrest is the author of *Isis Magic, Cultivating a Relationship with the Goddess of 10,000 Names* and *Offering to Isis, Knowing the Goddess through Her Sacred Symbols*.

Isidora has been devoted to Isis ever since the Goddess told her, in no uncertain terms, that she was not yet ready to be Her priestess. (Isidora respects a Goddess Who doesn't coddle.) More than twenty years—and a lot of research, ritual, agony and ecstasy—later, Isidora has earned the title of Prophetess in the House of Isis.

She is also a priestess of the international Fellowship of Isis, a Hermetic adept, a maenad for Dionysos, and a founder of the Hermetic Fellowship, a religious non-profit devoted to education in the Western Esoteric Tradition.

Isidora lives and works in the not-all-all-Egypt-like climate of Portland, Oregon with her husband, Adam Forrest, a very curious black cat, and both a Temple of Isis and a grape arbor sacred to Dionysos in the backyard.

Contact Isidora at www.isiopolis.com

The Fire Tablet Ritual

Introduction

by Darcy Küntz

This Enochian Fire Tablet ritual was written by Catherine Edith Hughes. She joined the Order of the Stella Matutina on 21 March 1908 and took the Latin motto L[ux] O[rta] E[st], which means, "The Light has arisen." She rose quickly through the Grades and took her 5°=6° Grade of Adeptus Minor on 6th December 1909. She became the senior Chief of Bristol Hermes Temple and served as Chief alongside such notable members as Dion Fortune and Israel Regardie.

This Ritual is important because it explains in further detail how the Golden Dawn and Stella Matutina performed Enochian Magic. The partial paragraphs and Enochian Calls have been fleshed out to make it easier to read.

There was another version of the formula that was published by Aleister Crowley, a renegade from the Golden Dawn. It was published in the article, "A Brief Abstract of the Symbolic Representation of the Universe: Part II: The Forty-Eight Calls". (See the Opening of the 4°=7° Grade) in *The Equinox*, Vol. I, No. 8.

Special thanks to Frater Enigma and to Fratres F.A. and Y.Sh.Y for their research with this article.

The Fire Tablet Ritual

by G.H. Soror L.O.E.

THREE GREAT HOLY NAMES OF GOD:
OIP TEAA PEOCE.

KING OF THE WATCH TOWER OF FIRE:
EDLPRNAA.

THE EARTH QUARTER OF THE FIRE TABLET.

THE NAME OF SIX LETTERS FROM THE VERTICAL OF THE SEPHIROTIC CROSS:
VABXDO.

THE NAME OF FIVE LETTERS FROM THE HORIZONTAL OF THE SEPHIROTIC CROSS:
SIADA.

SPECIAL NAME FOR THE TWELFTH SERVIENT SQUARE:
ZOOX.

COMPLETION FROM BITOM OF THE TABLET OF UNION:
BZOOX.

THE LIGHT EXTENDED

Enochian Vision

SUBJECT:— THE TWELFTH SERVIANT SQUARE IN THE AIR QUARTER OF THE FIRE TABLET.

1. *(Lesser Banishing Ritual of the Pentagram.)*

2. *(Circumambulate with CUP saying:)*

So therefore first the Priest who governeth the works of Fire must sprinkle with the Lustral Water of the Loud resounding Sea.

3. *(Circumambulate with INCENSE saying:)*

And when after all the Phantoms are banished thou shalt see that Holy and Formless Fire, that Fire which darts and flashes though the hidden depths of the Universe. Hear thou the Voice of Fire,

4. *(GREATER RITUAL OF THE PENTAGRAM. INVOKING [FIRE].[1])*

5. *(Take Pyramid from the Altar and place it in the South.)*

6. *(Make an Invoking Hexagram in the South. Vibrate the Great Name of the Tablet, thus:—)*

In the Three Great Secret Names of God borne upon the Banners of the South:

OIP TEAA PDOCE.

Powers of the Tablet of Fire, awake!

In the Name of EDLPRNAA, Great King of the South, I Invoke ye, Forces of the Tablet of Fire, to awaken the Powers of the Pyramid of Fire and Earth.

---

[1] It is interesting to note that Soror L.O.E. uses the title "Greater Ritual of the Pentagram" which is a term Crowley used in *Magick in Theory and Practice* (Paris, 1929) instead of the G.D. title "Supreme Ritual of the Pentagram" The later title was used in the G.D. and Stella Matutina.—D.K.

FIRE TABLET RITUAL

7. *(Enlarge the Pyramid before you and Invoke the Angel five times.)*

Arise! Thou Great Angel of the Pyramid Z in the Earth of Fire.

In the Great Name YOD HEH VAU HEH TZABAOTH, and

In the Great Name EL CHAI SHADDAI.[2]

I Invoke Thee:—

ZOD, BZOOX, BZOOX, BZOOX, BZOOX, BZOOX.

The Sixth Key (Enochian)

Gah s diu chis em micalzA pil zin sobam El harg mir babalon: od obloc samvelg dlagar malprg ar-caosgi: od Acam canal: so bol zar f-bliard caosgi: od chis a ne tab od miam: ta viv: od d Darsar sol peth bi en: B ri ta: od zacam g mi calzo: sob ha hath trian Lu ia he: od ecron MAD Q a a on.

The Sixth Key (English)

The Spirits of the fourth angle are Nine, Mighty in the Firmament of Waters: whom the First hath planted, a torment to the wicked and a garland to the righteous: giving unto them fiery darts to vanne the earth, and 7699 continual workmen, whose courses visit with comfort the earth; and are in government and continuance as the Second and the Third—Therefore hearken unto my voice! I have talked of you, and I move you in power and presence, whose works shall be a song of honour, and the praise of your God in your Creation!]

The Seventh Key (Enochian)

Ra-asa isalamanu para-di-zoda oe-cari-mi aao iala-piregahe Qui-inu. Enai butamonu od inoasa *ni* pa-ra-diala. Casaremeji ujeare cahirelanu, od zodonace lucifatianu, caresa ta vavale-zodirenu tolhami. Soba lonudohe od nuame cahisa ta Da o Desa vo-ma-dea od pi-beliare itahila rita od miame ca-ni-quola rita! Zodacare! Zodameranu! Iecarimi Quo-a-dahe od I-mica-ol-zododa aaiome. Bajirele papenore idalugama elonusahi--od umapelifa vau-ge-ji Bijil--IAD!

---

2 Crowley uses "ELOHIM" in *The Equinox*, Vol. 1, No. 8.—D.K.

The Seventh Key (English)

The East is a house of virgins singing praises amongst the flames of first glory wherein the Lord hath opened his mouth; and they are become 28 living dwellings in whom the strength of man rejoiceth; and they are apparelled with ornaments of brightness, such as work wonders on all creatures. Whose Kingdoms and continuance are as the Third and Fourth, Strong Towers and places of comfort, the Seats of Mercy and Continuance. O you Servants of Mercy, Move! Appear! Sing praises unto the Creator; and be mighty amongst us. For to this remembrance is given power, and our strength waxeth strong in our Comforter!

The Eighth Key (Enochian)

Bazmelo i ta pi ripson oln Na za vabh ox casarmg vran Chis vgeg dsa bramig bal to ha goho i ad solamian trian ta lol cis A ba i uo nin od a zi agi er rior Ir gil chis da ds pa a ox bufd Caosgo ds chis odi puran teloah cacrg isalman loncho od Vouina carbaf Niiso Bagle auauaga gohon Niiso bagle momao siaion od mabza Iad o i as mo mar poilp Niis ZAMRAN ci a o fi caosgo od bliors od corsi ta a bra mig.

The Eighth Key (English)

The Midday, the first is as the third Heaven made of 26 Hyacinthine Pillars, in whom the Elders are become strong, which I have prepared for mine own Righteousness, saith the Lord: whose long continuance shall be as bucklers to the Stooping Dragon, and like unto the harvest of a Widow. How many are there which remain in the Glory of the Earth, which are, and shall not see Death until the House fall and the Dragon sink? Come away! for the Thunders (of increase) have spoken. Come away! for the Crowns of the Temple and the Robe of Him that is, was, and shall be, crowned, are divided! Come forth! Appear! to the terror of the Earth, and to our comfort, and to the comfort of such as are prepared.]

8. *(In the Sign of the Enterer, enter the Pyramid and sit down.)*

FIRE TABLET RITUAL

9. *(Stabilize the Pyramid in the Great Name:)*
   VABXDO.

10. *(Awaken the Sphynx in the Great Name:)*
    SIADA.

11. *(On returning, rise and make the Sign of Silence.)*

12. *(Set all Spirits free in the Name of JEHESHUA.)*

[Depart ye in peace unto your abodes and habitations. May the blessing of] JEHESHUA [be upon you. Be there ever peace between us, and you and be ye ready to come when ye are called.]

13. *(Make the Banishing Ritual of the Pentagram.)*

About the Author

Darcy Küntz is the director of the Golden Dawn Research Trust which was founded in 1998. The Research Trust is preserving the teachings, ritual, history, practices, documents, letters, and books of the Hermetic Order of the Golden Dawn (as it existed between the dates 1887–1930). We are preserving this material so that the information may be available and remain accessible to scholars now and in the future.

Some of his published works includes: *Complete Golden Dawn Cipher Manuscript* (1996); *Golden Dawn Sourcebook* (1996); *The Historic Structure of the Original Golden Dawn Temples* (1999); *The Golden Dawn American Source Book* (2000); *Sent From the Second Order* (2005); *Ancient Texts of the Golden Rosicrucians* (2008). *The Golden Dawn Legacy: The Magical Writings of Florence Farr* (2012).

The Enochian Alphabet
Golden Dawn Versus Dee Purist Letter Forms

by Frater Yechidah

I have previously argued (in *Enochian Magic in Theory* and *Enochian Magic in Practice*) that the Golden Dawn's approach to the Enochian system is less divergent from its Dee roots than it would at first appear. While it undoubtedly explored new areas, much of it had precedence in the original material, and where great differences appeared, they were more often mistakes by modern magicians than errors made by Mathers and Westcott.

Since those books were written and published, I have found numerous other examples that further prove this argument. One of these is the Enochian alphabet, which I long suspected to be more unified among the various branches.

First, let us look at the form of the Enochian alphabet given in Dee's material. There was the blocky print form, which was delivered on 6 May 1583 as part of the Appendix to Dee's *Quinti Libri Mysteriorum* (which largely contains material for the Heptarchic system).

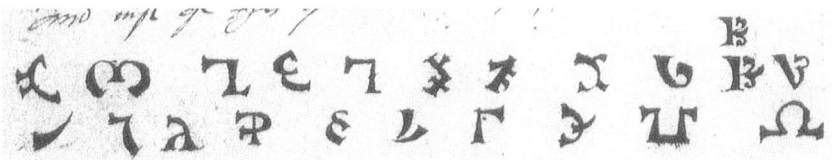

Then there was the more cursive script form, delivered earlier on 26 March 1583. This form was copied twice in quick succession, the second with the letter names, as shown overleaf from Sloane 3188.

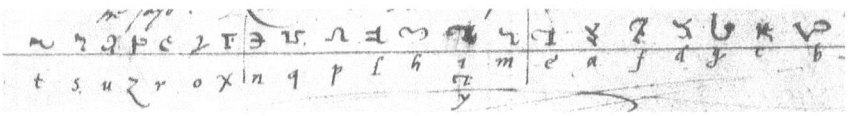

THE LIGHT EXTENDED

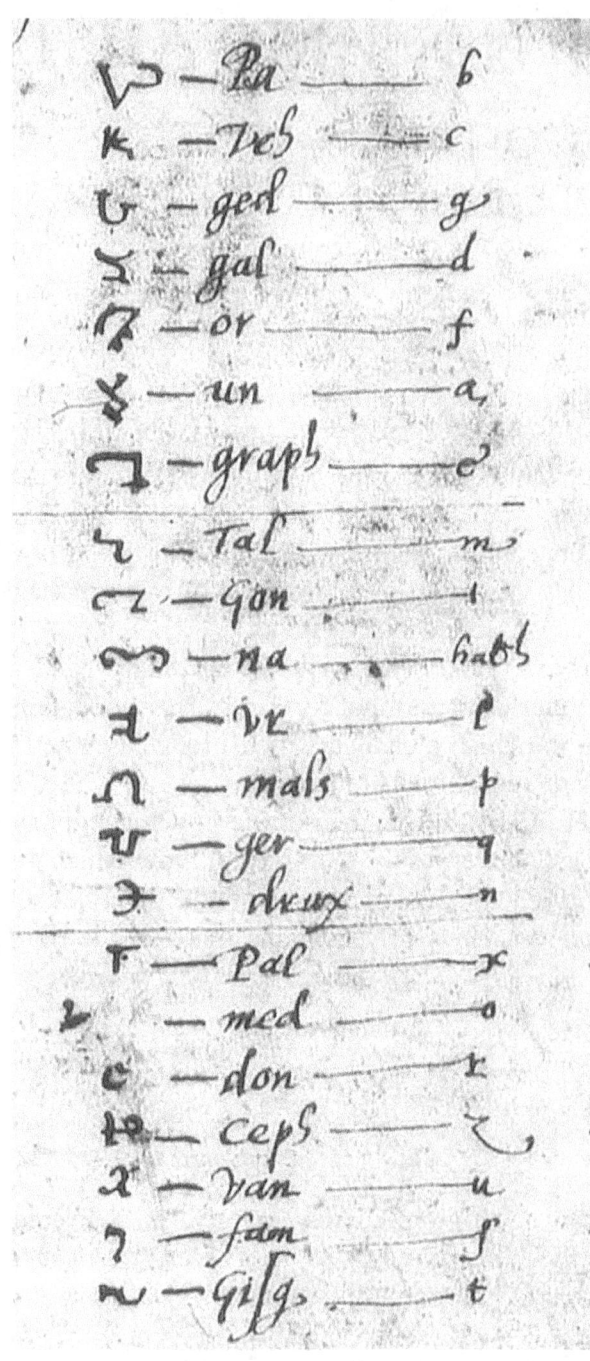

Enochian Alphabet Cursive (from Sloane 3188)

THE ENOCHIAN ALPHABET

The presence of two forms is similar to Hebrew, and, just like Hebrew, the print form is predominantly used for religious and magical purposes, while the script from is used in everyday records. For our purposes, the print form is all we need to be concerned with, as it is what we find in the various tables, on talismans, etc.

Centuries later, we add a third form, commonly called the "Golden Dawn" form, but arguably (as we shall see) the "Regardie" form, thanks to the popularisation of the Golden Dawn material—and, as a by-product, the Enochian system—from Israel Regardie's tome.

Those who have explored both variants have noticed significant differences between the Dee print form and the Golden Dawn print form, particularly with the letter *Veh*. The version found in Regardie's books shows the letter divided in two, a quite glaring error. There are additional small differences with many other letters.

There are also discrepancies with the names of the letters, most notably *Gisg*, which is rendered as *Gisa* in the Golden Dawn version. Other examples include the first letter, *Pa*, which is given as *Pe* in Regardie's work, as well as *Drux*, given as *Drun* in Regardie.

These errors have been touted as examples of the Golden Dawn's alleged poor understanding of the Enochian system, but the problem with this argument is that original manuscripts typically do not contain these mistakes. They are a product of more modern sources and magicians' dependence on published Golden Dawn material (which is often riddled with errors).

If we are to look to original sources, then we must look to Ritual X, *The Book of the Concourse of the Forces Binding Together the Powers of the Squares in the Terrestrial Quadrangles of Enoch*. This paper was supplied to members of the Zelator Adeptus Minor grade. We can find the Enochian alphabet elucidated in the first few pages, along with an Exhortation in Enochian lettering.

In R.W. Felkin's copy,[1] dated 14 October 1897, we not only find the print form to be a much closer match to the original (with *Veh* drawn in a single, connected form), but even the names of the letters better match Dee.

---

1 See *Ritual X - The Book of the Concourse of the Forces*, introduced by Tony Fuller, published by Hell Fire Books in 2017.

THE LIGHT EXTENDED

Elaborate	Cursive	Title	Power
		Pe	B
		Veh	C or K
		Ged	G
		Gal	D
		Orth	F
		Un	A
		Graph	E
		Tal	M
		Gon	I, Y, or J
		Na-hath	H
		Ur	L
		Mals	P
		Ger	Q
		Drun	N
		Pal	X
		Med	O
		Don	R
		Ceph	Z
		Vau	U or V
		Fam	S
		Gisa	T

Enochian Alphabet (from Complete Golden Dawn)

THE ENOCHIAN ALPHABET

Extract from Ritual X (R.W. Felkin, 1897)

This is identical or largely the same for many other original copies of Ritual X, including George Pollexfen's copy from 1895, as well as W.A. Ayton's and F.L. Gardner's versions from around the same year. Most of these were copied from Westcott's loan copy, made in 1893, so it is likely safe to say that Westcott had copied the alphabet accurately (or mostly so, as we shall see later).

There are, of course, some incidences where we start to see the form of the letter *Veh* drift slightly, so that it is maginally disconnected (often times with the correct, connected form given in the same manuscript). These, however, are clearly mere copying errors, likely made in haste, as evidenced in the inconsistent forms of *Veh* shown in Ayton's copy overleaf.

These kind of mistakes are similar to those made with regard to other mystical alphabets, like Hebrew and Coptic. We would, for example, distinguish between the square edge of Daleth and the rounded edge of Resh, and not permit one to be mistaken for the other. Likewise, just because the Enochian alphabet is less well-known should not mean we permit similar errors in form.

THE LIGHT EXTENDED

Enochian Mystic Characters or Sigils

Elaborate	Cursive	Title	Power	Elaborate	Cursive	Title	Power
V	VoP	Pa	B	G	z	Ur	L
B	K	Veh	C	Ω	Ω	Malo	P
U	U	Ged	G	25	25	Gon	Q
X	Y	Gal	D	)	)	Drux	N
↑	Z	Orth	F	Γ	F	Pal	X
¥	)	Un	A	L	2	Med	O
⌐	T	Graph	E	ξ	ε	Don	R
ξ	ε	Tal	M	P	P	Ceph	Z
⌐	Z	Gon	IY	n	2	Van	U
↔	∾	Na-hath	H	ζ	ζ ∾	Fam	S
				⌐	/ /	Gisg	T

Extract from Ritual X (F.L. Gardner, c. 1895),
from the Archives of the Golden Dawn Research Trust

Exhortation

Extract from Ritual X (W.A. Ayton, c. 1895)

THE ENOCHIAN ALPHABET

Interestingly, however, a 1935 typescript by Euan Campbell (a member of the Smaragdum Thalasses temple in New Zealand) shows the letters predominantly in the familiar Regardie style. Given Regardie's version wasn't published until 1937 onwards, this suggests they were both operating from the same, inaccurate source. Indeed, this is supported by the fact that Campbell was present at the Bristol Temple during the same period that Regardie was a member. Given the arguably butchered versions of the Stella Matutina rituals that Regardie published, having similarly poor source material for the Enochian system is not entirely unexpected. What is most surprising, however, is that Campbell did not use a more correct form of the letters, as he was known to have a particular interest in the Enochian system, studying the Dee material directly in the British Museum in 1934. This is doubly so when considering his warning about the danger of "inaccurate and carelessly worked Magical Rituals and Formulas."[2]

These more modern errors aside, there are some errors that *do* appear in original copies, the most notable being the name of the letter *Or* (given as *Orth* by the Golden Dawn). This is likely based on the pronunciation guide for the letters given to Dee, where it states "the voice sounded Orh." Given how difficult it is to read some sections of Dee's diaries, this is potentially a simple misreading of the text.

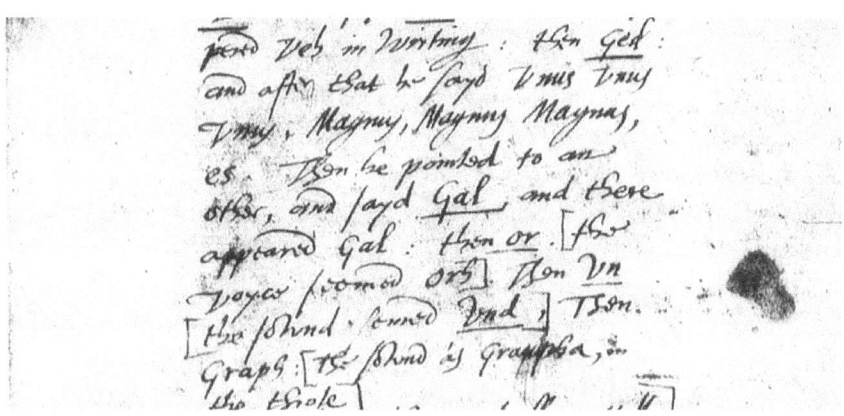

Extract of Enochian Letter Pronunciations (from Sloane 3188)

---

2 *Ibid.*, Introduction.

Another error is the letter *Van*, given as *Vau* in some original Golden Dawn copies (though this may be due to the similarity of 'n' and 'u' in the handwriting of many from that period). It is possible this mistake was not present in Westcott's original.

There is also the issue of the letter *Na*, given as *Na-hath* in original Golden Dawn material. This is clearly based on the chart given to Dee, where instead of giving 'h', he gives 'hath'. Some argue that this letter should therefore be called *Na-hath*—and there is certainly a reasonable argument for that—but it was given as *Na* elsewhere in Dee's diaries, so I think we can safely assume that the latter is the correct form.

These three genuine errors (down from the seven or more in Regardie) should be corrected by modern Golden Dawn magicians, as they are clearly misreadings or misunderstandings, and not, as some claim, a legitimate heterodox tradition.

When it comes to Regardie's copy, it is not entirely clear if there were errors in his source document, if he made the errors in his copies, or if the errors were made by illustrators for the publisher—though Campbell's copy suggests there were at least some problems with the source material employed by the Stella Matutina at the time. Regardless, they have become immortalised as the "Golden Dawn" form of the Enochian alphabet, rather erroneously. If anything, they should be known as the "Regardie" form—if only for the fact that his book has imortalised them—or some other such more accurate moniker.

That these errors occured is one thing (all of us make mistakes, myself included). That they remain is quite another. Unfortunately, these errors have not been corrected in the most popular Golden Dawn textbooks, including the most recent (seventh) edition of *The Golden Dawn* by Israel Regardie, where a new font containing these mistakes was used.[3] So long as this remains the case, new students—or those not exposed to original material—will continue to learn an inaccurate form of the letters, or come to think that the Golden Dawn messed up its documenting of the Enochian alphabet far more than it actually did.

I hope this essay proves a small contribution to addressing this long-standing misconception, and that more students will seek out

---

3 Israel Regardie, *The Golden Dawn (Seventh Edition)*, p. 808-809.

THE ENOCHIAN ALPHABET

the original source material for the Golden Dawn, as, indeed, they should do for the Dee diaries. In magic, details matter, and a small alteration can have significant effects. Let us, therefore, ensure we are armed with all the facts, and that, indeed, we have a full and accurate magical alphabet at our disposal.

About the Author

Frater Yechidah is a magician and author.

He has written on many occult topics, including articles for *Hidden Spirit*, *Hermetic Virtues*, and *The Gnostic*. He also blogs about topics related to the Golden Dawn and Gnosticism.

He established the occult publisher Kerubim Press and wrote two books on the Enochian system entitled *Enochian Magic in Theory* and *Enochian Magic in Practice*.

He has been involved with a number of esoteric groups, including the Order of the Sons and Daughters of Light, the Hermetic Order of the Golden Dawn, and the Ancient and Honourable Order of the Golden Dawn.

He lives in Dublin, Ireland.

CPSIA information can be obtained
at www.ICGtesting.com
Printed in the USA
FSHW010858160121
77757FS

9 781908 705167